The Global Sports Arena:
Athletic Talent Migration in an
Interdependent World

edited by

John Bale

and

Joseph Maguire

Frank Cass · London

First published in 1994 in Great Britain by
FRANK CASS & CO. LTD.
Gainsborough House, Gainsborough Road,
London E11 1RS, England

and in the United States of America by
FRANK CASS
c/o International Specialized Book Services, Inc,
5804 N.E. Hassalo Street, Portland, Oregon 97213–3644

British Library Cataloguing in Publication Data

The Global Sports Arena:Athletic Talent
Migration in an Interdependent World
I. Bale, John II. Maguire, Joseph
331.12791

ISBN 0–7146–3489–1 (cloth)
ISBN 0–7146–4116–2 (paper)

Library of Congress Cataloging in Publication Data

The Global sports arena : athletic talent migration in an
interdependent world / edited by John Bale and Joseph Maguire.
    p.   cm.
Papers originally presented during a colloquium at Keele
University, April 1991.
Includes bibliographical references and index.
ISBN 0–7146–3489–1   0–7146–4116–2
    1. Athletes--Relocation--Congresses. 2. Emigration and
immigration--Congresses. I. Bale, John. II. Maguire, Joseph, A.,
1956–   . III. University of Keele.
GV706.8.G575   1994
305.9796--dc20   93–24340
                                                                    CIP

Typeset by Photoprint, Torquay, Devon
Printed and bound in Great Britain by
Bookcraft Ltd, Midsomer Norton, Avon

The Global Sports Arena:
Athletic Talent Migration in an Interdependent World

Contents

For Ruth
and for Thomas

Notes on Contributors

Joseph Arbena teaches Latin American history and geography at Clemson University, South Carolina, USA. In addition to writing numerous papers on sport in Latin America, he edited *Sport and Society in Latin America* (1988) and compiled *An Annotated Bibliography of Latin American History* (1989). He is also editor of the *Journal of Sport History*.

John Bale is a senior lecturer in the School of Human Development at Keele University, UK. He has written many articles on geographical and historical aspects of sport. Among his books are *Sport and Place* (1983), *Sports Geography* (1989), *The Brawn Drain: Foreign Student-Athletes in American Universities* (1991) and *Sport, Space and the City* (1992).

Christian Bromberger teaches ethnology at the University of Provence at Aix-en-Provence, France, where he is director of the Laboratoire d'ethnologie méditerranéenne et comparative. His interest lies in the study of collective identities through different themes. His empirical research into the passion for football in Marseilles, Naples and Turin will be presented in a forthcoming book, written in collaboration with A. Hayot and J.M. Mariottini, titled *Le match de football. Ethnologie d'une passion partisane à Marseille, Naples et Turin*.

Vic Duke teaches in the Sociology Department of Salford University, UK. He has published several papers and essays on various aspects of sport, notably on the recent changes in sports in eastern Europe. He has a special research interest in football in Czechoslovakia.

Henning Eichberg, a cultural sociologist, researches at the Institute for Sport Research (Idrætsforsk), Gerlev, Denmark, and teaches at the University of Copenhagen. He is the author of *Der Weg des Sports in die industrielle Zivilization* (1973), *Leistung, Spannung, Geschwindigkeit* (1978) and *Leistungsräume: Sport als Umweltproblem* (1988). He has edited *Nordic Sports; History and Identity* (1989) and *Körperkulturen und Identität* (1989) and has written numerous articles on various aspects of sport.

Simon Genest is undertaking doctoral research in the Department of Geography at Laval University, Quebec, Canada. He is currently attached to the Maison de Geógraphie at the University of Montpellier, France.

Jeffrey Hill teaches in the Department of International Studies at Nottingham Trent University, UK. He has published various articles on working-class politics and society in Great Britain in the nineteenth and twentieth centuries, recent among which include studies of the development of popular sport in northern communities.

Alan Klein is Associate Professor of Sociology–Anthropology at Northeastern University in Boston, Massachusetts, USA. He has carried out extensive research on Latin American baseball in the Dominican Republic and is beginning fieldwork in Mexico on nationalism and baseball. He has also published *Sugarball: the American Game, the Dominican Dream* (1991) and *Little Big Men: Gender Construction and the Bodybuilding Subculture* (1992), as well as many articles on bodybuilding subculture and international baseball.

Pierre Lanfranchi is a post-doctoral researcher at the Centre for Research into European Culture at the European University Institute, Florence, Italy. He has written widely on several historical aspects of sport and is editor of *Il Calcio e il suo Pubblico* (1992).

Joseph Maguire is a senior lecturer in the Department of Physical Education, Sports Science and Recreation Management at Loughborough University, UK. He has published widely in the areas of football hooliganism, basketball, racism and the political economy of sport. He is co-editor of *The Sports Process* (1992), and co-author with Grant Jarvie of *Sport and Leisure in Social Thought* (forthcoming).

Tony Mason is Senior Lecturer in social history at Warwick University, UK. He is author of *Association Football and English Society* (1980) and *Sport in Britain* (1989), as well as many articles and papers on historical aspects of sport.

Fiona Miller is currently researching in the area of law and the international market for professional footballers. She is a lecturer in law at Manchester Metropolitan University, UK.

H.F. Moorhouse works in the Department of Sociology, University of Glasgow, where he is director of the Work and Leisure Research

Unit. He is editor of the journal *Work, Employment and Society* and author of *Driving Ambitions: a Social Analysis of the American Hot Rod Enthusiasm* (1991).

Kalevi Olin teaches in the Department of Social Sciences of Sport at the University of Jyväskylä, Finland. He has published research articles and reports on various topics in sport sociology, social planning of sport and sports policy-making. The author (in Finnish) of *Reference Groups of Decision Makers in Sport Policy of Cities* (1982), he has edited *Contributions of Sociology to the Study of Sport* (1984 – a festschrift to Kalevi Heinilä) and is the co-author of the book, *Sport: Change, Brake or Chaos?* (1992).

Matti Penttilä graduated in sport behaviour from the University of West Virginia, USA and is currently a post-graduate student at the Department of Social Sciences of Sport at the University of Jyväskylä, Finland. His previous research has focused on the issue of migration in professional sports.

Steve Redhead is Reader in Law and Director of the Unit for Law and Popular Culture at Manchester Metropolitan University, UK. He is the author of *Sing When You're Winning* (1987), *The End of the Century Party* (1990), *Football with Attitude* (1991), and *Unpopular Cultures* (1992) and many articles on British football.

Joe Sang is a doctoral student in the Department of Education at Keele University, UK. He is researching aspects of sport in Kenya, focusing particularly on the development of track and field athletics in that country.

Gareth Williams is Senior Lecturer in History at the University College of Wales, Aberystwyth, UK, and an editor of *The International Journal of the History of Sport*. He has written widely on the social history of sport, particularly rugby football, and his recent publications include *1905 and All That: Essays on Rugby Football and Welsh Society* (1991).

Acknowledgements

The majority of studies contained in the following pages were originally presented at an international, interdisciplinary colloquium held at Keele University in April 1991. Financial and other forms of support provided by the Departments of Education and Geography and the School of Human Development at Keele, the Department of Physical Education, Sports Science and Recreation Management at Loughborough University and the British Council, are gratefully acknowledged. We would also like to offer thanks to Maralyn Beech and Andrew Lawrence of the Keele Department of Geography for assistance with some of the illustrative material in the book and to the scholars who contributed to the colloquium and who provided their papers in publishable form with the absolute minimum of editorial coaxing.

John Bale
Joseph Maguire

1

Introduction: Sports Labour Migration in the Global Arena

Joseph Maguire and John Bale

Athletes are on the move. The migration of sports talent as athletic labour is a pronounced feature of sports development in the late twentieth century. The purpose of this book is to explore this phenomenon from a variety of perspectives. The book is divided into three parts: historical examples of such integration, some questions of contemporary concern about the international migration of sports talent and, finally, a section indicating some possible future global developments. This movement of elite sports talent – the subject of this collection – is referred to in terms of labour migration in order to convey to the reader how this process is interwoven with the commodification of sport within the capitalist world economy. Although it is not usual to think of sportspeople as workers, we argue that they are, in fact, not unlike other sectors of the workforce who, for various reasons, have to ply their trade in several national, continental or trans-continental locations. Again, not unlike their counterparts in other occupations, elite athletes as a group experience varying degrees of exploitation, but also enjoy some personal gains.

Such sports labour migration occurs within nation-states, between nation-states in the same continent and between nation-states in different continents (see Arbena's chapter in this book for a case-study based on this threefold division). In order to capture the complexity of this global movement of sports labour, it is perhaps appropriate to cite specific examples of its various dimensions.

DIMENSIONS OF SPORTS LABOUR MIGRATION

A socially and geographically mobile workforce is a feature of most modern industrial societies. The movement of athletes from their home town to their place of initial recruitment to elite or professional sport clubs can be seen as part of this same process. There is evidence to suggest that there are patterns to the recruitment and subsequent retention of athletes in sports such as American football, baseball, basketball, cricket, ice hockey, track and field and soccer (Bale, 1989). If UK sport is examined, it can be shown to highlight a number of both quite specific and more general features of sports labour migration. Although the UK is composed of England, Scotland, Wales and Northern Ireland, each of these nations has, for example, its own soccer league containing varying levels of indigenous labour and labour from other nations within the UK (in this connection see Moorhouse's chapter in this volume). Movement of Welsh rugby union players to English rugby league also occurs (for further discussion see the chapter by Williams). Because of its specific constitutional arrangements, the UK is anomalous in this regard. Nevertheless, it was also possible, at least until relatively recently, to point to countries such as the former Soviet Union and Yugoslavia as examples of the existence of similar processes at work; that is, sports talent from different republics such as the Ukraine and Georgia and Croatia and Bosnia moving within the overall nation-state to ply their trade for sports teams such as Moscow Dynamo and Red Star Belgrade.

Sports labour migration also occurs between countries located within the same continent. If one considers the states within the United States of America, inter-state migration of sports talent is extremely widespread and is not without controversy (Rooney, 1980). Also witness the involvement of citizens of the United States in Canadian baseball teams and athletes from the Dominican Republic in American baseball teams (for further discussion see the chapter by Klein). In Europe this sports labour migration takes place in a number of sports including soccer, ice hockey, rugby and basketball among others.

This migration process is arguably most pronounced in soccer. Professional players criss-cross the continent of Europe. In this case, the elite of soccer talent is purchased mainly by the national leagues of Italy and Spain. This labour is drawn from donor countries spread across Europe, including Germany, Holland, the UK, the Commonwealth of Independent States and the Balkan and Scandinavian countries. But this outflow of players is not confined to host countries such as Italy and Spain. Soccer labour movement flows across the continent with those more economically powerful leagues attracting a standard of player commensurate with their ability to pay transfer fees and the salary of the players concerned. Even in those countries where the outflow of talent is most evident (such as the Scandinavian countries) recruitment of lesser talented players also occurs (for the

Swedish, Norwegian and Finnish leagues). The opening up of eastern Europe, with Hungarian, Czechoslovakian and Romanian players to the fore, will further complicate this movement of athletic labour but will, we suspect, largely involve the outflow of talent from eastern Europe in the first instance (for further discussion see the chapter by Duke). This trend may be a precursor of a broader pattern of migration from eastern and central Europe to western Europe; for example, over 50 top Romanian rugby union players currently play in France. In this connection, as Arbena notes in his chapter, questions arise concerning athletes' rights and the free movement of labour on the one hand, and the deskilling of underdeveloped countries on the other.

A similar trend is also evident on a trans-continental level. Movement of sports labour occurs between North American and Europe in sports such as basketball, American football and ice hockey. Currently over 400 Americans play in Europe's professional men's basketball leagues, with the higher calibre players again found in Italy and Spain. Here the situation is further complicated by issues of ancestral links to specific countries and the imposition of quotas on foreign players by particular national sports organizations: some American citizens can claim dual nationality and reside in – and in specific instances play for – the European country from which his or her ancestors came, and French Canadians often ply their ice hockey skills in France or Switzerland (for further discussion see the chapter by Genest).

There is also a flow of sports labour in the opposite direction. Scandinavians have long been recruited by North American ice hockey clubs and American universities have actively recruited European men and women in sports such as track and field, soccer, rugby, basketball and swimming (Bale, 1991; Donnelly and Young, 1988). More recently, this trend has been the subject of critical debate within the United States with the establishment of a quota of non-US athletes being proposed (*US Today*, 2 January, 1992).

This movement of sports labour on a trans-continental level is not confined to that which takes place between Europe and North America. Africans are prominent in French, Belgian, Portuguese and Dutch soccer leagues (Maguire, 1991). Here issues of first- and second-generation migration patterns emerge. As Lanfranchi argues in his chapter, sport provides a means of integration into the host society, exemplified by the presence of a continual stream of foreign footballers into France. As Pooley discovered, however, sport does not necessarily assist in the cultural assimilation of ethnic groups. Rather, in certain instances, sport can serve as a symbol of identification with the cultural heritage of the group to which the individual belongs (Pooley, 1981).

The migration of labour and sports labour on a trans-continental level is also evident in the involvement of first- and second-generation Afro-Caribbeans in English soccer (Maguire, 1988). That is, with regard to English and mainland European soccer, a number of these players are the descendants of migrants who settled in the country that was formerly their colonial overlord. African track and field talent also appears in the American university scholarship programme (for further discussion of this see the chapter by Bale and Sang). Australian, Afro-Caribbean, Asian and South African cricketers figure prominently in English cricket, and, as Hill's chapter demonstrates, have done so for many decades.

In some of these examples the sports labour tends to be hired by a specific club or organization and is resident in the host country for a limited period of time. But this is not always the case. Some athletes stay on and make the host country their home. More usually this occurs either through marriage to a citizen of that country or by having resided in a country for a length of time sufficient to qualify for nationality status. Take, for example, the case of Chen Xinhua, a former citizen of the People's Republic of China who now plays table tennis for Britain. Indeed, the migration of Chinese table tennis players is not confined to Britain and, as a signal to others not to try to follow his example, the Chinese vetoed Xinhua's inclusion in the British Olympic team for Barcelona (*Guardian*, 28 January 1992). One might also recall the case of Sydney Maree, a South African runner who became a naturalized American citizen in order to run in international competitions. In some instances, such as in European basketball, individuals can play for the country in which they are then resident and for whom they can claim 'nationality'.

There are other aspects of this sports labour migration which need highlighting. In certain sports, such as cricket and rugby league, migration has a seasonal pattern. The weather patterns in the northern and southern hemispheres in effect offer certain sports two seasons of play per year. Other sports migrants experience a transitory form of migration. Take, for example, the experience of European, American and African athletes on the European track and field grand prix circuit or European and American skiers on the World Cup Alpine skiing circuit. Other examples include cycling and motor sports ranging from formula one to motor cycling. In some instances both seasonal and transitory migration patterns are evident. Here we can recognize the global travels of golf and tennis players; in fact, for golf and tennis players one could arguably say that they are the nomads of the sports labour migration pattern *par excellence* with a seemingly constantly shifting workplace and place of residence.

ISSUES AND QUESTIONS OF SPORTS LABOUR MIGRATION

In some ways, as the chapters in the first part of this collection highlight, these migration patterns are nothing new. It appears however, that the process is speeding up. The migration of sports labour is both gathering pace and occurring over a more widespread geographical area and within a greater number of sports subcultures. But before we attempt to locate sports labour migration within an overall framework, a number of questions arise from the patterns we have so far described. Why do athletes decide to leave their native lands? How do they cope with the experience of being in a foreign culture? How do people from their own culture and people from their host culture view their embarkation, arrival and settlement? What do these movements of athletes reveal about gender relations, the political economy of sports labour migration linked to broader trends regarding migration and globalization? These and other questions form the backcloth to this book. For now, let us concentrate on locating sports migration within an overall framework. In this regard its connection with the issue of globalization is seen as crucial.

Sports labour migration is arguably gathering momentum and appears to be closely interwoven with the broader process of global sports development taking place in the late twentieth century. In turn, this sports development is interwoven with a process of accelerated globalization which has been unfolding at least since the late nineteenth century. Significant features of this have included: an increase in the number of international agencies; the growth of increasingly global forms of communication; the development of global competitions and prizes; and the development of notions of rights and citizenship that are increasingly standardized internationally.

Several aspects of sports development highlight the interconnections between this migration and globalization. The last century and a half has, for example, witnessed the emergence and diffusion of sport, the establishment of international sports organizations, the global standardization of rules governing sports, the growth of competition among individuals and club teams from different countries and among the national sides of such countries, and the establishment of global competitions such as the Olympic Games, soccer's World Cup tournament and the athletics world championships.

There are at least five dimensions of social change that are produced in conjunction with global cultural flows (Appadurai, 1990). These are 'ethnoscapes' that are produced by the international movement of such people as tourists, migrants, exiles and guestworkers; 'technoscapes' that are created by the flow between countries of machinery and plant produced by corporations (trans-national as well as national) and government agencies; 'financescapes' that centre on the rapid flow of money and its equivalents around the world; 'mediascapes' in which the flow of images and information between countries is produced and distributed by newspapers, magazines, radio, film, television and video; and, finally, the 'ideoscapes' that are linked to the flow of ideas centrally associated with state or counter-state ideologies and movements.

All five dimensions can be detected in late twentieth-century sports development. Although this collection of readings concentrates on ethnoscapes, it is our contention that this dimension of global social change must be understood as interconnected with the other dimensions referred to. Thus, at the level of ethnoscapes the global migration of professional, elite and college sports personnel (players, coaches, teachers and administrators) was a pronounced feature of sports development in the 1980s and appears likely to continue to be so in the present decade. The flow from country to country, continent to continent, of sports goods, equipment and landscapes (sports complexes, golf courses, artificial playing surfaces etc.) has grown to the position of a multi-billion dollar business in recent years and represents a trans-national development in sports at the level of technoscapes. In terms of financescapes it is clear that the flow of finance in the global sports arena has come to centre not only on the international trade in sports personnel, prize money and endorsements, but on the marketing of sport along specific, that is, American, lines. Closely connected to these dimensions has been a development at the level of mediascapes. This 'media–sport production complex' projects images of both individual sports labour migrants (Ballesteros, Becker, Graf, Krabbe, Maradona and Navratilova) and specific cultural messages to large global audiences. At the level of ideoscapes, global sports festivals such as the soccer World Cup, the Olympics and the Asian games have come to serve as vehicles for the expression of ideologies that are trans-national in character.

STUDYING SPORTS LABOUR MIGRATION: CONCEPTUAL TOOLS AND THEORETICAL FRAMEWORKS

The decision to locate the issue of sports labour migration within the context of globalization itself rests on an assumption which the editors also believe to be true. Though one of the editors is a sociologist and the other is a geographer, neither discipline on its own has provided a comprehensive way of capturing the temporal, spatial and structural dimensions to migration. Indeed, we share share Giddens' assessment of the social sciences when he noted that they had 'failed to construct their thinking around the modes in which social systems are graduated across time-space' (Giddens, 1984: 110). Giddens notes the 'remarkable convergence' between geography and the social sciences on matters of social theory and this edited collection is in part a reflection of that. We hasten to add that we see a similar convergence occurring between history and sociology. Take Philip Abrams' remarks in this connection:

> In my understanding of history and sociology, there can be no relationship between them because in terms of their fundamental pre-occupations, history and sociology are and always have been the same thing. Both seek to understand the puzzle of human agency and both seek to do so in terms of the process of social structuring (Abrams, 1982: x).

We argue that this insight is particularly relevant in making sense of an individual's inter- or intra-societal movement. Indeed, with regard to the study of sports labour migration we are dealing not just with the positioning of individuals relative to one another, but also with the contexts of social interaction relative to one another. We are dealing with ethnoscapes and technoscapes, financescapes and ideoscapes. The advantages flowing from the convergence of the disciplines referred to are, for example, that in some geographical studies the concern is on locating people in time–space and on promoting a sensitivity for place and space, (Gregory, 1985 among others). In some studies in historical sociology there is a concern to discern and explain long-term structured processes of development (Mennell, 1990). Inherent within the approach we have advocated is the idea that social development involves spatial and temporal movement. This interconnection of time and space can be examined both in terms of the involvement of people in cycles of social interaction and, at the same time, at the level of societal and global transformation.

In both time-geography and historical sociology attention is given to what Hägerstrand has termed the 'time–space choreography of individuals existence over given time periods' (Hägerstrand cited in Giddens, 1984). For time-geographers social interaction can therefore be understood as the coupling of paths in social encounters or 'activity bundles' which occur at definite 'stations' such as buildings or territorial units. It is in these contexts that the paths of two or more individuals meet. Hägerstrand conjures up the essence of this process when he refers to this as a 'weaving dance through time' (Hägerstrand cited in Giddens, 1984). This imagery conveys the idea of a co-ordination of movement in time and space as involving a multiplicity of paths or trajectories.

Once more a significant convergence of thinking is evident between time-space geography and some forms of historical sociology. In writing the introduction to the 1968 edition of *The Civilising Process* (originally published in 1939 as an attempt to discern and explain long-term structured processes of development *par excellence*), Elias himself used the example of dance to capture the temporal and spatial interweaving of numerous interdependent individuals:

> Like every other social figuration, a dance figuration is relatively independent of the specific individuals forming it here and now, but not of the individuals as such. It would be absurd to say that dances are mental constructions abstracted from observations of individuals considered separately. The same applies to all other figurations. Just as the small dance figurations change – becoming now slower, now quicker – so too, gradually or more suddenly, do the large figurations which we call societies (Elias, 1978 [1968]: 262).

In thinking of these webs of interdependence, Elias provided some theoretical–empirical guidelines which can be useful in the study of labour migration. Based on his study of a specific space and place, that of court society, Elias provides some criteria by which to calibrate more accurately the various dimensions of social development. The details of this need not concern us here. However, given the preceding discussion of time-geography and historical sociology, his reference to the following is of especial importance:

> One of the simplest of these criteria is the number of routine contacts which people of different classes, ages and sex have at

one stage of social development as compared to another. Others are the number, length, density and strength of the chains of interdependence which individual people form with others within a time-space continuum at a certain stage as compared to earlier or later stages. A standard criterion that could be better calibrated than is the case at present is the central balance of tensions in a society: the number of power centres increases with a growing differentiation of functions (Elias, 1983 [1969] 221).

Here we have some indices by which to calibrate the movement of an individual, of groups of people and of societies. The number, length, density and strength of the chains of interdependence which individual people form with others in a time–space continuum is an extremely fruitful way of understanding both sports labour migration and the broader process of globalization within which it is enmeshed.

Taken in isolation, any one of this book's chapters probably contains only some of the qualities of convergence outlined, and indeed not all the contributors would necessarily share our convictions regarding convergence. Taken as a whole, however, we think that this book, representing as it does a variety of disciplines, reflects the convergence of thinking outlined above. Certainly it was our aim to provide some overall grasp of sports labour migration and we argue that, in order to do that, research from human geography and historical sociology is required. What these approaches provide are tools for thinking about the problem in question. In the following sections we attempt to summarize what these disciplines can contribute in this regard.

Human geography and theories of labour migration
Human geography has been slower than either sociology or history to embrace sport as a central area of enquiry. The fledgling subdiscipline of 'sports geography' has tended to be locked into a time-warp of 'cartographic fetishism' and has generally failed to embrace the more recent theoretical, post-positivist movement in which structuration and time-geography might be included. So while Hägerstrand's more recent ideas may have influenced Giddens, sports geographers have related more to his previously influential ideas (Hägerstrand, 1967) on innovation diffusion (Bale, 1984; Genest, 1991). Here, sport is interpreted as an innovation in time and space and the dominant variables taken to be distance from the origin of the innovation and the varying levels of economic development of potential adopters.

Most geographical studies of labour migration have assumed forms which range from the quantitative modelling of migrant flows to more behaviourally oriented studies. Migrations through space and over time are well accommodated by the notion of Hägerstrand's time-geography but although it provides an appealing conceptual framework for exploring international migration, its use has been to explore shorter-distance, often daily, movements rather than long-distance, migratory ones. In the case of sports talent migration, no work currently exists which employs this approach, though Pred (1981) has shown how important time–space 'prisms' are to an understanding of the changing nature of movements to spectate in nineteenth-century US baseball – an interesting case of sport being used to illuminate geography, rather than vice versa. Instead, sports-geographic studies have tended to adopt traditional positivist approaches which, in the context of sports talent migration, have mainly been at the national, rather than international, level. This is far from saying, however, that sports geographers should not embrace time–space concepts as a potential tool for research.

A first step in much geographical work on migration – and very well demonstrated in sports-geographic studies – is simply to map the information to show the pattern of migratory flows between origin and destination. In this way, some areas can be seen to be talent-deficit regions and others talent-surplus regions. The work of Rooney (1974), whose studies of the inter-state migration of elite high-school sports talent en route to universities or colleges in the USA is typical of this approach but tends to be weakly related to any theoretical base. This omission can be rectified by applying the well-known 'gravity model' to the number of migrants and the distance migrated. Given these basic variables it is possible to model the flows, and hence predict the number of migrants moving between two places. Such an approach has been undertaken by McConnell (1983; 1984), again at the national scale for high school–college footballer migration in the USA. Other such approaches to migration are reviewed in the chapter by Olin and Penttilä.

These approaches may be complemented by a more behavioural approach to migration which sees movement between two places as an outcome of a decision-making process. A model based on the needs and expectations of migrants (internal stressors) and the characteristics of their existing (sports) environment (external stressors) leads to an evaluation of the existing level of place utility. If a critical threshold level of such utility is passed, the decision is made to migrate. Bale (1991) has used this model in a study of foreign student-athlete migration to the USA. Also relevant in this context is the level of place utility achieved at the new location which will influence the decision to

"HE'S THE 'LONDON LINGO' CO-ORDINATOR — SOME GUY CALLED DEL-BOY"

Figure 1.1 Problems of global sport migration and adjustment?
(*Source*: *Quarterback*, 1, 24, 22 March 1986, p. 6)

stay or to return home. Concepts derived from research into culture-shock and adjustment to new locational situations (Furnham and Bochner, 1986) are also relevant to the study of sports talent, as are insights provided by educational research into overseas sojourn among foreign students (see, for example, Spaulding and Flack, 1984; see also Figure 1.1).

More promising, we feel, for geographers with research commitments to sport studies on a world scale, are approaches which embrace a global systems approach. Taking an analogy of Taylor's (1985) three-tier model of the world political system, Bale (1991) introduced his study of foreign student-athlete migration to American universities by noting scales of (1) reality (global-achievement sport), (2) ideology (national sport systems) and (3) experience (local sport situation). The point being made here is that the experience of sport in, say, Hungary, Kenya or Scotland cannot be fully understood without an awareness of the scale of reality, the nature of which is experienced via the mediation of national ideology. The reasons why Hungary loses its best footballers and why Kenya loses its best runners cannot be

explained by events in those specific countries. Given Taylor's influential interpretation of Wallerstein's work (see below), and the renewed
interest among geographers in global cultural experiences (Cosgrove
and Rogers, 1991), there is every reason to hope that more geographers might embrace the study of the global dimension of sport – *the
global experience* – as a legitimate field of enquiry.

Historical-sociology and theories of the global system

We have already suggested that in order to understand sports labour
migration processes more adequately there is a need to locate these
within the debate regarding sports development and the global system
(for further discussion see the chapter by Maguire). With regard to
both the origins of modern sport and its subsequent spread and
development there is a range of competing theoretical approaches.
This debate has been subject to extensive review (Dunning, Maguire,
and Pearton, 1993; Donnelly, (forthcoming); Gruneau, 1988; Maguire
and Jarvie, forthcoming; Stoddart, 1989; Stokvis, 1989). In this
context, the analysis is more concerned to review the main principles
underpinning theoretical approaches to the study of global systems. In
so doing, reference will be made to literature which illustrates how
these approaches have been applied to the study of sport.

Modernization theory

This approach, closely linked to functionalism, was the dominant
paradigm in sociology until the early 1970s. Essentially concerned
with how traditional societies reach modernity, modernization theory
has focused on the political, cultural, economic and social aspects of
this process. Consideration is given to the development of political
institutions which support participatory decision-making. The growth
and development of secular and nationalist ideologies is examined.
The emergence of a division of labour, the use of management
techniques, technological innovations and commercial activities are
also the subject of attention. These changes are accompanied by
urbanization and a decline of traditional authorities. In his review of
the emergence of modern sport, Gruneau (1988) points to a range of
literature which has utilized this approach. Its application has not been
confined to the origins of sport. Writers such as Baker (1982), Clignet
and Stark (1974), Krotee, (1979), Mandell (1984), Guttmann (1991)
and Wagner (1989; 1990) have all used ideas drawn from this approach
to account for aspects of global sports development. A number of

these ideas are implicit in the chapters by Genest, Lanfranchi and Olin and Penttilä.

Imperialism and neo-imperialism

This approach is more usually associated with Marxist writings which try to explain the colonialism of specific nation-states, especially western nation-states, in terms of its necessity for capitalist expansion. At least three dimensions of these colonial ventures have been noted. These include the search for new markets in which to sell products, the search for new sources of raw materials and the search for new sources of cheap or skilled labour. This process is seen to assist western economic development and, at the same time, impoverish the rest of the world. Large business corporations as well as state organizations have played and continue to play a leading role in these developments.

But while the formal possession of empires has largely disappeared, with the concomitant rise in self-governing countries, a form of economic neo-imperialism has developed in which western countries are able to maintain their position of ascendancy by ensuring control over the terms on which world trade is conducted. Though one of the first approaches within the field, it still has its devotees. Ideas of this kind have surfaced in the literature on sport. Consider Baker and Mangan's (1987) collection of papers on sport in Africa, Mangan's own work on the games ethic and imperialism (1986), Cashman's (1980) exploration of the phenomenon of Indian cricket, Eichberg's earlier work critically examining the neo-colonial aspects of the Olympic movement (1984) and Arbena's evaluation of literature relating to Latin America (1989). In the present collection, the chapters by Bale and Sang, Klein and Maguire illustrate aspects of this theme.

Dependency theory

In a number of respects dependency theory links with neo-imperialist accounts. Both are concerned with the uneven manner and form of global development; further, the origins and nature of the dependency of specific nations varies according to how far a country was colonized and by whom. There are, however, a number of strands evident in this metatheory. These include dependent underdevelopment, dependent development and dependency reversal (for further discussion see the chapters by Arbena, Bale and Sang, Klein and Maguire).

In the first strand it is argued that the global capitalist system, largely but not exclusively through multinationals, operates actively to under-develop the third world. Third world countries' impoverishment is the direct result of their subordinate position in relation to the industrial-

Figure 1.2 Baseball, development and dependency reversal

ized countries. The wealth of the industrial countries is at the expense of third world countries, the latter being economically dependent on the former. Exponents of this strand argue that no genuine development is possible as long as this system is in place.

But this dependent underdevelopment strand appears unable to account for the growth of some third world countries. Hence, advocates of this overall approach coined the idea of dependent development, that is, the growth of some third world countries is acknowledged, but is viewed as limited in nature. But while dependent development is conceived of as possible, such an approach still does not appear to allow for the fact that certain countries can break out of the 'double bind' of dependent development. In this context, a further revision of the basic approach is evident in which reference is made to dependency reversal. In this approach it is conceived possible that certain third world countries, and/or institutional sectors of third world countries, can escape and reverse the previous disadvantageous relations with developed countries (for a graphic illustration of the tensions that can be engendered by this, see Figure 1.2). At present, however, no one approach dominates within dependency theory.

Despite this, variants of dependency theory have been used extensively in the study of sport. A number of studies have, not surprisingly, examined Latin and South American (Arbena, 1988; Klein, 1989; Stoddart, 1986, 1988). This approach has also been taken up by Jarvie in his study of the Highland games (1991).

World system theory

Associated with the work of Wallerstein (1974) this approach argues that a world system of commerce and communication has developed dating from the sixteenth century. This world system has produced a series of economic and political connections based on the expansion of a capitalist world economy. For Wallerstein, the world capitalist economy is oriented around four sectors. The core states dominate and control the exploitation of resources and production. Their wealth derives from their control over manufacturing and agriculture and they are characterized by centralized forms of government.

Those states which are linked in various kinds of dependent trading are referred to by Wallerstein as being semi-peripheral to the core, while peripheral states are those which depend on selling cash crops directly to the core states and are seen as being at the outer edge of the world economy. For Wallerstein, however, these were states which were, until colonial expansion, relatively untouched by commercial development. Their dependency has been established and maintained by the legacy of colonialism. For Wallerstein, these nations are enmeshed in a set of economic relations which enrich the industrial areas and impoverish the periphery. As yet, this approach has not been taken up extensively by scholars studying global sports development.

Insights into sports labour migration

With each of these theories there are a number of insights which can be gained in terms of an understanding of labour migration. Theories of imperialism and neo-imperialism alert us to the extent to which hegemonic powers exploit other nations in their search for new markets to sell sport forms, products, equipment and merchandise. Further, in the context of sports labour migration, the activities of hegemonic states can be seen to centre on the search for new sources of 'skilled' labour whose early development was resourced by these former colonial countries. From a dependency perspective, the global sports system can thus be seen to operate largely, but not exclusively, through multinationals or organizations dominated by first world nations. This system operates actively to underdevelop the third world by excluding it from the centre of political decision-making processes and from the economic rewards derived from the world sports economy. Indeed, utilizing a world systems theory, it can be argued that the core states dominate and control the exploitation of resources and production. A deskilling of semi-peripheral and peripheral states occurs on the terms and conditions set by core states. The most talented workers, in whom peripheral or semi-peripheral states have invested time and resources, are lured away to the core states whose wealth derives from their control over athletic labour and the media–sport production complex. Non-core states are thus in a position of dependent trading: their athletic labour being the equivalent of the cash crops which they sell in other sectors of the world economy.

BREAKING NEW GROUND

The chapters contained in the following pages cover a wide range of sports and types of sport talent migration in and between Europe, North and Latin America, and Africa. Part One includes chapters which review aspects of the substantial amount of sports talent/labour migration which has taken place since around the turn of the century. As Gareth Williams points out, there has been a long tradition of Welsh rugby players making the move north to the professional ranks of English rugby league. More recently, English-born players are attempting to play for Wales and Scotland, as happened in the 1992 Five Nations Championship. Implications for the 'nationality' of Wales are clearly found here, as they are for that of Scotland in Bert Moorhouse's chapter on the extensive migration of Scottish footballers to England. Talent migration is part and parcel of the colonial legacy, as graphically demonstrated by Pierre Lanfranchi in the case of footballer migration in France and by Jeff Hill who traces the links between England's imperial past and the inter-war migration of foreign cricketers to north-west England. A fascinating antecedent of the current wave of English footballer migration to distant parts of the world is examined by Tony Mason in his chapter on the early 1950s moves of Neil Franklin and his colleagues to South America. Each of these chapters teases out broader questions relating to culture shock, family adjustment or foreign sojourn and attitudes of both sports-people themselves and members of the host community to the question of sporting migrants.

Part Two looks more explicitly at some contemporary case studies, though few ignore the legacy of the past or the space and time dimensions. Adopting an approach at a continental scale, Joseph

Arbena notes how sports talent migration may be classified on a scale ranging from those who move *within* a continent, those who move *out of* a continent, and those who move *into* a continent. His examples, taken from Latin America, illustrate both a wide range of sports and a wide range of nations which are involved in international recruiting.

Four national and sporting case studies follow Arbena's scene-setting chapter. A detailed geographical approach characterizes Simon Genest's treatment of the influx of Canadian ice hockey players into Europe. He illustrates how the wealth of quantitative data provides a ready source for time-series analysis of sports talent migration and the ways in which the geographer's traditional cartographic skills can be harnessed in order to display the varied migration flows between different countries. Kalevi Olin and Matti Penttilä examine trends in American basketball player migration to Finland. They are centrally concerned to explore the motivation of such sport migrants, predominantly American, and focus on issues such as the exploration of a new society, new life experiences, improvement as a player, better sporting and social status and more adequate monetary rewards.

The tension balance between freedom of movement and the deskilling of 'underdeveloped' sport economies is followed up in the chapter by Fiona Miller and Steve Redhead. In this regard the issue of European footballers' rights and the moves towards greater unification within the European Community are examined. In contrast to the predominantly American migration to Finland, the sporting implications of *glasnost*, *perestroika* and the break-up of the Soviet empire are traced by Vic Duke. Though he gives particular attention to developments in Czechoslovakia and Hungary, a number of the observations made appear pertinent to a wider examination of events in eastern Europe.

Many of the trends described in the first two parts of the book will probably continue into the future, and Part Three focuses explicitly on possible future global developments. Christian Bromberger explores the migration of foreign footballers to three major Mediterranean clubs – Marseilles, Naples and Juventus – and highlights the intriguing relationships between the cultures of these clubs and those of the type of migrant footballer attracted to them. As such, it also highlights the tension between localism, nationalism and globalization. In his chapter on talent migration and Dominican baseball, Alan Klein goes beyond charting the extent of such migration and raises questions about this process in the context of dependency and underdevelopment. Klein's study provides a timely critique of the impact which sports labour migration can have both on the individual and the society from which they come. These themes are returned to in the chapter by John Bale and Joe Sang who look at talent migration as simply one of a number of global influences on the development or underdevelopment of Kenyan track and field athletics. The chapter by Joseph Maguire more explicitly links the issues of American sports migration and the media–sport production complex to broader issues of globalization. In the final chapter Henning Eichberg reminds us that 'talent' can be interpreted in a relative sense, and that although the migration of elite, or achievement-oriented sports participants is the most commonly observed form of sports talent migration, other forms also exist. He raises several enticing questions, including that of the ideological bases of many of our assumptions about sports and athletic migration and that of possible post-modern forms of migration in a sports context.

One major omission from this book is that of women migrants in the world of sport. This subject is touched on in one or two of the chapters, but in most cases men form the principal focus. This is hardly surprising since it is men who have chiefly made up the various 'talent-pipelines' which have criss-crossed the world's sporting stage. But things are changing. Many European women now receive athletic scholarships in American universities; the burgeoning number of women now playing soccer has led to considerable flows of talented migrants. The same process is at work in other sports including golf and tennis, where issues arise concerning the commodification of women's bodies and athletic talent (Theberge, 1991).

Whether the patterns and experiences found in the analysis of women in talent migration are the same as those for men remains to be seen. The feminist literature on gender and sport more generally would suggest that this experience will, in certain respects, be significantly different. The study of gender and sports migration is one direction in which future research must go. Other areas include comparative analyses of the experience of athletes overseas, the ways of adjusting to change, the new perceptions athletes obtain of foreign countries as a result of temporary sojourn and the images they have of the countries they have left behind. Concern with the experiential aspects of sports migration must also be combined with consideration of issues of political economy and of what the process of sports labour migration reveals about broader questions of globalization. The migration of talent *per se* has attracted substantial interest over the years. This book points the way towards a research agenda on the migration of sports talent, a phenomenon which appears likely to increase in an increasingly interdependent world.

REFERENCES

Abrams, P. (1982) *Historical Sociology* (Newton Abbot: Open Books).

Appadurai, A. (1990) 'Disjuncture and Difference in the Global Cultural Economy', *Theory, Culture and Society*, 7, 295–310.

Arbena, J.L. (ed.) (1988) *Sport and Society in Latin America: Diffusion, Dependency and the Rise of Mass Culture* (Westport, CT: Greenwood Press).

Arbena, J.L. (1989) 'The Diffusion of Modern European Sport in Latin America: A Case Study of Cultural Imperialism?', paper presented at the annual meeting of the Southern Historical Association, Lexington, KY, November 1989.

Baker, W. (1982) *Sports in the Western World* (Totowa, NJ: Rowman & Littlefield).

Baker, W. and Mangan, J.A. (eds) (1987) *Sport in Africa: Essays in Social History* (New York: Africana).

Bale, J. (1984) 'Sports History as Innovation Diffusion', *Canadian Journal of the History of Sport* 15,1, 38–63.

(1989) *Sports Geography* (London: Spon).

(1991) *The Brawn Drain: Foreign Student Athletes in American Universities* (Urbana, IL: University of Illinois Press).

Cashman, R. (1980) *Patrons, Players and the Crowd: The Phenomenon of Indian Cricket* (Bombay: Longman Orient).

Clignet, R. and Stark, M. (1974) 'Modernization and the Game of Soccer in Cameroun', *International Review of Sport Sociology*, 9, 81–98.

Cosgrove, D. and Rogers, A. (1991) 'Territory, Locality and Place' in Philo, C. (ed.), *New Words, New Worlds: Reconceptualising Social and Cultural Geography* (St Davids University College, Lampeter), pp. 36–8.

Donnelly, P. (forthcoming) 'Subcultures in Sport: Resilience and Transformation' in Ingham, A.G. and Loy, J.W. (eds), *Sport in Social Development: Traditions, Transitions and Transformations* (Urbana, IL: Human Kinetics).

Donnelly, P. and Young, K. (1988) 'Reproduction and Transformation of Cultural Forms in Sport. A Contextual Analysis of Rugby', *International Review for the Sociology of Sport*, 20, 19–38.

Dunning, E., Maguire, J. and Pearton, R. (eds) (1993) *The Sports Process: Essays in Comparative and Developmental Sociology* (Urbana, IL: Human Kinetics).

Eichberg, H. (1984) 'Olympic Sport: Neocolonism and Alternatives', *International Review for the Sociology of Sport*, 19, 97–105.

Elias, N. (1978) [1968] *The Civilising Process*, Vol I (Oxford: Blackwell).

(1983) [1969] *The Court Society* (Oxford: Blackwell).

Furnham, A. and Bochner, S. (1986) *Culture Shock* (London: Methuen).

Genest, S. (1991) 'Etude Géographique du Processus de Diffusion du Hockey sur Glace dans le monde', unpublished MA dissertation, Laval University, Canada.

Giddens, A. (1984) *The Constitution of Society* (Oxford: Polity).

Gregory, D. (1985) 'Suspended Animation: The Stasis in Diffusion Theory' in Gregory, D. and Urry, J. (eds), *Social Relations and Spatial Structures* (London: Macmillan) pp. 296–336.

Gruneau, R. *(1988) 'Modernization or Hegemony: Two Views on Sport and Social Development'* in Harvey, J. and Cantelon, H. *(eds)*, *Not Just a Game: Essays in Canadian Sport Sociology* (Ottawa: University of Ottawa Press) pp. 9–32.

Guttmann, A. (1991) 'Sports Diffusion: A response to Maguire and the Americanization Commentaries', *Sociology of Sport Journal*, 8,2, 185–90.

Hägerstrand, T. (1967) *Innovation Diffusion as a Spatial Process* (Chicago: Chicago University Press).

—— (1975) 'Space, Time and Human Conditions' in Karlquist, A. (ed.), *Dynamic Allocation of Urban Space* (Farnborough: Saxon House).

Jarvie, G. (1991) *Highland Games: The Making of a Myth* (Edinburgh: Edinburgh University Press).

Klein, A. (1989) 'Baseball in the Dominican Republic', *Sociology of Sport Journal*, 6,2, 95–112.

Krotee, M. (1979) 'The Rise and Demise of Sport: A Reflection of Uruguayan Society', *Annals of the American Academy of Political and Social Science*, 445, 141–54.

McConnell, H. (1983) 'Southern Major College Football: Supply, Demand and Migration', *Southeastern Geographer*, 23, 78–106.

—— (1984) 'Recruiting Patterns in Midwestern Major College Football', *Geographical Perspectives*, 53, 27–43.

Mandell, R. (1984) *Sport: A Cultural History* (New York: Columbia University Press).

Maguire, J. (1988) ' "Race" and Position Segregation in English Soccer: A Preliminary Analysis of Ethnicity and Sport in Britain', *Sociology of Sport Journal*, 5, 257–69.

—— (1991) 'Sport, Racism and British Society' in Jarvie, G. (ed.) *Sport, Racism and Ethnicity* (London: Falmer Press) pp. 94–123.

Maguire, J. and Jarvie, G. (forthcoming) 'Historical Sociology and Sport: A Review and Critique', *Exercise and Sport Sciences Review*.

Mangan, J.A. (1986) *The Games Ethic and Imperialism* (London: Viking).

Mangan, J.A. (ed.) (1988) *Pleasure, Profit, Proselytism: British Culture and Sport at Home and Abroad 1700–1914* (London: Cass).

Mennell, S. (1990) 'The Sociological Study of History: Institutions and Social Development' in Bryant, C. and Becker, H. (eds), *What has Sociology Achieved?* (London: Macmillan) pp. 54–68.

Pooley, J.C. (1981) 'Ethnic Soccer Clubs in Milwaukee: A Study in Assimilation' in Hart, M. and Birrell, S. (eds), *Sport in the Sociocultural Process* (Dubuque, IA: Brown) pp. 430–47.

Pred, A. (1981) 'Production, Family and Free-time Projects: A Time-geographic Perspective on the Individual and Societal Change in Nineteenth-Century U.S. Cities', *Journal of Historical Geography*, 7, 3–36.

Rooney, J. (1974) *A Geography of American Sport* (Reading, MA: Addison Wesley).

—— (1980) *The Recruiting Game* (Lincoln, NE: University of Nebraska Press).

Spaulding, S. and Flack, W. (1985) *The World's Students in the United States* (New York: Preager).

Stoddart, B. (1986) *Saturday Afternoon Fever: Sport in Australian Culture* (Sydney: Angus and Robertson).

(1988) 'Cricket and Colonialism in the English-Speaking Caribbean to 1914: Towards a Cultural Analysis' in Mangan, J.A. (ed.) (1988) *Pleasure, Profit, Proselytism*, pp. 231–57.

(1989) 'Sport in the Social Construct of the Lesser Developed World: A Commentary', *Sociology of Sport Journal*, 6, 125–35.

Stokvis, R. (1989) 'The International and National Expansion of Sports' in Wagner, E. (ed.), (1989) *Sport in Asia and Africa*, pp. 13–24.

Theberge, N. (1991) 'Reflections on the Body in the Sociology of Sport', *Quest*, 43,2, 123–34.

Taylor, P. (1985) *Political Geography* (London: Longman).

Wagner, E. (ed.) (1989) *Sport in Asia and Africa: A Comparative Handbook* (Westport CT: Greenwood Press).

(1990) 'Sport in Africa and Asia: Americanization or Mundialization?', *Sociology of Sport Journal*, 7, 399–402.

Wallerstein, I. (1974) *The Modern World System* (New York: Academic Press).

Part One:
Sports Migration:
Tradition and Change

2

The Road to Wigan Pier Revisited: The Migration of Welsh Rugby Talent since 1918

Gareth Williams

The road to . . . Wigan is a long one, and the reasons for taking it are not immediately clear.

(*Orwell, 1963: 106*)

Jim Sullivan was born within a few months of George Orwell, in Cardiff, in December 1903. Such was his prowess in rugby league football as an outstanding full back and an unparalleled points-scoring goal-kicking phenomenon, in a playing career extending from 1921 to 1946, that he became known as 'the Wigan peer'. He made his debut for Cardiff RFC at the age of 16 in 1920, even then clearly destined for every honour in the game. At 17 he appeared in a Welsh trial but later that year Wigan offered him £750 plus match fees of £5 for a win, £4 15s (£4.75) for a draw and £4 10s (£4.50) for defeat, when the average wage was around four pounds a week. Some years after (in 1936) he wrote:

> I was serving my apprenticeship to a boiler-maker, and I seemed to have little prospect of securing another job. The first of the post-war industrial depressions had settled its sinister shadow over South Wales, and the Cardiff club could do nothing to help although I have not the least doubt it would have done so if it had been possible . . . the Cardiff club would have done anything to keep me, but it just had to keep within the rules, and when I broached the subject, officials said that I could have been given a job on the ground, but that would have meant me being classed as a professional. Then, the day after I had attached my name to

a form for Wigan, they did offer me a job, but it was too late
(Gate, 1986: 28).

Those words could also serve as the epigraph to this chapter.

Since its foundation in 1895 the Rugby League (RL), or the Northern
Union as it was called until it officially changed its name in 1922, has
been a source of magnetic attraction to Welsh rugby union players. Of
the 227 home rugby union internationals who changed codes between
1895 and 1990, 7 were Irish, 14 Scottish, 50 English and 156 Welsh.
These are *international* players only: the total number of ordinary
uncapped club players who 'went north' remains unknown, but
preliminary researches indicate that the proportion of uncapped to
capped Welsh players is in the order of at least 12 to one. In other
words, we are effectively dealing with an out-migration of around
2,000 Welsh rugby players to the north of England since 1895. More
especially, between 1919 and 1939, 70 Welsh internationals turned
professional compared with, in that same period, 5 English, 5 Scottish
and 1 Irish. We need hardly look far to explain why Wales failed to win
the Grand Slam or Triple Crown between 1911 and 1950: between
1919 and 1939 the equivalent of nearly five international XVs and
around 900 players overall took the road to Wigan Pier and points
north.[1] This must be our starting point.

From 1921 to early 1940 the United Kingdom suffered mass
unemployment on an unprecedented scale, with never less than 1
million – the economist A.C. Pigou's 'intractable million' – out of
work. By the winter of 1932–33 they were almost 3 million, or nearly a
quarter of the working population of the UK, and these official
statistics are safely reckoned to be underestimates.

In the last few decades revisionist historians have painted a determi-
nedly cheerful picture of these years (Pollard, 1962; Richardson, 1967;
Stevenson and Cook, 1977; Constantine, 1983). They point, in the
1930s in particular, to advances in economic growth, the extension of
the social services, the rise in consumerism, the coming of domestic
electricity and the family car, the growth of the leisure industry, the
popularity of the radio and the dream palace, the provision of paid
holidays, the building boom, and the rise in real incomes for the
majority who were *in* work. For South Wales, however, this version
'cannot possibly be accepted': here was a society in large measure
'crucified by mass unemployment and near starvation' (Morgan, 1981:
230; Hopkin, 1988).

The distinguishing features of this society stand out stark and clear,

for Wales was the only one of the Ministry of Labour's administrative
divisions

- where the number of insured workers between 16 and 64 was
  actually smaller in 1939 than 1923, a fall of 9 per cent as opposed to
  an increase of over 27 per cent for the country generally;
- where the monthly unemployment rate was consistently higher
  than for any other division between 1928 and 1939, never lower
  than 20 per cent and reaching 38 per cent;
- where unemployment was consistently 10 per cent above the
  national average between 1927 and 1931, and 16 per cent above it
  between 1931 and 1936;
- where in 1932, the worst year, the monthly unemployment average
  in the county (now three counties) of Glamorgan was 40.4 per cent
  and in Monmouthshire (now Gwent) 42 per cent;
- where in 1938 a quarter of all unemployed workers in Wales had
  been out of work for more than three years;
- where, in consequence, out-migration was persistent and heavy.
  Fifty thousand people left the Rhondda between 1921 and 1931, 20
  per cent of its population; 27,000 left Merthyr between 1921 and
  1937, an average of 1,000 a year. Nearly half a million people left
  Wales between the wars, to put a new gloss on Cecil B. de Mille's
  filmed version of Exodus, *The Ten Commandments*.

Of this loss, 85 per cent was borne by the old counties of Glamorgan
and Monmouthshire, and half of these migrants were in the 15 to 29
age group, the most active, adaptable and productive. In fact, two-
thirds of all outmigrants from South Wales between 1921 and 1931
were under 30 (HMSO 1932; NIDC, 1937; Fogarty, 1945; Thomas,
1988). Emigration was clearly a selective process, the age and skill
structure of the population being deeply affected. It led to a deterio-
ration both in the quality of life and in the determination and capacity
of the area to attract new industries, and brought about a decline in
human capital that is measurable by indicators as varied as trades
union membership, religious attendance and sporting achievement.

Symbolically, the fistful of world champion boxers to emerge from
the self-confident, economically buoyant South Wales of the prewar
period suffered defeat and early death in the 1920s. 'Peerless Jim'
Driscoll, tubercular and needy, was defeated by Charles Ledoux at the
National Sporting Club in 1919; Jimmy Wilde lost his world flyweight
title to Pancho Villa at New York's Polo Grounds in 1923; former
world flyweight champion Percy Jones died aged 30 in 1922; Driscoll

followed him to a premature grave three years later; and former world lightweight champion Freddie Welsh died in a dingy New York hotel in 1927. The greatest boxing hero of the inter-war period was Tommy Farr, whose defeat by Joe Louis in 1937 was almost historically necessary as the gutsy Tonypandy former miner became the embodiment of the gallant loser tag which was attached to South Wales as a whole in the 1930s (Smith, 1990). And of course we have the consistently poor performances of the Welsh rugby team, un-manned by migration as much as by the selectorial myopia, administrative obsolescence and technical bankruptcy which were themselves reflections of the increasing insolvency of Welsh club rugby.

In 1926–27, the year of the seven-month coal stoppage following the General Strike, the Welsh Rugby Union was inundated by requests from clubs for financial assistance. Ebbw Vale, Cross Keys, Blaenavon and Pontypool wrote for help. Cross Keys' appeal is both representative and poignant: 'We are forced to appeal to you to again kindly consider granting us financial assistance to enable us to carry on'. Several clubs do not merely teeter on the rim of the abyss of closure, they actually fall in. Rhymney RFC ceased to exist from 1924 to 1933; Machen was forced to withdraw from the Union in 1926, Cwmbran closed in 1927, the run-down of the local iron works between 1924 and 1926 led to the collapse of Tredegar RFC; that year too Ebbw Vale came within a hair's breadth of enforced closure when the cessation of steel-making threw 10,000 out of work; Pontypool, with an overdraft of £2,000 similarly hovered on the edge of bankruptcy (Williams, 1983).

For it is the western valleys of Monmouthshire and the eastern valleys of Glamorgan, highly dependent on iron and coal, that bore the brunt of the Depression. By the early 1930s unemployment rates in the valleys of east Glamorgan ran to 76 per cent in Pontypridd, 73 per cent in Dowlais, 59 per cent in Merthyr and 43 per cent in the Rhondda. In Monmouthshire, the figures for 1934 were 74 per cent of the insured male workforce in Brynmawr, 80 per cent in Abertillery and 72 per cent in Blaina. These areas were rich pickings for the Rugby League: in November 1936 Brynmawr lost to Wigan the 17-year-old Roy Francis, sensationally good as a three-quarter and later as coach; internationals Jack Gore in 1925 and Emlyn Watkins in 1926, both colliers, went from Blaina to Salford and Leeds respectively; in 1931 Welsh international forward and former miner Trevor Thomas left Abertillery for Oldham.

It is from Monmouthshire, particularly, that there was a haemorrhage of players going north that could not be staunched. In 1921 the whole Pontypool pack went north. Of the seven internationals who joined the RL that year, four were from Monmouthshire (Wilf Hodder and George Oliver of Pontypool, Archie Brown and Jerry Shea of Newport). Nor should we overlook the submerged mass of the iceberg, those uncapped players who often went on to greater northern fame than their more illustrious international contemporaries, like Fred Roffey (to Wigan from Pontypool), or the massive contribution of the small second-class Gwent valley club of Talywain whence migrated stars like Percy Coldrick (via Newport to Wigan in 1912) and Danny Hurcombe (to Wigan in 1919), to be followed in the next two decades by Hodder and Oliver, Tommy Flynn, George and Stan Lewis, Stan Donovan, Billy Rhodes, Alf Higgs, Tommy James, George Baynham, Andrew Hurcombe, Billy Targett, Wilf Sulway, Tom 'Wild Man' Davies, J. Thomas, W. Price and S. Price (Salter, 1973).

While 1927 may not be altogether typical, with the industrial areas still feeling the crippling effects of the prolonged coal stoppage, the internationals who went north that year included George Andrews, a 23-year-old ship's painter who joined Leeds from Newport for £600; Dai Jones, who went from Newport to Wigan for £300 (his clubmate, Ernie Dowdall, uncapped but a half-back, joined him for £500); W.A. (Billy) Williams, a collier, went from Crumlin to Salford for £250, while Dan Pascoe, another miner, had a couple of international caps but no job, and went to Leeds for £600.

An international player could command a lump sum of anything from £250 upwards, on top of which there were match payments of £3 for a win, £2 for a draw, and £1 15s (£1.75) for a defeat; cup-ties might be worth £7-8, semi-finals £10 and a cup finalist might be rewarded with £15. These were considerable inducements for playing rugby when the average weekly wage of a South Wales collier was £2 3s 9d (less than £2.20) in 1930; when unemployment benefit for a single man, before 1931, was 17s (85p), and even less afterwards; and when nearly 80 per cent of main breadwinners in South Wales, according to one estimate of 1934, were earning less than £4 per week.

In these circumstances an immediate cash sum of £200 could be the equivalent of a year's wages; to a collier on £1 15s (£1.75p) a week a down payment of even £50 was a lifeline. It is surely understandable that Joe Thompson, after winning the international cup that enhanced his value in 1923, could later that year be lured from Cross Keys to Leeds for £300. A collier from the age of 13, he was promptly found employment by Leeds Corporation Tramways and went on to enjoy a famous career as an outstanding forward and prolific goal-kicker. Then there was Idris Towill, an uncapped apprentice electrician from

Bridgend, who went to Huddersfield for £500 in 1931. As well as match bonuses of £4 10s for a win, £3 10s a draw, and £2 10s for a defeat, he was found a job as a meter reader. Neath's Arthur Lemon, with 13 caps to his name, went north in 1933 to practise the two skills he knew best, playing rugby (professionally for St Helens) and plying his trade as a carpenter (in the job found for him at Greenall's Brewery).

The financial attractions of going north were enhanced by such job opportunities. Many RL club directors, like Sir Edwin Airey in Leeds, were prominent local businessmen, and several clubs had links with local councils. Salford director Lance Todd found a job for Gus Risman as clerk with a local firm, then at Shell-Mex in Manchester. Risman was perhaps the greatest bargain RL ever made when the 17-year-old Cardiff youngster was signed by the Central Park club in 1929 from under the noses of Cardiff RFC and Spurs for a mere £77 plus match fees (Risman, 1958). Versatile, athletic, cunning, brilliant and unemployed, he went on to enjoy a prodigious 25-year career, the longest known in the game next to his fellow product of the Cardiff docklands, Jim Sullivan.

While it would be artificial to try to impose too rigid a pattern on this northward migration, certain common factors regularly assert themselves. Half-backs, for instance, were valued more highly than forwards, preferably in pairs. Though there have been many notable Welsh successes at forward in RL, from Jack Rhapps, the Rhondda collier who went from Penygraig in 1897 to become the 'Lion of Salford', to John Mantle from Newport to St Helen's in 1965, it is half-back pairings that have attracted the attention and the money: the legendary James brothers of Swansea at Broughton, Wigan's own Swansea duo of 'Dodger' Owens and Syd Jerram, Halifax's Pontypool pairing of Stuart Prosser and Bobbie Lloyd, Leeds' inter-war international partnership of Bill Bowen and Raymond 'Dickie' Ralph, Huddersfield's Eddie Williams and Gwyn Richards, Swinton's Billo Rees and Ivor Davies and, most gifted of all, Emlyn Jenkins, who in 1930 went uncapped from Treorchy to form a brilliant link with Billy Watkins of Cross Keys, for Salford and the Great Britain touring team (Gate, 1988). Again we are struck by the preponderance of Monmouthshire valley products in that list, from Crumlin, Risca and Pontypool, all within a stone's throw of Ebbw Vale and its long tradition of involvement with professional rugby, always in the forefront of attempts to launch RL initiatives in South Wales from 1907–12 through the inter-war period to the 1980s.

Yet to speak of the whole of Wales, even industrial South Wales, as an undifferentiated region uniformly affected by the Depression is too facile, for the anthracite valleys and ports of west Glamorgan and east Carmarthenshire were less severely blighted. In the summer of 1927, when unemployment stood at 40 per cent in Ferndale in the Rhondda, it was 10 per cent in Ammanford in the anthracite; 1934, when east Glamorgan had 46 per cent of its adult males unemployed, was the peak production year in the western coalfield. This contrast had implications across a wide spectrum, from the literary, musical and artistic vitality of the inter-war Swansea of Dylan Thomas and Vernon Watkins, the composer Daniel Jones, and the painters Mervyn Levy and Alfred James, to sporting success. When in September 1935 the Swansea 'All Whites' beat the New Zealand All Blacks, and provided the nucleus for Wales to do the same three months later, unemployment was at a modest 13.8 per cent in the Amman Valley but 51 per cent in Merthyr. Unquestionably, the most striking example of a club that successfully resisted the siren song of the Rugby League was Llanelli. After losing a clutch of stars in the immediate postwar period (Ike Fowler and Bryn Williams to Batley in 1919 and 1920, and Frank Evans to Swinton and Edgar Morgan to Hull in 1921, all internationals), Llanelli withstood further depredations and retained its brightest and best to become the most successful side in Wales in the 1920s. That manual workers like Albert Jenkins and Dai John were able to resist offers in excess of £500 says something for the imaginative strategies devised by the Llanelli club to retain them, strategies made possible by a club whose prosperity in turn reflected the economic wellbeing of tinplate, anthracite and west Wales overall, relative to stricken east Wales (William, 1983; Smith and Williams, 1980; Hughes, 1986).

If Llanelli's 'Scarlets' were the dominant club in Welsh rugby in the 1920s, their equivalent in the northern professional game was Wigan, which brings us to another feature of the Welsh migration: the preponderance of Welsh players in some clubs as opposed to others. Without doubt what helped Central Park's 'Red Devils' acquire the mantle of glamour club worn pre-1914 by Harold Wagstaff's Huddersfield (though without quite attaining the Fartown club's prewar dominance) was the liberal sprinkling of Welshmen in its ranks (Gate, 1988). The list of Wigan's recruits would have to be headed by Jim Sullivan and the speedy Johnny Ring who joined in 1922 from Aberavon for the then record fee of £800, and of the side that won the Lancashire cup final in 1922 only two had not been recruited from South Wales. What gave Wigan its 'particular mania' for raiding the Welsh market was its readiness to find positions for many of the new arrivals as ground staff and pay a small wage for odd jobs like boot repairing on top of match payments. Leeds, Salford and Huddersfield were the other big clubs with a pronounced Welsh flavour: Leeds attracted more Welsh international players (17 in the inter-war period) than any other, though Huddersfield was also a virtual Welsh home from home during the 1930s and other clubs had periodic Cymric concentrations – Halifax, for instance, had 11 Welshmen playing for them in 1931/32. At the same time, there were clubs that seem not to have attracted any Welshmen at all; traditionally homespun clubs like Castleford and Featherstone, for instance, whose preference for home-grown talent in the inter-war years was reinforced by financial necessity, for these were coal-mining areas experiencing much the same problems of structural unemployment and social distress as their counterparts in South Wales.

This brings into focus the second half of the equation, the destinations as well as the points of departure of these rugby-playing exiles, for they were not leaving for Slough, Dagenham, Croydon or Coventry. Of the 1.7 million registered unemployed in July 1931, the north of England accounted for 0.75 million of them. The north of England, like South Wales, was a low-income area where high levels of unemployment were afflicting the ailing giants of coal, iron and steel, with cotton an added casualty. Wales' unemployment figures may have been consistently worse than all other regions in these years, but the next worst were invariably the north of England's.

The incidence of Rugby League is such that its main centres are in south Lancashire and west Yorkshire. In prewar Lancashire the largest employers were cotton, the textile finishing trades, coal and engineering, and the number of jobs available in these groups fell by about 200,000 between 1923 and 1937. The heyday of industrial Lancashire, as of industrial South Wales, spanned the years between the mid-nineteenth century and the First World War, on the eve of which the county's worldwide supremacy in cotton remained intact. Postwar, it suffered from antiquated technology, outdated organization and stiff foreign competition. Cotton's travails had a knock-on effect on engineering as the replacement rate of old machinery slowed and fell. Coal, too, declined in Lancashire in the inter-war period, the 110,000 miners of 1922 falling to 70,000 in 1937, and low wages brought undoubted poverty to those pit villages around Wigan that George Orwell visited in the 1930s.

Lancashire cotton, moreover, is no more an economic monolith than South Wales coalmining. The division here is north–south, between weaving and spinning. The main weaving areas – Blackburn, Burnley, Rossendale, Nelson and Colne – are soccer areas. Further south are the spinning districts in rugby league country, a belt running west from Salford through to Leigh, Warrington, Widnes, and north to St Helens and Wigan. The Depression was more severe in the weaving districts which suffered more in terms of population loss; but they still did not qualify for special area status, a matter of controversy at the time. We ought not to underestimate the poverty, insecurity and suffering among the working population in the old weaving towns and industrial villages of the north and north-east of the county, nor minimize the distress further south in concentrated pockets like Oldham and Wigan. Other industries, like shipbuilding, also had problems, but these were largely offset by substantial increases in the service industries, building, road transport and chemical engineering, so that the number of insured workers, and insured workers in employment in Lancashire, actually increased by 10 per cent between 1927 and 1937 (Fogarty, 1945; Kirby, 1974; Walton, 1987).

This is the crucial difference from the Welsh situation. Though a low-wage county – the average male cotton worker earned £2 7s 9d (£2.38) a week in 1935 – Lancashire was better able to attract new industries than was South Wales. It may well be that the most rapid growth in new industries took place outside the districts that needed them, but Lancashire was able to exploit certain advantages absent in South Wales: a ready supply of labour accustomed to factory life, a large local market, a good communications network, and commercial facilities; even disused textile factories could be converted without too much difficulty to new industrial purposes, say boot- and shoe-making. The Depression brought intense poverty to traditional single-industry communities, but while unemployment in Wigan was 27 per cent in the mid-1930s, there was some relief in the form of industrial development in nearby Leigh; and since most of the county's coal output was consumed locally, even coal was not as dependent on those export markets whose loss South Wales felt so hard.

In Lancashire, there was little to compare with the sustained mass unemployment of South Wales, or for that matter the north-east of England, because losses in the traditional industries were offset by new developments. If heavy chemicals felt the strain in St Helens and Widnes (home of the 'Chemics') there was compensation in the rise of glass manufacture at Pilkington Brothers. One-third of St Helens' workforce was employed there in the 1930s as demand increased from the building, motor and electrical industries: there was even a Pilkington's works professional RL side, the St Helens' Recs; in this period Warrington and the surrounding area was relatively prosperous too, thanks to economic diversity in the form of soap, textiles, brewing and metalworking (Fogarty, 1945). The decline in heavy engineering around Manchester and Salford – 'perhaps the largest urban centre in Britain never to produce a professional soccer team' (Russell, 1988: 189) – was offset by the growth of electrical engineering and a wide variety of industrial concerns, from manufacturing to service industries, so that the insured population in Greater Manchester, with unemployment constantly below the national level and little affected by the trade cycle, rose faster than that of Lancashire as a whole. Lancashire's experience of the inter-war years is by no mean all dole queues, hunger marches and the means test.

If we cross the Pennines to Yorkshire we find a comparable but different pattern of regional variation, economic diversity and sporting preference. Here south Yorkshire, where coal and steel dominate, was and is predominantly a soccer stronghold: Rotherham, Doncaster, Barnsley and especially Sheffield (Fogarty, 1945). Unemployment was markedly higher here than in the rugby league-playing West Riding, where Castleford and Featherstone, closer in character to south Yorkshire's pit villages, were exceptions to west Yorkshire's general ability to attract Welshmen to the 13-a-side game.[2]

Otherwise the West Riding was not much worse off than the national average. Here again we find textiles, but not cotton so much as wool, Leeds, Batley and Dewsbury specializing in woollens, and Bradford, Keighley and Halifax in worsteds, with a scattering of engineering as well. In Leeds, Halifax and Huddersfield, unemployment was consistently below the national level. Leeds gained from industrial diversification ranging from tailoring to engineering and miscellaneous smaller industries; Bradford benefited from increased employment in electrical engineering and rayon; while a thriving machine-tool industry made Halifax a prosperous community amidst the surrounding woollen towns.

Generally speaking, therefore, the situation in the rugby league-playing areas of Lancashire and Yorkshire was far from being all gloom and doom, and there is clear evidence of a climb out of depression by the end of the 1930s. There is little such relief in South Wales, however. In the South Wales special area in July 1938 the unemployment rate was still 25 per cent, over a quarter of whom had been unemployed for at least three years. There was still no brake on the drift of players north, either. The six internationals who turned professional in 1939 – including Arthur Bassett to Halifax for a record £900 and W.T.H. (Willie) Davies to Bradford Northern – establish that year as one of the worst for inter-war defections, comparable to 1921 (seven international losses), 1924, 1926 and 1931 (five each) and

1934 (six), and brings to 68 the total of Welsh capped players who went north in the years 1919–39.[3]

⌐In the 45 years following the Second World War, 56 international players took the road to Wigan Pier, a lower figure than in the inter-war years in a period more than twice as long⌐ RL would continue to make the occasional headline-making signing like Lewis Jones to Leeds for £6,000 in 1952, David Watkins to Salford for £16,000 in 1967, and Clive Griffiths to St Helens in 1979 for £27,000, and there was still a persistent migration of uncapped players who went north for far less than the established golden boys but who proved worth their weight in gold for all that, like Billy Boston (Wigan), Tommy Harris (Hull), Dickie Williams (Hunslet), Ray Price (Warrington) and Clive Sullivan (Hull).

Nevertheless, until recently it has been a slow drain rather than the haemorrhage of the 1920s and 1930s – a reflection of the better health of the Welsh economy to which the postwar boom restored optimism, capital investment and employment. The long-delayed diversification of Welsh industry and new investment, especially in steel at Ebbw Vale and Aberavon (hence the supremacy of those clubs in the 1950s and early 1960s) enabled rugby union in Wales to retain most of its players. In the 1960s and 1970s, increased social and geographical mobility and a new affluence that generated new aspirations and made possible the breaking of political and cultural moulds, proved the catalysts which made possible Welsh supremacy during the so-called 'second golden era' of the 1970s, when a galaxy of extraordinarily gifted players were able to etch their names on the public conscious-ness far beyond the confines of Wales itself (Smith and Williams, 1980). Significantly, hardly half a dozen Welsh internationals went north in the 1970s. Of the 56 who have taken that route since 1945, it is equally striking that 18 have done so since 1980. This reversion to the pattern established in the 1920s and 1930s is in evidence less in the expensive 'star' signings – like the figures in excess of £100,000 paid for David Bishop (Pontypool to Hull KR) and Adrian Hadley (Cardiff to Salford) in 1988, Jonathan Davies (Llanelli to Widnes) and John Devereux (Bridgend to Widnes) in 1989 and David Young (Cardiff to Leeds) in 1990 – than in the strong supporting cast of highly accomplished non-international players like Mike Carrington (Neath to St Helens for £60,000 in 1988), Gerald Cordle (Cardiff to Bradford Northern for £80,000 in 1989) and Kevin Ellis (Bridgend to War-rington for £100,000 in 1990).

How may we account for this renewed migration on a scale so reminiscent of the inter-war years? A cluster of particular and personal reasons can fairly readily be adduced: ⌐the hard-luck stories of those like Bishop who incurred the disciplinary attentions of the WRU (not to mention the law), or of the disillusioned victims of selectorial whim and arbitrariness⌐At a deeper level, however, for all the self-serving propaganda of government ministers and the overblown rhetoric of the Welsh Office's 'valleys initiative', the 1980s have seen the massive deindustrialization of the Welsh economy. Consider some of the features of this last decade of allegedly unprecedented prosperity in the history of Wales:

- the remorseless decline of coal mining which has left Wales with fewer than 1,000 men in the three remaining pits – in 1981 there were 27,000 at work in 36 pits;
- in steel, the current workforce of 25,000 is a third of its 1979 level, and 20,000 job losses are forecast;
- tinplate, after reorganization and job-shedding, is at a third of its 1979 employment level;
- manufacturing output has fallen by 25 per cent in the same period;
- unemployment has risen dramatically since 1979. In 1978 the Welsh jobless figure stood at 75,000, around 6 per cent of the working population. By January 1982 the figure was 176,000 or 16.2 per cent – the highest level since September 1938 when it reached 185,000 or 17.4 per cent and it was still over 175,000 in June 1986 (George and Mainwaring, 1987; 1988; Thomas, 1991).

In brief, despite the diversification that took place in the 1950s and 1960s, the Welsh economy has still been heavily dependent on its traditional industries of coal and steel. The decline in these has been a major blow, for combined job losses in these sectors amount to more than 70,000 or over half the growth of post-1960s unemployment. Once again, as in the inter-war period, new manufacturing industry has failed to fill the jobs vacuum. The decline of an old industry like mining in the Aberdare area, which had a recorded unemployment rate of 20 per cent in 1986, is accentuated as before by factors such as inaccessibility, an inadequate social infrastructure and an unattractive urban environment which discourages new investment. It is a grim reminder of an earlier period that Wales still lags behind the other regions of Britain in several key indicators including weekly household income, average gross weekly earnings and annual average employment rates. Out-migration is once again the response of those of working age who have the means and the inclination to move.[4]

It was actually 'the road from Mandalay to Wigan' that Orwell described as 'a long one, and the reasons for taking it . . . not immediately clear'. From Mandalay maybe not, but for the Welsh rugby union player from Merthyr, Mountain Ash or Maesteg, the road is shorter, and the reasons for taking it in the 1980s and 1990s little different from what they were in the 1920s and 1930s, when the road to Wigan Pier was indeed well-traversed.

NOTES

1 Figures derived from information generously put at my disposal by Robert Gate, whom the Rugby League have had the good sense to appoint as their official historian and archivist. Others whose help I am pleased to acknowledge in gathering material for this chapter are Timothy Auty, John Jenkins, Tony Lewis and Dennis Thomas.

2 It is as well to bear in mind that amateur rugby league greatly exceeds the professional version in both numerical strength and geographical extent; their boundaries have never been coterminous.

3 Two Welsh international players turned professional in this period without actually 'going north': James Brown (Cardiff) to the short-lived Pontypridd RL club in 1926, and Con Murphy (Cross Keys) to Acton and Willesden RLFC in 1935.

4 The deindustrialization of the Welsh economy in the 1980s is only one among an array of factors, ranging from educational change to structural weaknesses in the administration of the game in Wales, which account for the plummeting rugby fortunes that reached their nadir when the national side made a humiliating first-round exit from the 1991 Rugby World Cup. While it would be simplistic to attribute this failure solely to northern defections, it was nicely symbolic that, in the very month when the World Cup tournament was in progress, a Wales RL side played, and beat 68–0, Papua New Guinea at Swansea (27 October 1991). The Welsh squad included 12 former RU internationals who had only recently 'gone north'.

REFERENCES

Constantine, S. (1983) *Social Conditions in Britain 1918–1939* (London: Methuen).

Fogarty, M.P. (1945) *Prospects of the Industrial Areas of Great Britain* (London: Methuen).

Gate, R. (1986, 1988) *Gone North: Welshmen in the Rugby League*, 2 Vols (Sowerby Bridge: Gate).

George, K.D. and Mainwaring, L. (1987) 'The Welsh Economy in the 1980s' in Day, G. and Rees, T. (eds), *Contemporary Wales: An Annual Review of Economic and Social Research*, Vol. I (Cardiff: University of Wales Press), pp. 7–37.

(1988) (eds) *The Welsh Economy* (Cardiff: University of Wales Press).

Hopkin, D. (1988) 'Social Reactions to Economic Change' in Herbert, T. and Jones, G.E. (eds), *Wales Between the Wars* (Cardiff: University of Wales Press), pp. 53–83.

HMSO (1932) *An Industrial Survey of South Wales* (London: Board of Trade).

Hughes, G. (1986) *The Scarlets* (Llanelli: Llanelli RFC).

Kirby, M.W. (1974) 'The Lancashire Cotton Industry in the Inter-War Years: A Study in Organisational Change', *Business History*, 16, 145–55.

Morgan, K.O. (1981) *Rebirth of a Nation: Wales 1880–1980* (Oxford: Oxford University Press and Cardiff: University of Wales Press).

NIDC (National Industrial Development Council of Wales and Monmouthshire) (1937) *The Second Industrial Survey of South Wales* (Cardiff: University Press Board).

Orwell, G. (1962) (ed.) [1937] *The Road to Wigan Pier* (Harmondsworth: Penguin).

Pollard, S. (1962) *The Development of the British Economy 1914–50* (London: Arnold).

Richardson, H.W. (1967) *Economic Recovery in Britain 1932–39* (London: Weidenfeld & Nicolson).

Risman, G. (1958) *Rugby Renegade* (London: Stanley Paul).

Russell, D. (1988) 'Sporadic and Curious: The Emergence of Rugby and Soccer Zones in Yorkshire and Lancashire c. 1860–1914', *International Journal of the History of Sport*, 5,2, 185–205.

Salter, J. (1973) *Talywain RFC 75th Anniversary Brochure: Talywain v. Monmouthshire 4 September* (Talywain: Talywain RFC).

Smith, D. (1990) 'Focal Heroes: A Welsh Fighting Class' in Holt, R. (ed.), *Sport and the Working Class in Modern Britain* (Manchester: Manchester University Press), pp. 198–217.

Smith, D. and Williams, G. (1980) *Fields of Praise: The Official History of the Welsh Rugby Union 1881–1981* (Cardiff: University of Wales Press).

Stevenson, J. and Cook, C. (1977) *The Slump* (London: Cape).

Thomas, D. (1988) 'Economic Decline', in Herbert, T. and Jones, G.E. (eds), *Wales Between the Wars* (Cardiff: University of Wales Press), pp. 13–46.

——— (1991) 'The Welsh Economy: Current Circumstances and Future Prospects' in Day, G. and Rees, G. (eds), *Regions, Nations and European Integration: Remaking the Celtic Periphery* (Cardiff: University of Wales Press). pp. 39–59.

Walton, J.K. (1987) *Lancashire: A Social History 1558–1939* (Manchester: Manchester University Press).

Williams, G. (1983) 'From Grand Slam to Great Slump: Economy, Society and Rugby Football in Wales during the Depression', *Welsh History Review*, 11, 339–57 (reprinted in Williams, G. (1991) *1905 And All That: Essays on Rugby Football, Sport and Welsh Society* (Llandysul: Gomer Press), pp. 175–200).

3

The Bogotá Affair

Tony Mason

To most football people in Britain the phrase 'Bogotá affair' has a very clear meaning. In 1970, en route with the England team for the Mexico World Cup, Bobby Moore, captain of the side, was arrested on suspicion of stealing a bracelet from a local jeweller's shop. He spent a few very uncomfortable days in a local jail before the evidence against him was proved to be feeble. But 20 years earlier, in 1950, Bogotá was the location for another football sensation when seven British players, including Neil Franklin, the centre-half who had played for the English national side in their last 38 matches, broke the contracts they had with British clubs and in an atmosphere of excitement and intrigue went to Bogotá in Colombia to ply their trade. Many more players allegedly expressed an interest in going and were thought to be watching carefully to see how the seven pioneers got on. For a brief moment, in the summer of 1950, the core of the British game appeared to be threatened.

The professional footballers who went to Bogotá were part of a long tradition of mainly skilled workers taking their trade overseas in the hope of better prospects and better pay. Artisans not only tramped around the nineteenth- and early twentieth-century United Kingdom looking for work but crossed the seas both west and east to the Americas and Europe. Professional footballers were no exception. Before the war of 1914–18 they had journeyed to a variety of destinations as players and coaches. After that war, the United States proved an attraction for several prominent Scottish footballers. There were also small colonies of British referees in a number of South American countries, including a group of five in Colombia, in the early years of peace after 1945. So the syndrome of 'have boots will travel' was not new in 1950. But why should this new 'ripple' have begun then, and why should Colombia have been the improbable destination?

There is no doubt that the main reason for going was money. A good proportion of British professional footballers felt an acute sense of grievance in the years immediately following 1945. These were boom years for many commercial leisure activities including sport and particularly football. There had never been such crowds. Yet the pay of the players did not reflect the money coming in at the gate. A maximum wage was in operation as well as a highly restrictive retain-and-transfer system. It is true that the maximum wage had been increased to £12 a week in the season and £10 in the summer, but many of the players were not paid the maximum and many of those who were felt that it was not enough (Fishwick, 1989). The top players increasingly thought of themselves as part of the entertainment industry and could only be disappointed by the large gap which existed between the salaries earned by the stars of the stage, screen and radio and the pay and conditions of football players. Moreover, they felt that they were treated like workmen rather than the professionals they increasingly thought of themselves as being. Neil Franklin was not only upset when his request for a transfer from Stoke City was turned down: he also felt humiliated at being kept waiting for three hours while the club's board of directors discussed the matter. They then refused to see him (*Sunday Empire News*, 28 May 1950).

It is difficult to discover how much was on offer to those players prepared to go west and south but Franklin claimed at the time, in June 1950, that £1,500 had been paid into his bank account in dollars on signing for Santa Fé of Bogotá – in England the signing-on fee was £10 – and that he was then paid £150 per month with bonuses of £7 for a win and £5 for a draw. And all this for only 28 matches instead of the 42 plus he would have had to play at home. And each time he signed another one-year contract he would be paid a further £1,500. Charlie Mitten, another member of the mercenary seven, claimed to have cleared £3,500 in his year with Santa Fé, as against the £600–800 he might have earned with his club, Manchester United, over the same period. His salary was £5,000 a year with a bonus of £25 for a win and £8 for a draw and he claimed this meant that he was making more money than in all his previous 14 years as a professional which had included a benefit of £750 less tax. Half his salary had been paid into his English bank in dollars and the rest paid to him in local currency. Franklin told a reporter at the time that in a reasonably successful season a player could live on bonuses and perks without touching his salary. And if a player was playing well he could go to the board of directors and have his contract revised. It must have sounded too good to be true to the hard-bitten British professionals reading their *Sunday Empire News* and *Sunday Despatch* (*Sunday Empire News*, 4 June 1950, *Manchester Evening Chronicle*, 29 June 1950).

Why Colombia? Even by the standards of the adventurous minority of British workers who had travelled abroad in search of work and excitement, Colombia was a particularly exotic destination (Romoli, 1941). It was an adventure in itself just to get there. Franklin flew from London on a Sunday and went via Shannon, Goose Bay, New York – an overnight stop – Miami, Havana, Kingston, and Barranquilla before finally touching down in Bogotá on the Tuesday. Colombia certainly fitted the parochial description of a far-away country of which most British people – and almost all footballers – knew nothing (Franklin, 1956). At least the *Daily Mail* helpfully published a small map pinpointing it and informed its readers that it was a former Spanish colony bordering the Caribbean and the Pacific, five times the size of Great Britain but with only one-fifth of the population (*Daily Mail*, 19 June 1950). What appeared to concern no one in this country was that in 1950 Colombia had entered its second year of civil war – admittedly mainly by then fought in the countryside – as a crypto-fascist dictator, Laureano Gomez, who called liberals 'communists', seized power and attempted to crush by force all opposition (Fluharty, 1957). Franklin did write in his autobiography, however, that never a day passed without some form of political demonstration: 'and when the Colombians demonstrate they really demonstrate . . . so electric was the political atmosphere that during the time we were there a curfew was in force' (Franklin, 1956: 101). There are hints of the dictatorship trying to exploit footballers' popularity with the urban masses, for example, by paying for the staging of an extra 'derby' game between Santa Fé and Millionarios for which admission was free (*Manchester Evening Chronicle*, 15 August 1950).

Because I have been unable to look at any Spanish sources, it is not clear to me how far Colombian football was affected by the political situation. But the reasons why some Colombian clubs were able to induce foreign players to break contracts and come to play there was that they were not members of FIFA, the world governing body of football. The Colombian Football Association *was* affiliated to FIFA but was in dispute with the Division Mayor del Futbol professional de Bogotá (the Colombian league), which was *not*. It was clearly a struggle, of sorts, for control of the Colombian game. Both Santa Fé and the other leading Bogotá club, Millionarios, took advantage of the situation to sign foreign players without having to pay transfer fees to their previous clubs. Argentina provided most of the recruits including the famous Alfredo di Stefano who helped make Millionarios one of the best club sides in the world in the early 1950s (see *Miroir du*

Football, 19 June 1961), and who later won fame and fortune in Europe with Real Madrid. But most Latin American countries were scoured for players and so was Europe. It was in November 1949 that Neil Franklin received a letter from the chairman of Santa Fé, Luis Robledo, a wealthy Cambridge-educated, English-speaking rancher, setting out the enticing prospects for those prepared to take a chance. As we have seen, Franklin was unhappy at Stoke, approaching 30 and the twilight of his career, and felt that here was a real opportunity to assure his financial future which could not, after careful consideration, be turned down. It seems certain that he talked to another Stoke player, George Mountford, and persuaded him to go along as well, no doubt providing Santa Fé with a good reference. The two families began that adventurous flight on Sunday 7 May 1950.

Perhaps a brief summary of the Franklin case will be in order here before looking in more detail at the problems identified by the British players who went to Colombia and how they coped, or failed to cope, with them. The retain-and-transfer system meant that British players were not free agents even if they had failed to agree terms with their clubs. This meant that Franklin and Mountford had to keep secret the fact that they had signed contracts to play for Santa Fé. They told Stoke City that they were going to coach. The club had agreed to that but the players also had to obtain permission from the Football Association. Neither had done this. The main reason for this omission had been that Franklin had told the Football Association earlier that he did not wish to be considered for either the coming England matches in Lisbon and Brussels, or the approaching World Cup in Brazil. His wife was expecting their second child and Franklin had told the FA that he did not wish to be separated from her during this stressful time. It was unthinkable for wives to accompany footballers on international tours (Franklin, 1956), but she could and did go to Colombia. Franklin had been assured that medical facilities were available in Bogotá and the anxieties of the parents that a child born in Colombia would not be British seemed to have been overcome.

In fact, Mrs Franklin obviously felt that she would prefer the baby to be born in England and to be with her own family and friends during this time. She decided to go home, and after two months and six matches for Santa Fé, the club gave Franklin permission to fly with her as far as New York. He claimed in his autobiography, written six years later, that he always intended to return to Bogotá to honour his contract, but that on arriving in New York hotel bookings and flight reservations promised by the club had not been made and, in a fit of last-straw impulsiveness, he flew on to London with his wife (Franklin,

1956). He still intended to return, but on learning of the furore his action had caused back in Bogotá he decided, in the words of his ghost writer, that he would rather be unpopular in England than in Colombia and never went back (Franklin, 1956: 94).

Of course it *was* a great step to leave family, friends, one's own country and a familiar way of life and embark on a life which was very different. Most British professionals were young, ill-educated, with little experience of the world. Adapting to a new way of life was going to be hard, and it is notable that even Charlie Mitten and George Mountford, both of whom stayed for a year in Bogotá, do not seem to have made many friends among the local people, although Mitten speaks warmly of one of the Argentinian players in the Santa Fé team, Hector Real.

Wives were likely to be particularly vulnerable to loneliness and we have already seen the important role which Mrs Franklin (who does not seem to have liked Bogotá much) had in her husband's actions. All the more important to discuss the matter beforehand, it would seem; yet Mrs Mitten had first heard about her husband signing for Santa Fé from the newspapers – he was on tour with Manchester United in the United States – and was quoted as saying she couldn't believe it: 'I'll still maintain he won't sign without first coming home and discussing it with me. I'm still going ahead with plans for a holiday at Scarborough in two weeks' time' (*Manchester Evening News*, 24 June 1950).

Roy Paul went to Colombia without even telling his wife. The *Daily Mail* reporter quoted her as saying it was deliberate because ' "they" know I don't like the idea of Bogotá. I'll certainly join Roy when he sends for me . . . but I know I won't like it. Gelli [in the Rhondda] is good enough for me. I don't think Roy is wise in going. What's going to happen to him in a couple of years?' (*Daily Mail*, 12 June 1950). Fortunately Paul was back home in ten days. There was some doubt as to whether Millionarios would pay for the trip but Beryl Paul said: 'At the worst he could work his passage on a cargo ship. He's big and strong and it will do him good'. His mother-in-law added: 'And I hope they make him scrub the deck from end to end. That will teach him to fly off to the other side of the world without saying a word' (*Daily Mail*, 17 June 1950). John Kelly (Barnsley) was also prepared to go without telling his wife but literally missed the bus and never made the trip. Charlie Mitten's wife, however, liked Colombia and stayed for six months. She had no regrets at having tried life in Bogotá. A Manchester paper quoted her as saying that it had been a 'wonderful experience. We had everything we wanted – a lovely villa, two maids and a gardener. There were no shopping worries, in fact the conditions for English people in Bogotá were perfect' (*Manchester Evening News*, 28 March 1951).

Roy Paul, on the other hand, thought Bogotá lousy, the food was dreadful and so was the drink (*Daily Mail*, 19 June 1950; Paul, 1956). Franklin echoed the unease about the food which occasional outbreaks of 'Bogotá belly' can only have reinforced. 'It took us a couple of weeks to teach them how to cook bacon and eggs' (Franklin, 1956: 100). As against this, though, Mitten wrote how he and Mountford had been invited to a country house and put through what sounds like a food endurance test – soup, fish, chicken, steaks, rice, fried bananas, fruits and coffee. He also noted that unlike in Britain, where wartime austerity measures were still in force, in Bogotá there was rationing of neither milk nor eggs (*Manchester Evening Chronicle* 15 August 1950). In his autobiography, Franklin complained about the high cost of living. He was well paid, but prices four times as high as in the United Kingdom soon eroded the extra money. Mrs Mitten disagreed: the additional income more than compensated for the higher prices; her husband later claimed he had bought a Chevrolet for $2,000.

Of course none of the players spoke Spanish or, it seems, had any intention of learning it. As Franklin's biographer later wrote, not speaking the language of a country is all right if you are only on a short holiday, but to live there for any length of time without being able to speak to people or read the newspapers makes you feel an outcast. It was not surprising that when soup was asked for porridge was brought. The young children of the British players apparently had less inhibitions about learning Spanish, but interestingly Franklin, Mitten and Mountford all pointed to inadequate education as an obstacle to long-term residence in Bogotá. It is surprising that there was, apparently, no English/American school.

Of course the altitude was a problem. Bogotá is about 9,000 feet above sea level. One 'minor cultural object' who visited it in 1948, Christopher Isherwood, described what this could be like. It produced a lightening of the muscles around the heart, 'a vague irrational sense of anxiety, as if you had forgotten some important obligation. In the mornings I feel tense, restless and uneasy; in the afternoons lazy, exhausted and sad' (Isherwood, 1949: 46). But everyone usually adapted: Franklin and Mountford actually played their first match for Santa Fé against Medellin, on the Sunday following their arrival on the Tuesday. The British, of course, are obsessed by the weather and Bogotá can be wet. Weekend rain is so legendary that it is called *Lluvia de los Empleados* – 'the employers' day-off spoiling shower'. (*Sunday Empire News*, 11 June 1950). Franklin claims to have been told that the climate was spring-like all the year. When it rained throughout most of his stay he felt this was another example of Colombian perfidy. And then there were the distances between towns to get used to. These were much greater than in England and involved air trips to most away games.

Finally there was the problem of the job itself. The British found a different style of football being played in Colombia and different sorts of players playing it. Having no Spanish cannot have helped. There was some suggestion that the Argentinian players on the Santa Fé side resented the British and were reluctant to pass to them. In that first match against Medellin Mountford found himself being starved of the ball, but near the end threw himself forward at a speculative cross which happened to pass close by and scored the winning goal (*Staffordshire Evening Sentinel*, 23 January 1950; 25 June 1950). The supporters christened him Bald Arrow on the spot and forever after. Franklin claimed that the Argentinian players were jealous and lazy. They did not take training as seriously as the imports from Britain and were too individualistic. There was very little first-time passing or teamwork. In his autobiography Franklin wrote that Santa Fé and Millionarios were of only third-division standard but Charlie Mitten believed standards were much higher, although perhaps not as high as the best teams in division one in England. Everyone was impressed by the ball control of the South American players, though, and even Franklin felt that the training there was more advanced than in England with more variety and greater emphasis on practice with the ball. Mitten, who was already a qualified coach, reckoned he learned a lot about the game from his year in Bogotá (Franklin, 1956; *Manchester Evening Chronicle*, 29 June 1950; 19 July 1951).

One final issue of some interest is how this secret flight to footballing foreign parts was viewed by the great British public. When Franklin unexpectedly returned to Stoke in July 1950 opinion in the town seemed to be more or less equally divided between those who thought he had seriously blotted the English escutcheon and ought to be banned from playing again and those who did not blame him for wanting to better himself and felt that the sooner he was back in the Stoke defence the better. In his autobiography Franklin claimed that he and his wife received many abusive and anonymous letters about their failure to honour their Colombian contract. Unfortunately he did not give any examples. (Franklin, 1956; *Sporting Chronicle*, 8 June 1950).

On 16 May 1950 the *Daily Mail* devoted the whole of its front page comment column to the Franklins' tale. Their verdict was that no wonder a 'star' like Franklin had decided to seek his fortune elsewhere.

> It seems totally unfair that a man whose skill attracts thousands of paying customers to the gates should be so meagrely rewarded . . . What is he after all? He is a performer in no different category from the top-of-the-bill music hall artist who gets hundreds of pounds a week . . . It is not unethical for a businessman to 'better himself'. Nor would his firm expect a transfer fee.

Although they did not come right out and say so it was clear that they felt the maximum wage had to go. It was one of the few things on which the *Daily Mail* and the *Daily Worker* agreed.

But the men at the FA and the Football League who ran the game were not amused. To them it was a simple matter: the players who went to Bogotá had broken their contracts and in other respects brought the game into disrepute. All four players who had actually taken part in matches in Bogotá – Franklin, Mitten, Mountford and Higgins – were fined and suspended. Mitten received the longest suspension and was not reinstated as a registered professional until January 1952. The Joint FA/Football League Commission of Inquiry clearly thought his case was the worst both because he had broken two contracts and, it is clear, because he was the player who showed least regret at his excursion and was most outspoken about the financial benefits it had brought. The Commission agreed that Mountford's evidence had shown that the promises made by the Colombian negotiators for his services had not been fulfilled and 'that the conditions in Bogotá were in fact, very different from what he had been led to expect' (*FA Minutes and Proceedings*, October–November 1950, June–September 1951). This conclusion doubtless comforted the members of the Commission and helped mitigate Mountford's penalty but seems of doubtful veracity in both his and Mitten's cases.

In one of four articles published in his name during his stay in Bogotá Franklin had proclaimed 'I'll never come crawling home' (*Sunday Empire News*, 18 June 1950). But he did, and the commissioners were impressed by Franklin's statement that he had no intention of going back to Bogotá and by his expression of regret at the way he had behaved (*Daily Herald*, 3 October 1950). Perhaps it was because he came home so quickly that other players who might have been encouraged by his attractive accounts of life in Bogotá decided that discretion was called for. In his autobiography, published in 1956, Franklin concluded his account of the Bogotá adventure by calling it a 'ghastly mistake' and admitted that he had returned 'sadder but wiser'. In that account, he could hardly find anything positive to say about Bogotá and his experiences there. But that was not what he apparently told the man from the *Sunday Empire News* in May and June 1950. Far from Colombia not being as good as Stoke-on-Trent it was 'picturesque and Swiss like'. Far from all promises being broken 'the climate, the people, facilities, social status – everything is better than we expected . . . and in striking contrast to the shabby treatment at home'. Far from Bogotá not being like Rio 'we have not come to an uncivilised primitive, end-of-the-world spot in South America . . . Bogotá is not an ancient narrow streeted city of hovels. Neither is it true that there are no cinemas, or that martial law closed everything down after dusk'. Instead, he emphasized that he had had a lucky break, linking up with a good club run by a president 'educated at Cambridge and reared in the British way of sportsmanship'. But he also confessed that he was able to 'take the risk of disillusionment on this trip because I had a few thousand in the bank and was independent of football as a living'. This was also omitted from the autobiography. (The articles in the *Sunday Empire News* appeared on 28 May, 4, 11 and 18 June 1950).

British football, like the British people, thought it had done well in the war. British was still best. In 1950, the flight of a handful of professionals to an unknown South American destination and the World Cup defeats by the USA and Spain a few weeks later served notice to the complacent. But the Bogotá episode was significant in at least two other respects. It provided a cautionary tale for any other British players thinking of seeking their fortunes through a spell on a foreign football field. It also suggests that British players put up the strongest cultural resistance to life in a foreign land. This reluctance to adapt to a changed world may make it difficult for British star players to succeed abroad; and in 1992 it prompted the question: would Paul Gascoigne be any more impressed with Lazio and Rome than Roy Paul was with Millionarios and Bogotá?

ACKNOWLEDGEMENTS

I am grateful to Pierre Lanfranchi for the reference to the *Miroir du Football* and to Ian Ward for material from Ian Austers' interview with John Kelly.

REFERENCES

Fishwick, Nicholas (1989) *English Football and Society 1910–1950* (Manchester: Manchester University Press).

Fluharty, Vernon Lee (1957) *Dance of the Millions, Military Rule and the Social Revolution in Colombia 1930–1956* (Pittsburgh: University of Pittsburgh Press).

Franklin, Neil (1956) *Soccer at Home and Abroad* (London: Stanley Paul).

Isherwood, Christopher (1949) *The Condor and the Cows* (London: Methuen).

Paul, Roy (1956) *A Red Dragon of Wales* (London: Robert Hale).

Romoli, Kathleen (1941) *Colombia: Gateway to South America* (New York: Doubleday, Doran).

4

Cricket and the Imperial Connection: Overseas Players in Lancashire in the Inter-war Years

Jeffrey Hill

The global migration of sports talent in first-class cricket is now commonplace. Since the late 1960s England, with the world's most developed form of professional cricket, has become a magnet for star players from the world's major cricket-playing countries. With the exception until recently of Yorkshire all the English county clubs have felt it necessary to include one or more such stars in their teams (Sandiford, 1985). This process, however, has not been without its critics. The importation of overseas sports talent has frequently been held responsible for the apparent decline of English test teams in international competition, particularly in the 1980s (*Guardian*, 1986). Indeed, the problems of cricket have often become subsumed in the wider discourse of 'decline' that has been a characteristic feature of British national life in recent years. But what is often overlooked when such ideas are voiced is the fact that players from overseas – from various parts of the Commonwealth and, before that, the Empire – have long been a feature of the game in England. For example, a glance through the *Wisden Cricketers' Almanack* for the 1953 season reveals a total of 17 Commonwealth players employed by nine of the 17 county clubs, at least 10 of them occupying leading batting or bowling places (*Wisden*, 1954). Not, admittedly, as great a number as were to figure in more recent seasons but a significant proportion none the less.

This imperial connection in English cricket has a long, if not always very conspicuous, history. It started with the migratory activities of W.E. Midwinter, who played for both England and Australia in the 1870s and 1880s (Midwinter, 1981). It continued through W.I. Murdoch, A.E. Trott, Alan Marshall and E.A. McDonald – all Australians who exercised a powerful influence in county cricket before and just after the First World War. Following the Second World War the connection expanded to include such leading players as George Tribe, Colin McCool, Bruce Dooland and the West Indian Roy Marshall, as well as a range of less famous names. It reached its fullest extent in the period after the 'Packer revolution', when county clubs were seeking to maximize income from television coverage of cricket and were trusting in overseas players to provide the necessary star quality to ensure the game's appeal. By the late 1970s, it has been suggested, the game had become 'unashamedly commercialized' (Sandiford, 1985: 276).

But alongside this developing network in county cricket there was another, and in some ways more significant, imperial connection in the English game. Until the influx of the 1970s and 1980s the most concentrated presence of overseas players in English cricket was to be found, not in county cricket, but in the league cricket of the north, in particular that of Lancashire.

The role of league clubs in recruiting Empire and Commonwealth cricketers was probably first brought to the attention of a wide public in 1952. It was then that the Lancashire League club Nelson signed the Australian fast bowler Ray Lindwall, one of the best known players in world cricket at that time, to play for them for one season (Lindwall, 1954: 101–2). Far from being an isolated event, the signing of Lindwall was part of a continuing process that had started in the northern leagues back in the inter-war period. At that time there had developed a steady migration of star players, chiefly from Australia and the Caribbean. This process is an interesting one for its consequences were not limited to the field of play. The players themselves, their clubs, the type of cricket played in the leagues and the communities whose champions the overseas stars became, all were affected in a variety of ways by the migration.

In this part of the country cricket had become one of the major pastimes of the inhabitants of the industrial towns and villages by the end of the nineteenth century. Saturday afternoon leagues, staging competitive and partisan matches, were firmly installed in the cultural life of these communities. 'Cricket in this district', reported an Australian observer of Nelson in the early 1920s, 'is a live force.' (*Sydney Daily Telegraph*, 1921). In most places a hierarchy of skill had developed. In the lowest stratum was the rough-and-ready cricket of church, Sunday school or even street teams often playing on ill-prepared pitches, sometimes of concrete or cinders (Williams, 1990). At the highest level of the local cricketing world was the team which usually bore the community's name, and with that a good deal of the pride and hopes of the local population. At this level the ethos of professionalism was strong, no doubt as a consequence of the remarkable playing success of the professional clubs of the Football League, several of which were to be found in the north-west of England. Some cricket clubs in the late nineteenth century were employing as many as three 'pros' to assist with coaching, ground maintenance and, of course, playing (Hill, 1986). In 1900 the premier league in the region – the Lancashire League – agreed to restrict the number of professionals to one per club, chiefly in order to control the spread of professionalism and to encourage amateur talent (Barlow, 1922). By the time of the First World War it had become customary for the club professional in the Lancashire League sides to be a figure of some standing nationally in the cricket world, usually as a result of having played county cricket. Willis Cuttell, who played several seasons for Nelson, is a good example. Cuttell had served both Lancashire and Yorkshire with distinction and even played for England on a couple of occasions in the 1890s, but became disillusioned with county cricket following a disappointing benefit from Lancashire in 1906 (Cuttell, 1924).

Very occasionally overseas players would make an appearance in the leagues, though always through the same channel – county cricket. The South African C.B. Llewellyn played just before the war, and again in the 1920s, though he was in effect an English county professional by virtue of a dozen seasons with Hampshire from the turn of the century. Similarly the Australian bowler Alex Kermode played in the League after a spell with Lancashire (*Cricket*, 1913). But at this time the most celebrated, successful and notorious of all the professionals in league cricket, first in Lancashire and then in north Staffordshire, was undoubtedly the Englishman S.F. Barnes, most of whose 27 test match appearances occurred while he was engaged as a league professional (Duckworth, 1967).

This pattern changed in the Lancashire League in the 1920s with the gradual acquisition of an overseas cadre of professionals. The change was triggered by Nelson CC, who signed the Australian fast bowling star E.A. McDonald for the 1922 season (Hill, 1990). McDonald stayed at Nelson for three seasons, before becoming the subject of an early cricket 'transfer deal' between Nelson and the Lancashire county club. He was replaced by another Empire player, the South African J.M. Blanckenberg, an experienced international who, like McDonald, had recently appeared with success in test matches in England. But at this time few other clubs in the Lancashire League saw reason to depart from their traditional practice of hiring English players. Indeed, strong doubts about both the financial and sporting validity of Nelson's strategy were raised in the local and national press.

Apart from the immense financial costs involved in hiring overseas stars – McDonald cost Nelson almost twice the wages paid to their previous professionals (Nelson Cricket and Bowling Club, 1920–24) – one of the chief complaints registered against the practice was that it would denude the colonies of scarce sporting talent. League clubs were accused of exploiting the rest of the world as a nursery for the development of star players whilst at the same time preventing local players from maturing. Criticisms of this kind continued well into the 1930s, even though by this time the practice being objected to was very firmly entrenched (*Nelson Leader*, 1922; Brooking, 1921–22; Rice, 1934; Gregson, 1934). What, as much as anything, served to dispel many of these doubts and to gain more general acceptance for the idea of overseas players was the remarkable success of Nelson's third such professional – the Trinidadian Learie Constantine. Under Constantine's influence Nelson won the Lancashire League championship seven times and came second twice in the years from 1929 to 1937. It was largely in order to be in a position to compete on reasonably equal terms against this dynamic cricketer that other league clubs were drawn into a scramble to sign star players. With the contemporary English big names usually tied to the county and test circuit the attention of league committees was turned overseas. During the 1930s a clutch of Empire cricketers was drafted into the Lancashire League: from Australia Arthur Richardson, Bill Hunt, Alan Fairfax, Syd Hird and, after retiring from county cricket, Ted McDonald once more; from New Zealand Bill Merritt, who later played in the Birmingham League; from India Amar Singh and Lala Amarnath; and from the Caribbean Manny Martindale, George Headley, Ellis Achong, Edwin St Hill and Constantine himself. There continued to be a sprinkling of well-known English players: Fred Root, for example, who had recently retired from county cricket; Nobby Clarke, the Northants fast bowler, who played in the League in the early 1930s following a disagreement with his county, which he later rejoined; and the everlasting Barnes, who continued to play (and to be unplayable) until well into his fifties. But the chief subject of attention was the overseas star (*The Cricketer Spring Annual*, 1937:105).

Underlying the immediate need to compete with Nelson under Constantine there was a deeper reason for the scramble for overseas talent. Unlike club cricket in the south of England, that of the northern leagues had always possessed a strong spectator appeal. Although, of course, the length of a cricket match, and its susceptibility to bad weather, prevented its having football's potential as a mass spectacle, there were nevertheless several occasions on which league cricket matches drew large crowds. Given the passion for cricket in these small communities, there was an inbuilt incentive for clubs to provide an attractive game and to pursue the quest for cups, league titles and the all-conquering professionals who might make what was frequently termed 'big cricket' possible. Club treasurers usually found themselves in an upward financial spiral as they signed the players who would produce success and then sought to recoup their costs through increased gate and membership receipts.

All this is exemplified in Nelson's going after Ted McDonald in 1921. The club had become accustomed to success as one of the League's leading teams before the Great War, but had failed to reproduce this position in the seasons immediately after. Support from both club members and the general public was proving difficult to sustain, and the idea of persuading a leading personality to come and play for Nelson was a compelling one. The club's chairman, T.E. Morgan, freely admitted in an article written some years later that the current professional, George Geary of Leicestershire, was 'a most competent cricketer, but he did not attract the crowds' (Morgan, 1937). The signing of McDonald, who was one of the stars of the all-conquering Australian touring team of 1921, was astutely timed to achieve maximum publicity, and had an instantaneous effect. Membership subscriptions, particularly among women revived; so, subsequently, did gate receipts for both home and away matches (Brooking, 1922–23), McDonald's presence had a stimulating effect throughout the League, so that the Nelson secretary could report with a mixture of satisfaction and regret in 1925, when the player left for Old Trafford:

McDonald's departure is not only a loss to Nelson, but to the whole of the Lancashire League. Every club in the League has benefitted [sic] as a result of our enterprise in signing McDonald, and he brought new interest and enthusiasm into the League when there was a tendency for it to be weakening (Ashton, 1924).

In spite of all this, however, Nelson did not win the Lancashire League with McDonald, nor with his successor; which explains the club's determination to secure Constantine in 1929, a decision which was amply rewarded.

As for the professionals themselves, the attractions of employment in the leagues were strong. In no part of the Empire was professional cricket strongly established and it was impossible even for players of high repute to earn their living by cricket alone. Bradman himself needed a patron, which explains his move from New South Wales to South Australia in 1935. Whether or not he was tempted to accept a reportedly generous offer from Accrington in 1934 (Sissons, 1988: 238) is difficult to assess, but if even Bradman felt the lure of the Lancashire League it is hardly surprising that others succumbed. In Australia cricketers were technically amateurs and unless very famous were unlikely to make much money from the game. Players' attempts to secure a better deal had failed. As recently as 1912 the Board of Control in Australian cricket successfully rebuffed an attempt by leading players to control the profits from lucrative tours to England. Henceforward their touring fees were to be strictly regulated by the Board in the manner already well established for English touring teams (Sissons, 1988: 119–20). One of the factors prompting Mc-Donald to sign for Nelson was his inability to command regular earnings in Australia, and this was also the reason for Syd Hird's long association with Ramsbottom (and, in fact, his later migration to South Africa). As punishment for his decision to leave Australia, McDonald was subjected to a test-match ban by the Board of Control, although he had doubtless estimated that at the age of 30 his time as an Australian test player was in any event limited. As it worked out, McDonald probably made the correct decision in migrating to England. The move served to extend his playing career and enabled him to make business contacts which secured reasonably comfortable post-playing prospects as a publican in Blackpool, though a road accident brought about his untimely death in 1937 (*The Cricketer*, 1937).

For cricketers from the West Indies the attractions of league cricket were stronger still. Professional openings in the Caribbean were severely limited for black players, who suffered also the odious discriminations of the colour bar. West Indies cricket was rigidly stratifed on both colour and class lines in all the islands, but especially in Barbados. It was impossible for black people (and some whites) to join the elite clubs – Queen's Park in Trinidad, Georgetown in British Guyana or Wanderers in Barbados. Most of the black cricketers who represented the islands in inter-colonial matches were drawn from clubs like Shannon (Constantine's club) in Trinidad or the rather higher-status Spartan or Empire clubs in Barbados, which drew socially from the western educated elite. Employment opportunities were circumscribed too, especially for men who wanted time off to play cricket (Constantine, 1966; James, 1969; Stoddart, 1988). Learie

Constantine, for example, was favoured by the patronage of H.B.G. Austin, the captain of the West Indies team at the time, in terms of his *cricket* career. But he was unable to secure similar patronage in his search for regular employment. It was not until an oil company manager – ironically a South African – offered him a job that Constantine was able to get time off to play. His acceptance of the professional's post at Nelson in 1929, following a successful tour of England with the West Indies in 1928, has to been seen against this background of racial discrimination in the Caribbean. It was not simply a career move, as in the case of the Australians. It was a revolt, in C.L.R. James' memorable phrase, against 'the revolting contrast between his first-class status as a cricketer, and his third-class status as a man' (James, 1969: 110).

Nevertheless, earnings were an important element in the overseas players' decisions to join the League and it would be misleading to underestimate this factor. Uniquely, Constantine was receiving upwards of £1,000 a season from Nelson as his basic wage in the early 1930s, a greater sum, no doubt, than any paid to contemporary British footballers (Howat, 1975). McDonald's wages ten years earlier had been around £700 a season. Even relatively modest performers in some of the lesser leagues could earn weekly wages well in excess of those of most working men. In the Durham Senior League, for example, former English county players of no particular distinction were receiving around £5 a week in the 1920s (Hill, 1987). In addition to the basic wage there were, of course, other sources of income. 'Collections' for outstanding performances (when a collection box would be sent around the ground) could increase the earnings of a good professional significantly. Bill Alley, the Australian who played for Colne in the immediate post-Second World War period estimated that a professional could earn between £30 and £50 from collections in a local derby match (Alley, 1969: 37), S.G. Barnes, another Australian, who played for Burnley at about the same time, also did very well out of collections, though it was typical of his truculent nature that he complained of having to carry home a heavy bag of copper coins after matches (Barnes, 1953: 108–9). For truly outstanding, long-serving professionals there might be benefit matches arranged. Constantine was the beneficiary of such an event in 1936, when all the clubs in the League donated money for the staging of the match in recognition of his value throughout the League as a crowd-puller (*Nelson Leader*, 1937a). He took home around £500 from the proceeds of this event. For a skilful performer league cricket could offer handsome rewards. S.F. Barnes, a rational calculator in most things, spent only three seasons in county cricket in the whole of his long career. He had estimated that in the leagues, playing at most on only a couple of occasions each week, the lesser physical demands would allow him to play longer and thus increase his overall earnings (Duckworth, 1967: 167). The descriptions of Constantine's lifestyle in Nelson by both James (who knew him well) and Howat make it clear that the league professional could expect substantial material benefits (James, 1969: 127–8; Howat, 1975: 79–80).

In addition to financial privileges, playing cricket in the leagues bestowed a respect, accorded by employers and public alike, that it would have been difficult to find in other walks of life, or even in other forms of sport. In the inter-war period professional sport was a subordinated form of labour. The inferior status of the paid sportsman as *worker* was no more clearly illustrated than in the notorious retain-and-transfer system of the Football League clubs (Mason, 1981; 111–15). Yet in first-class cricket the position of the paid player was, if anything, yet more lowly. It was subtly inscribed through a variety of forms in the very fabric of the game – from matters of pay and discipline to the separation of amateurs from professionals in changing-rooms and hotels, and even in the use of surnames only for professionals on scorecards.

In the leagues, on the other hand, the 'pro' was a far more liberated figure. He was valued for his intrinsic skills on the field, where he was a specific focus of attention for players and spectators alike ('the players in his team instinctively look to him when in difficulty', according to Constantine [1933: 139]). And he was respected as a man who somehow carried the reputation of the local community on his shoulders, much as Stanley Matthews in the 1930s was the embodiment of Stoke-on-Trent (Mason, 1990). In fact, the identification of the league professional with his adopted community made him a local celebrity in a way that first-class cricketers were probably unable to emulate. Their community – the county – was a far more artificial one than that of the small, tightly knit and sometimes rather isolated industrial towns in which league cricket was played. Famous county and test players like Jack Hobbs were, to be sure, *national* figures by this time, especially as a result of the growth of advertising (Sissons, 1988: 211–12), but they were unlikely any longer to have close sporting contacts with a specific community. It was the special relationship that existed between player and town which was so evident in the case of league professionals. It particularly impressed a visitor from New Zealand who attended a match at Nelson in 1937 when the League title was won for yet another time:

I shall never forget the scene on that famous ground when the last wicket fell. Everyone went mad, hats, sticks and caps were thrown high in the air and 'Connie' (Constantine) was hoisted shoulder high and carried off the field . . . His personality is tremendous, wonderful . . . to say that he has been a 'godsend' to Nelson is to put it mildly. He has, to all people, both living in and out of Nelson, *been Nelson itself* (*Nelson Leader* 1937d).

For black cricketers like Constantine, Headley, Martindale and the others, to receive the adulation of the local white population in this way was a stunning contrast to the prejudice they had experienced in their native land. In spite of the prevailing ideologies of 'white superiority' in British society at this time, there seems to have been remarkably little racial hostility displayed towards these men. Alan Tomlinson has recorded a former Colne player as saying: 'a black chap, it didn't matter . . . 'e were an attraction as a cricketer if 'e were a good 'un' (Tomlinson, 1984: 78).

Of course it is significant to note that, in contrast to the present-day population patterns of east Lancashire, there was no black immigrant community in the 1930s. When C.L.R. James went to Nelson in 1932 he claimed that, 'apart from someone who went around collecting refuse in an old pushcart, Learie and I were the only coloured men in Nelson' (James, 1969: 127). Such ethnic hostility as had existed in east Lancashire was directed at the Irish, though this had moderated considerably since the nineteenth century, and in any case had never been as marked in the small Pennine towns as in larger industrial centres of mid- and west Lancashire, particularly Liverpool (Holmes, 1988: 37, 59–60). On one occasion Constantine admitted that he had been the victim of some 'shots' (snubs) because of his colour (*Nelson Leader*, 1937c), but even after leaving the Nelson club to play for Rochdale in 1938 he continued to live in the town, and did so until 1949. The environment was obviously congenial. There was, it is true, a certain degree of benevolent racial patronizing to be endured, of a kind that would be frowned upon in a later age, but nothing of the outright discrimination encountered by Constantine in London during the war, when the Imperial Hotel cut short his stay there in an attempt to appease the sensibilities of white American guests (Holmes, 1988: 202–3).

Ironically, the most prejudiced attitudes seem to have been present in professional cricket circles. In the mid-1930s, when it was being rumoured that Constantine might join the Lancashire county club (as McDonald had done before him), the idea was not warmly greeted by the county players. Len Hopwood, a Lancashire professional of the time, later recalled:

> In those days, the thought of a coloured chap playing for Lancashire was ludicrous. We Lancastrians were clannish in those less enlightened days . . . We wanted none of Constantine . . . We would refuse to play . . . In all fairness I must say we had nothing against Learie Constantine personally. He was, in fact, very popular with us. There was no personal vendetta. But the thought of a black man taking the place of a white man in our side was anathema. It was as simple as that (Hopwood, 1975; Bearshaw, 1990: 271).

This, it is worth noting, was at a time when one of the leading boxers in the country was prevented from competing for the British title because he was a black man (Cashmore, 1982: Ch.2).

In complete contrast to this the admirers of league cricket usually prided themselves on their tolerance, even though this sometimes came across in a fashion which smacked of the 'honorary white man': 'Constantine has proved that a man need not necessarily be possessed of white parents to claim the title of gentleman' (*Nelson Leader*, 1937b); 'I could not help but notice, when the League officials presented the Cup to Nelson on the balcony after the match, and made their speeches, what a pleasant change it was to hear Constantine's beautiful English compared to all the Presidents, past and present, with their broad Lancashire accent' (*Nelson Leader*, 1937d). But the sense of pride was justified. As one correspondent to the local press claimed, Constantine, Headley and the others were being given a chance by league clubs that might never have come their way in the counties, on account of their colour (*Nelson Leader*, 1938). Bearing in mind Hopwood's recollections, this was a fair point.

Does all this have any significance in a broader social context? Sport as an agent of imperial bonding is not to be underestimated, as recent work by both Brian Stoddart and Richard Holt has revealed (Stoddart, 1986; Holt, 1990). Sporting activity probably was an important means through which the idea of Empire was articulated, though imperial influences did not flow in an unproblematical, top-downwards fashion from elite to masses. Sport, and Empire, possessed different meanings for different people. The presence of so many Empire cricketers as local sporting champions in industrial Lancashire may well have served as confirmation for local people of a united British Empire. For the players themselves, however, sport was probably seen differently – as a route out of an ordinary life and an opportunity to secure a better future. Ric Sissons' phrase 'upwardly mobile professionals' (Sissons, 1988: 254) aptly describes the careers of many overseas players in the leagues. For black cricketers sport meant something more: a chance to assert their worth as men in a way that was never possible in the Caribbean. If (and it seems very likely) there was a link between the success of West Indies cricketers and the development of black nationalism in the Caribbean, then it might be suggested that this process was first launched in the 1930s by the activities of Constantine and his fellow professionals in Lancashire.

As far as the communities themselves are concerned, there is a sense in which the sporting star might be seen as fulfilling, not so much an idea of Empire, as a collective need for *local* identity. Some of these towns were of relatively recent origin. Nelson, for example, had only been incorporated as a borough in 1890 after a mushroom growth from virtually nothing in the 1860s (Bennett, 1957: 175ff). Most inhabitants were therefore of one or another variety of immigrant stock, usually from not too far away but still looking for something to give their lives a focus. Sometimes it was the local football team that supplied this (Holt, 1986). But the communities under discussion here were usually too small to sustain successful teams. Only Burnley could point to real soccer success, though not in the 1930s when the club was in the second division and unable to hold on to its rising star Tommy Lawton in the face of big club competition (Lawton, 1946: Ch.4). And so the cricket club served as one of the chief institutions of cultural identity. Its deeds encapsulated the worth of the community and were the subject of avid attention and speculation. Perhaps more is revealed about the community of Nelson through the local paper's full-page spread of 12 April 1929, *heralding* with 'testimonials' from leading figures in the cricket world the arrival of Constantine, than in anything else reported in that particular edition (*Nelson Leader*, 1929). It was as if the whole prestige of the community rested on the shoulders of this new messiah.

Yet the sporting champion also helped to give these small communities a place in a bigger firmament. When Ted McDonald went to Nelson in 1922, the town became for a time the centre of attention in the cricket world; a world which, to all intents and purposes, was the Empire, for cricket was not seriously played outside it. The Empire was an idea constantly promoted in everyday life; from ubiquitous press reports of speeches which evoked the British Empire as a cricket team playing the game, through the flag-waving celebrations of Empire Day each May, and not least to the posters on the walls of the local Co-op proclaiming imperial trade (Constantine, 1986). But cricket did not simply connect these communities to the Empire. It made of them a leading partner in the imperial enterprise, capable of attracting the Empire's foremost sportsmen.

And is it stretching credulity too far if we align this sporting migration with certain other aspects of the region's popular culture? There was in the popular culture of the north a peculiar sense of *modernity*. League cricket was sometimes accused by the traditionalists of having a 'circus' mentality towards the sport (Root, 1937: 185). There was some truth in this. Popularity and novelty were important considerations in the presentation of the game. The cultivation of an image of Constantine as a dazzling virtuoso was entirely consistent with the 'star' fixation of that other manifestation of northern pleasure – Blackpool, the favourite holiday destination of many of those people whose other summer pastime was watching league cricket. Tony Bennett, in an intriguing discussion of 'Blackpoolness', has argued that the place represented a self-consciously northern culture, which cocked a snook at metropolitan pretentiousness and constantly refreshed itself with up-to-the-minute American style. To southerners, who rarely visited, it was synonymous with vulgarity. But to the northern working class it was the last word in modern pleasure – beach, ballrooms, theatres, sideshows and 'the lights' (Bennett, 1986).

It is no coincidence that the word most frequently used to describe Constantine was 'electric'. He too was a symbol of this New World modernity, a 'turn' come to thrill the people of the north with eccentric skills, in his case on the sports field rather than the variety theatre. Through him, and the other 'pros', the community was not merely on the map – it was there in neon lights. There is more to sporting migration than simply play. It can form an important part of a society's identity.

REFERENCES

Alley, W.E. (1969) *My Incredible Innings* (London: Pelham Books).

Ashton, E. (1924) Nelson Cricket and Bowling Club Balance Sheet, season 1924.

Barlow, W. (1922) in *Athletic News* 10 April.

Barnes, S.G. (1953) *It isn't Cricket* (London: William Kimber).

Bearshaw, B. (1990) *From the Stretford End: The Official History of Lancashire County Cricket Club* (London: Partridge Press).

Bennett, T. (1986) 'Hegemony, Ideology, Pleasure: Blackpool' in Bennett, T., Mercer, C. and Woollacott, J. (eds), *Popular Culture and Social Relations* (Milton Keynes: Open University Press). pp. 135–54.

Bennett, W. (1957) *The History of Marsden and Nelson* (Nelson: Nelson Corporation).

Brooking, G.A. (1921–22) 'Northern Notes' in *The Cricketer Winter Annual* (London: The Cricketer) p. 124.

(1922–23) 'Northern Notes', in *The Cricketer Annual* (London: The Cricketer) pp. 94–6.

Cashmore, E. (1982) *Black Sportsmen* (London: Routledge & Kegan Paul).

Constantine, L.N. (1933) *Cricket and I* (London: Philip Allen).

(1966) 'Cricket in the Sun' in Constantine, L.N. and Batchelor, D. *The Changing Face of Cricket* (London: Eyre & Spottiswoode) pp. 69–140.

Constantine, S. (1986) *Buy and Build: The Advertising Posters of the Empire Marketing Board* (London: HMSO).

Cricket, 2 August, 1913.

The Cricketer, 31 July 1937.

The Cricketer Spring Annual (1937) (London: The Cricketer).

Cuttell, W. (1924) interview in *Nelson Leader* 23 May.

Duckworth, L. (1967) *S.F. Barnes – Master Bowler* (London: The Cricketer/ Hutchinson).

Guardian, 8 and 15 February 1986.

Gregson, W. (1934) in *The Cricketer* 2 June.

Hill, J. (1986) 'The Development of Professionalism in English League Cricket c. 1900–40' in Mangan, J.A. and Small, R.B. (eds), *Sport, Culture, Society: International Historical and Sociological Perspectives* (London: Spon) pp. 109–16.

(1987) ' "First Class" Cricket and the Leagues: Some Notes on the Development of English Cricket, 1900–40', *International Journal of the History of Sport*, 4,1, 68–81.

(1990) 'League Cricket in the North and Midlands' in Holt, R. (ed.), *Sport and the Working Class in Modern Britain* (Manchester: Manchester University Press) pp. 121–41.

Holmes, C. (1988) *John Bull's Island: Immigration and British Society 1871– 1971* (London: Macmillan).

Holt, R. (1986) 'Working Class Football and the City: the Problem of Continuity', *British Journal of Sports History*, 4, May, 5–18.

(1990) *Sport and the British* (Oxford: Oxford University Press).

Hopwood, L. (1975) in *Manchester Evening News*, 9 July.

Howat, G. (1975) *Learie Constantine* (London: George Allen & Unwin).

James, C.L.R. (1969) *Beyond a Boundary* (London: Stanley Paul).

Lawton, T. (1946) *Football is my Business*, ed. Peskett, R. (London: Sporting Handbooks).

Lindwall, R. (1954) *Flying Stumps* (London: Stanley Paul).

Mason, T. (1981) *Association Football and English Society, 1863–1915* (Brighton: Harvester).

(1990) 'Stanley Matthews' in Holt, R. (ed.), *Sport and the Working Class in Modern Britain* (Manchester: Manchester University Press). pp. 159–78.

Midwinter, E. (1981) *W.G. Grace: His Life and Times* (London: George Allen & Unwin).

Morgan, T.E. (1937) interview in *Nelson Leader* 23 July.

Nelson Cricket and Bowling Club (1920–24), Annual Report and Balance Sheet.

Nelson Leader (1922) 17 March.

(1929) 12 April.

(1937a) 14 May.
(1937b) 20 August.
(1937c) 27 August.
(1937d) 10 September.
(1938) 16 September.
Rice, C. (1934) in *The Cricketer*, 19 May.
Root, F. (1937) *A Cricket Pro's Lot* (London: Edward Arnold).
Sandiford, K.A.P. (1985) 'The Professionalization of Modern Cricket', *British Journal of Sports History*, 2,3, 270–89.
Sissons, R. (1988) *The Players: A Social History of the Professional Cricketer* (London: Kingswood Press).
Stoddart, B. (1986) 'Sport, Cultural Imperialism and Colonial Response in the British Empire: A Framework for Analysis' in British Society of Sports Historians *Proceedings of 4th Annual Conference*, July 1986, pp. 1–28.
  (1988) 'Cricket and Colonialism in the English-Speaking Caribbean to 1914: Towards a Cultural Analysis' in Mangan, J.A. (ed.), *Pleasure, Profit, Proselytism: British Culture and Sport at Home and Abroad* (London: Cass) pp. 231–57.
Sydney Daily Telegraph (1921) 9 July.
Tomlinson, A. (1984) 'Good Times, Bad Times, and the Politics of Leisure: Working Class Culture in the 1930s in a Small Northern England Working Class Community' in Gruneau, R.S. (ed.), *Leisure, Sport and Working Class Cultures: Theory and Practice*. (Working Papers in the Sociological Study of Sports and Leisure Studies (Kingston, Ontario: Queen's University) pp. 54–97.
Williams, J. (1990) 'Recreational Cricket in the Bolton Area Between the Wars', in Holt, R. (ed.), *Sport and the Working Class in Modern Britain* (Manchester: Manchester University Press) pp. 101–20.
Wisden Cricketers' Almanack (1954) ed. Preston, N. (London: Sporting Handbooks) pp. 325, 403, 423, 441, 480, 499, 540, 582, 602.

5

The Migration of Footballers:
The Case of France, 1932–1982

Pierre Lanfranchi

A professional football league was established in France in 1932. From the first day, one of its deepest characteristics was, without any doubt, its multi-ethnic composition. If we consider a period of 50 years, football has always had a large attraction-potential for newcomers to France. The example of the first revelation of French football at international level, the third place at the Swedish World Cup in 1958, is symptomatic. The star of the national team was the Real Madrid winger Raymond Kopa. His partners included Maryan Wisnieski, Casimir Hnatow, Celestin Oliver, Roger Piantoni and Claude Abbès and one of the two coaches, Jean Snella, was born, the son of Polish miners, in Germany. All of them were second-generation immigrants. Kopa himself was born Raymond Kopaszewski to Polish parents in the miners' district, in Noeux les Mines on the Belgian border, and received French citizenship at the age of 21 (Wahl, 1988; Rethacker, 1955).

In this sense the development of football in France seems very different from the growth of another popular team-sport, rugby union, as well as from the simultaneous development of football in the neighbouring countries of Britain, Italy or Germany. To focus on the migration of football players in France it seems relevant to inquire first if football ever was a 'national' object. Before the First World War, Italy changed the name of the game to *Giuoco Calcio* (Marri, 1983) recording the game's potential origins in the medieval Florentine game, it became *Voetbal* in Dutch, *Fußball* in German and *Fútbol* in Spanish. Only in French did the English word remain; and the people continued to play 'football'. In the inter-war period, the technical debates between national styles such as the Austrian system, the Italian method, the English and Scottish games illustrated the distinction between different national conceptions of football, but there was no word to characterize a French style. The first rhetorical use, in the press, of a 'French game' (*jeu à la française*) followed the 1958 World Cup and was more associated with players than with a tactical or technical interpretation of the rules or a national and autonomous style. The expression disappeared for about 20 years, re-emerging with the Platini, Tigana, Fernandez generation (also all sons of immigrants) of the 1980s.

The discourse about migration in football is, in Europe, strongly connected on one hand with the idea of national style and tradition (Do we need foreign players? Are they able to play football as played here? Are they bringing something new, something better? Are they modifying the very essence of the game? Won't they restrain the promotion of our young local talent?), and on the other hand with the global discourse about migration (Is football a vector of integration of immigrants? Are the immigrants, as part of the community, an improvement factor at the national level? As outsiders are they more motivated than the established locals?). The idea of a national style is well accepted in other countries, like Italy. From the 1930s on, the emphasis was on a Latin model with a name change to *Metodo* in the 1930s and 1940s; while *Catenaccio* in the 1960s and 1970s gave football the character of a national symbol (Milza, 1990; Lanfranchi, 1991). And the role of the foreign players is considered, often negatively, in respect of this national 'tradition'. Bonizzoni (1989) noted, for example, 'that, all things considered, Italian football was more damaged than helped by imports. The foreign players are an insult to our talent-scouts and youth trainers'. According to Archetti (1990), the general idea of a national style does not depend only on victories or ethnic identity, giving the example of a country like Argentina whose team was based on second- or third-generation immigrants:

> It is important to keep in mind that the consolidation of an Argentinian style happened in a context of international defeat for the national team. The myth of the Argentinian superiority was never history. The history of Argentinian victories was related to something abstract, 'a style', 'a way of doing', 'a way of playing', or to concrete names, the great players in exile (Archetti, 1990: 9).

There is no similar discourse in France. The lack of national identity and myth of any national superiority in football allowed a different level of discussion, football was generally connected with the discussion about the insertion of immigrants, which referred always to the 'original' nationality of the players.

THE LIMITS OF THE 'FRENCH GAME'

In an article published recently, Stéphane Beaud and Gérard Noiriel (1990) noted that one of the essential functions of football match commentaries was to diffuse among the working-class the idea of a 'national community' in concrete terms. French football can therefore be seen as the definitive example of a melting pot. In the 1930s, a fictional football team of Lyons was described as 'a mixed society in which the German-speaking Swiss was together with the Italian, the Englishman with the Egyptian, the man from Lyons with the one from Marseilles' (Jolinon, 1932: 83). In reality, the situation was not fundamentally different. In Sète, every second professional player was born outside France for the 30 years the team was professional (see Table 5.1). And, the quality of the *jeu à la sétoise* (Sète's style) came from an Englishman Victor Gibson, the team having up to nine British players at the same time in the 1920s (Dupont, 1973). Nantes, famous for a particularly technical style in the 1960s and 1970s, was trained by José Arribas, who left Spain during the civil war. Another Spanish immigrant after the civil war, Salvador Artigas, gave Bordeaux a defensive and virile style in the 1960s. In a similar way, the 'Nîmes school', a team playing a 'typical' strong physical football for decades, was invented and improved by Kader Firoud, an Algerian Muslim who coached the side from 1956 to 1978, but the commentators compared the way Nîmes played at this time with

Table 5.1 Birthplace of all professional football-players FC Sète (1932–60)

Place	N	%
Hérault	47	22.7
South-East France	34	16.5
Other French areas	39	18.9
North Africa	39	18.9
Black Africa	3	1.5
Foreign Countries	45	22.4
Total	207	100.0

Source: Les Sports du Sud-Est 1930–38, L'Information Sportive 1932–58, Les Cahiers de l'Equipe – Football, 1953–60

the Corrida, referring to the local importance of the bull-fighting phenomenon.

French football is a singular field of contradictions in the matter of national stereotypes. It is hard to speak about French identity in football, partly because French teams had long eclipses and partly because they were never representing *la France profonde* (the deep France). French roots are idealized in rugby union: 'Rugby is our country, is our youth' (Lacouture, 1979: 17; Pociello, 1983: 54–79). A national self-defined style exists in rugby (the *rugby-champagne*) and the national team is called the 'Quinze de France' (fifteen *from* France). Such a definition is unthinkable for football; football is a symbol of acculturation. In the perspective of the 'national-romantic' sporting social sciences, football is too urban, too permeable to minorities: sons of immigrants, sons of the colonies, mercenaries from all parts of the world are unable 'to reflect the soul of a population, its moral and physical qualities, its sense of individualism or community sociability, [or] preserve traditions saving the originality and virtues of the "race" ' (Eché 1984).

Deep-rooted actors with low mobility seem necessary for a symbiosis, and adoption of a sport as a patrimonial element. The example of the city of Béziers in Languedoc is interesting in this sense. During the 1960s Béziers had, at the same time, a fairly good second-division professional football team and an excellent first-division rugby team. Comparing the birthplaces of the players of both groups, the difference is extreme (see Table 5.2). While all the rugby players were born in a 100-kilometre radius, mainly in rural zones, only one-third of the football players came from the area and few of them from the countryside. Football in Béziers was the game of the Spanish immigrants and the *pieds noirs*, the white population returning from Algeria. Regarding the attendance at the two sports (they used the same stadium) there was no substantial difference, but only rugby was and is considered as a popular and local game, though a contradictory case was found in Bordeaux (Augustin, 1990).

The first intellectual criticism was the lack of connection between football and the local realities: 'The rejection of football could be the reaction against a game characterized by the rationalization of the organization, deterritorialization, cosmopolitism, mass recreation' (Laurens, 1985). On the other hand, the widespread use of migrant players and the general mobility of the actors, was seen as a negative factor for the national unity of football. In January 1961, *Miroir du Football*, a monthly journal close to the Communist Party, began a campaign for autarky: 'For the general interest and the technical

Table 5.2   Birthplaces of the Beziers rugby and football players

A

Rugby players

Place	1961	1967	1970
Béziers	8	7	4
Arr. Béziers	14	8	9
Hérault	–	4	3
Aude	2	1	4
Other – Languedoc	5	3	3
Other – France	1	–	–
Foreign Countries	–	–	1
N =	30	23	24

Source: Les Cahiers de l'Equipe – Rugby, 1961, 1967, 1970

B

Football players

Place	1961	1967	1970
Béziers	3	3	3
Arr. Béziers	2	1	3
Hérault	–	1	2
Aude	–	1	–
Other – Languedoc	–	1	2
Other – France	8	5	6
Northern Africa	5	3	3
Black Africa	1	1	1
Foreign Countries	3	3	–
N =	22	19	25

Source: Les Cahiers de l'Equipe – Football, 1961, 1967, 1970

progress of our football, foreign players are not essential'. They succeeded for a short period: from 1962 to 1966 the use of new foreign players was banned. But nationalization of football had to deal in France with three main elements of strong social significance: the question of nationality and the acquisition of a past, a culture; the biological argument about racial specialization; and the passage to integration from the individual to the group.

The assimilation of the two groups, foreign players and players with foreign origins, is related less to the sporting sphere than to the national community. French football lives in a dilemma, according to Beaud and Noiriel (1990) between 'race fusion' and 'chronic weakness' to find its own identity in a discursive perspective.

The question of the influences was always central. In the 1930s the professional clubs had two quite different strategies. The first, particularly in northern France, was to play like the British; the other had a Central European influence. This lack of unity in style is still present today, shown by the supporters and present in the stadia. In Marseilles, Toulouse and Bordeaux, the stadium has a *vélodrome* or an athletics track. It is not used only for football. In the same towns, the supporters call themselves *ultras* referring to an Italian model. In western and central France, the reference is British. The stadia are smaller, more connected to the industrial working life, and used only for football. The terraces are filled by groups of *fans* or the word *kop* is used. The French public, as well as French stadia, are not specific. They do not refer to French football culture or tradition; French football still needs models (Charroin, 1992).

SEEKING FORTUNES IN FRANCE

From the 1930s to the 1980s, over 1,000 players came to France to play football as professionals or semi-professionals. This is a little under 20 per cent of the total number of first- and second-division players for the period. This number is much higher than the 351 foreign players coming to Italy from 1929 to the closing of the borders in 1965 and than the 207 foreigners who played in the first 20 years of the Bundesliga. The French first division, in the first seven years of its existence (1932–39), saw 329 foreign players. The preceding paragraph was about national styles and here again France differs a good deal from its neighbours. The so-called 'Latin' countries traditionally use a lot of migrant players from South America. Of the foreigners in Italy, 176 came from Brazil, Uruguay and mainly Argentina, over half had Italian origins (*Guerin Sportivo*, 11 July 1979). In the 1970s, 70 per cent of the foreign players in Spain came from South America. From 1963 to 1983, only seven South Americans played in the Bundesliga, none of them having any success (*Kicker*, 1984). The 'guest players' in Germany came almost exclusively from (former) Yugoslavia, Austria, Scandinavia and Holland, countries which play a 'European' game and where the player market is not particularly expensive. In France, footballers come from everywhere. In the inter-war period, the biggest colonials were British, Austrian, Hungarian, Czech, Spanish and Argentinian. In the 1950s, British players disappeared. It was the time of Dutch, Swedish, Argentinian, Uruguayan and Paraguayan players. After the 1960s, the majority were Yugoslavian followed by the Argentinians, the Polish, the Senegalese and the Germans.

The countries of origin

In the 1930s the idols of Marseilles were the Brazilian goalkeeper Vasconcellos and the Hungarian winger Kohut; in the 1950s the Swedish forward Andersson and the Moroccan midfield player Ben Barek; in the 1960s and 1970s the duo Magnusson (Swedish winger) and Skoblar (Yugoslavian striker); and in the 1980s Bell, the Cameroonian goalkeeper, Waddle (from England) and Pelé (the midfield player from Ghana). Marseilles is certainly an extreme case of variety by the use and adoption of foreign players (see Table 5.3d), but diversity remains a constant variable in recruitment of foreign players in France. For the season 1976–77, the 63 foreign players in division one came from 21 different countries.

French clubs did not have a real recruitment policy in foreign countries. Some big clubs were able to spend money on international stars, the rest of the clubs contracted old players or second-division ones. The economic situation of football was always the most important element. England being out of FIFA, the clubs contacted a lot of British players in the 1930s because they did not have to pay any transfer fees. In the same period the economic situation of the central European countries was so bad that the clubs were obliged to sell their best players. After the Second World War, Holland, Sweden and Denmark, countries in which football was still amateur, offered good players for little money. The relatively low level of salaries in Yugoslavia and Argentina in the 1970s contributed to brake the inflationary tendency of the French football market. The rich footballing countries – Italy, Spain, England or Germany – were too expensive to be attractive, and the African continent was supplying the league with prices challenging any competitor.

There was never hegemony of a group of immigrants. On a social basis, football had long since ceased to be considered as exclusively the sport of the working-classes; it was a place for compromise. The same happened in the use of foreign players with a majority of clubs having at the same time a 'Latin' player and one from *Mitteleuropa*.

Positions on the field

If you need a goalkeeper, the Yugoslavs are perfect; for the wingers, Africans and South Americans will be excellent; to choose a striker

Table 5.3

A

Native country of foreign players – FC Sète (1932–60)

Country	
Britain	10
Hungary	9
Yugoslavia	7
Spain	6
Argentina	2
Egypt	2
Czechoslovakia	2
Austria	1
Ukraine	1
Armenia	1
Sweden	1
Finland	1
Not defined	1
Total	44

B

Native country of foreign players – RC Lens (1934–82)

Country	
Poland	11
Austria	8
Brazil	3
Uruguay	3
Britain	1
Armenia	1
Czechoslovakia	1
Holland	1
Iceland	1
Sweden	1
Yugoslavia	1
Total	32

you have two alternatives: the technically adept South American or the smart Yugoslavian. If you prefer an artist in the midfield, you must have a look at Austria or Hungary. To discover a tireless runner, the best place to look is Holland, and for a strong defender, the

Table 5.3 *continued*

C

Native country of foreign players – FC Nantes (1945–82)

Argentina	8
Austria	5
Yugoslavia	4
Denmark	4
Spain	1
Poland	1
Czechoslovakia	1
Ukraine	1
Germany	1
Mali	1
Total	27

D

Native country of foreign players – Olympique Marseille (1932–82)

Hungary	9
Britain	8
Argentina	8
Austria	7
Yugoslavia	7
Sweden	6
Brazil	4
Italy	4
Senegal	3
Switzerland	3
Cameroon	2
Denmark	2
Czechoslovakia	2
Germany	2
USSR	2
Eire	1
Greece	1
Holland	1
Congo	1
Ivory Coast	1
Luxemburg	1
Mali	1
Poland	1
Togo	1
Tunisia	1
Uruguay	1
Zaïre	1
Total	81

German is expensive but reliable; at a cheaper price, there is the Dane.

These stereotypes are important in the recruitment policies for football players. It is hard to say if they reflect any truth. In France, foreign players were recruited to play in any position. The striker, the centre forward, is certainly the position in which the highest number of foreign players are found and from 1971 to 1986 the top scorer in the league was always a foreigner. According to Beaud and Noiriel, it is not surprising that generosity, fighting spirit and aggressiveness are found in those who have a need for revenge.

In Italy, foreigners are found playing in all positions except in goal. (The exception to this rule is the first and only foreign goalkeeper, Taffarel, who has played for Parma since 1990. Surprisingly, he is the crowd's favourite player.) There is a general opinion in Italy that Italian keepers are the best in the world, and that the position demands loyalty to the team, self-confidence and experience, all of which are considered to be Italian qualities. In France there is a tendency to deploy foreign players as half-backs and centre forwards, and players from the Maghreb or Poland as wingers or full-backs. It is impossible at this stage to be more precise, but accurate empirical research about the hierarchy on the field in different countries could give interesting results.

A long-term emigration
If you ever have the chance to go to the harbour of Sète on the Mediterranean, you may certainly visit the 'See-cemetery', one of the most famous monuments of the city. The poet Paul Valéry lies here with many other local notables. There is another lesser known cemetery in Sète, where the two best players of Football Club de Sète (champions in 1934 and 1939) are buried in the middle of an anonymous population. Their names were Ivan Beck and Désiré Koranyi. The first was born in Belgrade and the second in Szeged (Hungary). Like many other foreign football players they married French wives and remained, after their sporting careers, on the scene of their footballing feats.

Marriage has been a central factor of integration for a number of foreign football players. Answering a questionnaire, Camille Passi, a winger from Congo wrote: 'The most important for me has been to meet, through football, my future wife with whom we had two fantastic boys'; these two boys are now famous players and the elder played for France some years ago. The marriage strategies seem a key point for research about migrant athletes. Football made it possible for this young man to improve his social position, to marry a French girl and to seek an established situation (he is now an insurance agent). Of the five foreign players of Montpellier in 1934, four married Frenchwomen, took French citizenship and remained in France. The widow of one of these four mercenaries, the Hungarian keeper Ernö Nemeth, testifies to their degree of integration: 'I am still using every day the silver cutlery the supporters gave us as a present for our wedding in 1934. They collected money to buy this gift' (Lanfranchi, 1992).

In 1966, the two foreign players in the Nantes team which won the championship were Bakou Touré from Mali and Ramon Muller from Argentina. In the Nantes team which again won the championship in 1980 and 1983, two of the midfield players were their sons, José Touré and Oscar Muller. Nantes is a conformist club (see Table 5.3c) which tried to keep its best players for a long period. In Lens, the mining community is largely of Polish origin and the majority of foreign players come from Poland (see Table 5.3b). This recruitment may be considered as the acceptance of the cultural background of the local working-class population. The import of Polish internationals began in 1970 and helped to create a myth of bi-national culture. This happened after the total assimilation of the Polish population (Weil, 1991: 365–75).[1] Polish football stars symbolized the long-term emigration of the Polish miners but reconciled those naturalized French like Kopa, who did not speak Polish, with their memories of home. There was no suspicion any more. There was no longer any risk in claiming that your favourite players were those working-class players who, like Szepan and Kuzorra in Nazi Germany, had identified Schalke 04 as 'The team of proletarians and Polacks' (Gehrmann, 1988). Such differences had now ceased to matter.

A SPECIFIC CASE: THE AFRICANS

Along with the school education, sporting education of our black brothers must give marvellous results. Initiation to football is less arid, I think, than initiation to literature or rhetoric, but sporting education is highly civilizing, without a doubt (*Match*, 20 August 1929).

According to Chartier (1987) and Ehrenberg (1991), the 'sportization' phenomenon is, in our societies, based on egalitarian values. Inequality does result, in sport, from a struggle between equals. The inequality is not a natural or just one; but, the representations of the

Table 5.4   Players who have migrated to France, having played in the World Cup for another nation

Country	1930	34	38	50	54	58	62	66	70	74	78	82
Algeria	–	–	–	–	–	–	–	–	–	–	–	10
Argentina	3	1	–	–	–	–	–	2	–	4	3	7
Austria	–	–	–	–	2	2	–	–	–	–	–	–
Belgium	–	–	–	–	–	–	–	–	3	–	–	2
Brazil	–	–	–	–	1	1	–	1	3	2	–	–
Cameroon	–	–	–	–	–	–	–	–	–	–	–	10
Chile	–	–	–	1	–	–	2	2	–	–	–	–
Czechoslovakia	–	3	1	–	–	1	4	–	–	–	–	4
Egypt	–	1	–	–	–	–	–	–	–	–	–	–
England	–	–	–	–	–	–	–	–	–	–	–	3
Germany (West)	–	–	–	–	–	–	–	–	1	1	2	5
Haiti	–	–	–	–	–	–	–	–	–	1	–	–
Holland	–	1	1	–	–	–	–	–	–	5	6	–
Honduras	–	–	–	–	–	–	–	–	–	–	–	1
Hungary	–	3	2	–	–	–	1	1	–	–	5	5
Israel	–	–	–	–	–	–	–	–	3	–	–	–
Morocco	–	–	–	–	–	–	–	–	2	–	–	–
Paraguay	–	–	–	2	–	1	–	–	–	–	–	–
Poland	–	–	–	–	–	–	–	–	–	8	5	4
Portugal	–	–	–	–	–	–	–	2	–	–	–	–
Romania	1	–	–	–	–	–	–	–	–	–	–	–
Spain	–	1	–	1	–	–	–	–	–	–	–	–
Sweden	–	–	–	6	–	1	–	–	1	1	2	–
Switzerland	–	4	2	3	1	–	2	–	–	–	–	–
Tunisia	–	–	–	–	–	–	–	–	–	–	1	–
Turkey	–	–	–	–	1	–	–	–	–	–	–	–
USSR	–	–	–	–	–	–	–	–	–	–	–	2
Uruguay	–	–	–	–	–	–	–	–	2	–	–	–
USA	–	–	–	1	–	–	–	–	1	–	–	–
Yugoslavia	3	–	–	–	1	4	10	–	–	8	–	9
	7	14	6	14	6	10	19	8	16	30	24	62

African players (Table 5.4) in France focus on their 'natural' characteristics. Their success in sport is not the result of their work, of their abnegation. They became stars of the sporting show only with their innate talent. Their biographies refer to supernatural elements to explain the success. Dahleb had 'a magical left foot', Mahjoub 'spoke with arabesques', Keita 'recalled conjuring' (Mahjoub, 1988) and Ben Barek, the 'Black Pearl' of French football 'gave to Madrid spectators, who loved to see it, a recital of feints like a juggler' (Ben Barek, 1954).

This irrational dimension attached to the coloured players is given as the only plausible explanation for success – a divine origin.

Players are categorized in different types. In every team you will find some physically strong players, some team players, some runners, some technical players. Africans are considered, almost unfailingly, as instinctive players. They are nice to see but not really efficient. They don't think about tactical schemes. The restrictive identity of the footballer from Africa (or of African origins) is evident, in view of the careers they have in the football world. Except for Kader Firoud, who was a well-educated schoolteacher from Algeria, no black or Maghrebian has been a trainer or manager of a professional football club in France, a similar situation to that in the USA (Edwards, 1986). The public is delighted by the qualities of the African artists. In Marseilles in 1985 the two favourite players were Bell, 'the Black Panther', and Diallo, the Senegalese winger with a disconcerting but not always efficient style (Bromberger, 1987).

The discourse on African players is binomial: gift and immaturity. They use instinctive qualities but easily give up. They play the game but are not skilled. In spite of this prejudice, French authorities tried from the first days of professional football, to encourage a policy of integration, not in domestic life but on the football field. Native Algerians, Moroccans and Senegalese played in the French national team during the 1930s. Indeed the first president of the Algerian Republic, Ahmed Ben Bella, played professionally for Marseilles in 1941 (Pecheral and Grimaud, 1985: 112–15). In 1958, 25 Algerians were playing as professionals and presaged the shape of the future brotherhood. When they left France to create an independent national team in April 1958, 'the football public was sensitive to the disappearance' of Mustafa Zitouni and Rachid Mekhloufi, members of the French national team (*Le Monde*, 17 April 1958), and for the first time, the challenge, the confrontation between natives and colonial power, entered the scene of French football. Ever since that time, football continues to have a central but ambiguous place in the relations between France and its old colonies in Africa. No country in Europe gives such access to professional football for Africans as France, but at the same time this access is limited to secondary roles: and when France was the nation with the highest number of nationals (38) at the recent African Championship in Senegal, over half of them did not play in the first division.

French football is a difficult subject. Football is certainly the most popular sport in France, but it does not reflect many of the values which are attached to the game in other countries. The challenge between centre and periphery in such a centralized country is limited. In the same way, the integration of minorities, one of the central problems of France in the last 20 years, is accepted in football but does not create any major problems. Hooliganism is very limited when football represents a quite efficient multi-cultural society. For the last 50 years football has provided an important access to integration for minorities without being really considered as such by the public and the authorities. It is a territory to take hold of.

NOTE

1. The Polish population in France grew from 46,000 in 1921 to 508,000 in 1931. They were 423,000 in 1946, 177,000 in 1962, 93,000 in 1975 and 64,000 in 1982. The fall is explained mainly by naturalizations (Weil, 1991: 365–76).

REFERENCES

Archetti, E. (1990) *In Search of National Identity: Argentinian Football and Europe* Colloquium Paper No. 101/90 (Florence: European University Institute).
Augustin, J.P. (1990) 'La percée du football en terre de rugby', *Vingtième siècle*, April–June, 97–109.
Beaud, S. and Noiriel, G. (1990) 'L'immigration dans le football', *Vingtième siècle*, April-June, 83–96.
Ben Barek, L. (1954) 'Les mémoires de la perle noire', *But et Club, Le Miroir des sports*, nn. 486–92.
Bonizzoni, L. (1989) *Calciatori stranieri in Italia, ieri e oggi* (Rome: Società Stampa Sportiva)
Bromberger, C. (1987) 'La passion du football à Marseille et à Turin', *Terrain*, 8, 8–41.
Charroin, P. (1992) 'Il pubblico del Saint-Etienne' in P. Lanfranchi (ed.), *Il calcio e il suo pubblico* (Naples: Esi), pp. 301–12.
Chartier, R. (1987) 'Sport, religion et violence', *Le Débat*, April, 67–9.
Dupont, Y. (1973) *La Mecque du Football ou les mémoires d'un Dauphin* (Nîmes: Bène).
Eché, G. (1984) Introduction to the special issue 'sport et société' of the journal *Midi, revue des sciences humaines et de littérature de la France du Sud*, 2.
Edwards, H. (1986) 'Au-delà des symptômes: absence d'éthique, barrière raciale dans le sport américain', *Les Temps Modernes*, 42,12, 135–51.
Ehrenberg, A. (1991) *Le culte de la performance* (Paris: Calmann-Levy).
Gehrmann, S. (1988) *Fußball, Vereine, Politik: Zur Sportgeschichte des Reviers 1900–1940* (Essen: Hobbing).
Grimaud, L. and Pecheral, A. (1985) *La grande histoire de l'O.M.* (Paris: Robert Laffont).

Jolinon, J. (1932) *Le joueur de balle* (Paris: Ferenczi).
Kicker Sportmagazin (1984) Special Issue, '20 Jahre Bundesliga'.
Lacouture, J. (1979) *Le rugby, c'est un monde* (Paris: Seuil).
Lanfranchi, P. (1991) 'Bologna: "The Team that Shook the World" ', *International Journal of the History of Sport*, 8,3, 336–46.
    (1992) 'Il calcio dei calciatori', in P. Lanfranchi (ed.), *Il calcio e il suo pubblico* (Naples: Esi) pp. 103–16.
Laurens, G. (1985) 'Football, rugby et identité occitane', *Amiras, Repères occitans*, 12, 84–103.
Mahjoub, F. (1988) *Trente ans de Coupe d'Afrique des nations* (Paris: Jeune Afrique).
Marri, F. (1983) 'Metodo, Sistema e derivati nel linguagio calcistico', *Lingua Nostra*, 44, 70–83.
Milza, P. (1990) 'Le football italien, une histoire à l'échelle du siècle', *Vingtième siècle*, April–June, 49–58.
Pociello, C. (1983) *Le rugby ou la guerre des styles* (Paris: A.M. Matailié).
Rethacker, J.P. (1955) 'Raymond Kopa', *Nos Champions*, 5, 105–60.
Wahl, A. (1988) 'Raymond Kopa, une vedette de football, un mythe', *Sport Histoire*, 1,2, 83–96.
Weil, P. (1991) *La France et ses étrangers* (Paris: Calmann-Levy).

6

Blue Bonnets over the Border: Scotland and the Migration of Footballers

H.F. Moorhouse

March! March! Ettrick and Tiviotdale!
Why my lads dinna ye march forward in order?
March! March! Eskdale and Liddesdale,
All the Blue Bonnets are over the border.
Many a banner spread, flutters above your head,
Many a crest that is famous in story.
Mount and make ready then, sons of the mountain glen,
Fight for your king and the old Scottish border.

Come from the hills where your hersils are grazing,
Come from the glens of the buck and the roe.
Come to the crag where the beacon is blazing,
Come with the buckler, the lance and the bow.
Trumpets are sounding, war steeds are bounding,
Stand to your guns and march in good order.
England shall many a day, tell of the bloody fray,
When the Blue Bonnets came over the border.

(Evans, 1824).

HOME AND AWAY

Study of a who's who of Scottish internationalists (Lamming, 1987) reveals that, of the 947 players listed who played for Scotland between 1872 and 1986, only five gained caps while playing for clubs outside Britain. This total compares very unfavourably with those won by Scots playing for just *one* of any number of English clubs. It is small relative to, say, the 25 Scots capped while playing for Newcastle

United (making this the eleventh ranking 'Scottish' club in the provision of internationalists), and stands even with unfashionable Coventry City, who can also list five Scottish internationals. Moreover, consideration of the 'continental caps', and excluding the unhappy year Law spent with Torino in the early 1960s, shows that the excursions of Souness, Bett, Archibald and Jordan were features only of recent years, especially the 1980s. In the years since 1986, we could add probably another three or four Scots who have played for their country while with teams such as Nantes, Boroussia and Bayern, but still the overseas total remains sparse.

Cap-winning is only one measure of the voyages of the Scottish player. There is an interesting account of an atypical (and non-capped) 1930s player, Sandy MacLennan, which recounts the wanderings of an Elgin lad along the byways of football. By 1934 he had got as far as Glasgow with the Scottish first-division side Partick Thistle and, because of troubles in the club, was retained by them without pay but with a transfer fee on his head. He was drawn to Excelsior de Roubaix, in France:

> At this time there was no affiliation between British and Continental football, so any 'tied' British player could always chance his luck in the unknown realms of the game abroad without restriction. Apparently 'feartie' (another player) had been approached at the end of the season by John Docherty, a former player acting as a Glasgow agent for the French club (MacLennan, 1974: 65).

After haggling he got £10 a week plus bonuses and a signing-on fee of £300. In France he approved of the system of a basic wage *plus* win and draw bonuses *plus* about 50 pence for each of the positive balance of goals for and against. MacLennan claims that, all in all, this was about double what he was being offered to join Sheffield Wednesday in the English first division at the same time. Then there was the super-stadium owned by the local millionaire: 'It was in magnificent contrast, when compared with the many threadbare and hard-up looking dreich headquarters of many Scottish football establishments back home, where more than a few were only gaunt, unpainted spectres, except for a few hours weekly' (MacLennan, 1974: 68). In France Sandy found, among other amenities, a six-lane running track, tip-up seats in the covered stand, tennis courts, athletic areas, billiard rooms, skittle alleys, shooting galleries, a fully equipped gym, a restaurant and a café.

Generally, at Roubaix he entered a more cosmopolitan world than is to be found along Glasgow's Maryhill Road. Among the 20 professionals were two Austrians, two Algerians, a Hungarian, a Belgian and a German. There, too, he experienced much more enjoyable training than the three mornings a week 'football-less' sessions with Partick. In France there was five-day, full-day, training, with stamina and sprint work in the mornings and individual ball practice in the afternoons. However, he was most dismayed at being hugged and kissed by his team-mates when he scored, an overt emotion that sat ill with his Scottish style, which a contemporary French paper described as: 'qui fonce à la manière d'un boulet' (MacLennan, 1974: 76). He was extricated from the soppiness, the continental referees who didn't know a dangerous, knee-high tackle when they saw one, and team mates who were always trying to lure him into brothels or dubious picture shows, by a letter from the Scottish Football Association (SFA) stating that his application for a free transfer from Partick had been granted, and by news that top Scottish clubs were now interested in him. A sudden 25 per cent devaluation of the franc meant that the Scot invoked a clause of his canny contract:

> the hardened player produced his ace card when he said he intended to send a copy of his contract to the French Football Federation for an independent ruling on the dispute. This was a real sickener for the club officials, as they would be caught with their pants down on two counts. First, there was the club's signed agreement to pay wages in British currency if required by the player and there was another, significant detail that the Scot had received £2 per week over the £8 permissible.
>
> He told Roubaix he would sever all connections for a free transfer and £300. (MacLennan, 1974: 83).

MacLennan was not the only not-quite-out-of-the-top-drawer Scot to carry his boots abroad. There are those many engineers and amateur coaches who fetched up in ports in Uruguay, in Austria and just about everywhere else, and taught the world to play in 'the Scottish style'. Escapades in Danish nightclubs, Norwegian hotels, Argentinian bars and Australian bedrooms dot the unofficial history of Scottish football and have meant the interruption, if not complete cessation, of many international careers (Cosgrove, 1991). A whiff of foreign air has often provided just the charge a Scottish player has needed to light the short fuse and start the fireworks. More recently some Scots have made their way to the USA or the Far East to add a few seasons to their playing careers, a fistful of dollars to their bank accounts, but my basic point remains: when talking about the Scottish footballer going 'abroad' England is the premier destination.

SOUTH OF THE BORDER

Some readers may demur. England 'abroad'? How can this be? No visas are required to cross the border and there are no language barriers (though plenty of English jokes about the 'impenetrable' Scots accent). The only documentation that has ever been needed for the player to move south is a one-way ticket. Still, as I will argue, the movement of Scottish footballers to England – surely the oldest and steadiest migration of sports talent in the world – does contain elements which may have a more general applicability. And crossing Hadrian's Wall can certainly be traumatic for players, spectators and country alike.

The kind of yearly flow shown in Table 6.1 (of course, by no means all these players were or became internationals) is no new thing. For over a century the English League and the Scottish League have stood in the relation of buyer and seller. The first Home-Scots versus Anglo-Scots international trial match was played in 1896. On 18 October 1926 a writer in *Athletic News* measured the tide quite precisely: 'in little more than a season 10 fully fledged internationalists, two inter-league players who would have had a cap if the Scotsmen could have played more than one centre-forward in a team, and a member of an international trial eleven have passed into English football'. In December of the same year, the Scottish correspondent of the paper declared that without too much deliberation he could list more than 70 front rank players who had moved south since the war and lots more who still had their names to make. Nearly 50 years later research showed that in the five seasons from 1968/9 to 1972/3, 61 players moved from the Scottish to the English League, and over £2.3 million had been paid by English clubs (Commission on Industrial Relations, 1974: 11–12). Moreover, and especially in the 1960s, English clubs signed young Scots direct, so transfers trace only part of the tide. Lay (1984) studied the origins of players in the English game from 1946 to 1981 and found 1,653 Scots had played in the English League in that time. On a population basis, Scotland just about held its own as an 'English region' producing players for the English professional game, while also supplying virtually all the players for its own League. In 1955–56 Accrington Stanley, then an English third division league side, set the record for using Scots when they often fielded a side made up

Table 6.1 Examples of the Movement of Scottish Players to England: Transfers between Leagues in Two Years of the 1960s

Player	Clubs	Approximate Fee
	1963	
A. Scott	Rangers to Everton	£ 39,000
P. Crerand	Celtic to Manchester United	£ 50,000
J. Ower	St Johnstone to Workington	
T. Burke	Clyde to Barnsley	
M. Gray	Third Lanark to Manchester City	£ 30,000
A. Kerr	Kilmarnock to Sunderland	£ 30,000
W. Penman	Rangers to Newcastle	£ 12,000
S. Colrain	Clyde to Ipswich	£ 12,000
J. Thorburn	Raith Rovers to Ipswich	£ 8,000
E. Brodie	Dundee United to Shrewsbury	
B. Friel	Dumbarton to Southend United	
J. Hutton	Hamilton Academicals to Scunthorpe	£ 8,000
G. Marshall	Hearts to Newcastle	£ 15,000
J. McLaughlin	Morton to Millwall	
J. Bolton	Raith Rovers to Ipswich	£ 6,000
J. Cassidy	Stirling Albion to Oxford United	
B. King	Rangers to Southend United	£ 8,000
E. Connachan	Dunfermline to Middlesbrough	£ 18,000
I. Ure	Dundee to Arsenal	£ 62,500
A. Brown	Partick Thistle to Everton	£ 25,000
D. Fraser	Aberdeen to West Bromwich	£ 25,000
B. Roberts	Motherwell to Leicester	£ 40,000
B. Cummings	Aberdeen to Newcastle	£ 5,000
C. Halliday	Dumbarton to Cardiff City	£ 7,000
M. Slater	Montrose to Southend United	
J. Byrne	Hibernian to Barnsley	
G. Kinnell	Aberdeen to Stoke City	£ 25,000
G. Baker	Hibernian to Ipswich	£ 17,000
N. Gillespie	Falkirk to Wrexham	
E. Yard	Partick Thistle to Bury	£ 12,000
	1969/70	
P. Marinello	Hibernian to Arsenal	£100,000
T. Craig	Aberdeen to Sheffield Wednesday	£100,000
J. Smith	Aberdeen to Newcastle United	£100,000
R. Barry	Dunfermline to Coventry City	£ 40,000
A. Thomson	Hearts to Oldham	£ 4,000
P. Cormack	Hibernian to Nottingham Forest	£ 90,000
G. Queen	Kilmarnock to Crystal Palace	£ 35,000
P. Bartram	Morton to Cyrstal Palace	£ 18,000
R. Hynd	Rangers to Crystal Palace	£ 12,000
W. Lawson	Brechin City to Sheffield Wednesday	£ 7,500
G. O'Brien	Clydebank to Southampton	£ 16,000
A. Rae	East Fife to Bury	£ 2,000

Source: *The Scotsman*, 2 August 1971

entirely of Scottish-born players. Fifteen of the 19 players the club used that season were Scottish (Taylor, 1970: 73–4).

This steady outflow of players has meant that a characteristic preoccupation of virtually all Scottish supporters has been whether and when their club would succumb to the lure of English silver and sell their favourites. Of course, such sales did not always pass without a commotion. Early Scottish football history contains plenty of demonstrations and even 'kidnaps' with players snatched back to Scotland from the waiting rooms of Lancashire railway stations and the like but, in modern times, the movement has seemed so natural that until very recently people in England have scarcely bothered to think about it except, to Scottish disgust, when scanning a map for the town of 'Raith' (the club is in Kirkcaldy) to find out exactly where their latest acquisition has come from. What has been an ever-present topic of discussion north of the border (at the time of writing around McStay of Celtic) – 'will McX stay?', 'who will McY go to?', 'who will replace McZ?' – has not been so pressing a preoccupation of the football culture around English clubs, the major ones at least. All migration, sports migration included, connotes different things at the points of embarkation and arrival.

Once they leave even the best players tend to 'disappear' from Scottish view (and, remember, many famous Scots – Liddell, Law, Bremner, etc. – have played only a handful of professional games 'in their own country'), aided both by the routines of the Scottish media and, in recent decades, by the restrictions placed on TV coverage of the English game by the Scottish football authorities. Moreover, real dangers (as well as monetary benefits) are perceived to lurk in the short trip. There are constant possibilities of a dislocation of moral stability, but a major effect of this exodus has been to put into question the national spirit of 'the Anglo'. When the Scot crosses the border there has, apparently, been an attendant danger not only of an unhinging of common sense and personal balance but also, even more pernicious, of a loss of national identity. Like the thistle, the feeling of being Scottish seems to be a flower that flourishes best in adverse circumstances and on stony ground, it can often fade when planted in softer southern soil.

Booze, blondes and bonanzas

Of course, the Scottish footballer has never needed to leave Scotland to squander talent and scatter sanity but, shaken out of his 'nation', out of his usually West-of-Scotland manual working-class community, the young Scot is seen as very vulnerable to the perils of the flesh.

available in ever increasing profusion the further south he travels. This cultural preoccupation has been given dramatic form. In 1947 Glasgow Unity Theatre, a company devoted to plays about and performed by the Scottish working class, first performed G. Munro's *Gold in His Boots* (Munro, 1947), revived by another socialist company, 7:84 (Scotland), in 1982 as part of their 'Clydebuilt' season. The play, which had a successful run on both occasions, concerns Tommy Craig, son of a means-tested miner, who becomes 'the uncrowned king of Scotland' through football ability. Despite the protestations of his father: 'Tommy'll stay in Scotland. We've exported enough brain to England', the boy is transferred south; but in England things do not go well for Tommy, he strikes his oppressive manager, and the press picks on him with stories of booze, blondes and bonanzas. The star takes to drink at the injustice of it all and, though he finds redemption and a place in the Cup Final team at the end of the play, plenty of real Scots stars have not found that 'birds, booze and bets', in whatever combination, lead to a happy ending (Moorhouse, 1990). One of the quintessential Scottish players – Hughie Gallagher – lived out this kind of tragedy in real life and, in a different way, the Scottish media looked at Kenny Dalglish in early 1991, and read his resignation as manager of Liverpool, not just some indiscriminate 'pressure of the modern game', but as a case of a gifted but inarticulate Glaswegian boy out of his depth in a strange world. The prognosis was that a return 'home' (but, for added spice, would that be Rangers, would that be Celtic?) had to be the best pick-me-up.

Let me note the case of Charlie Nicholas. Charlie (Celtic–Arsenal–Aberdeen–Celtic) has had a most interesting Scottish trajectory. Hailed in the early 1980s as 'the next Dalglish' (Kenny having moved to Liverpool), he was about as near as Scottish football got in that decade to having a genuine superstar. In those years it was not unusual to see his picture on three pages of the popular papers, many days a week. The story that a Scottish commentator on an international match against England cried out: 'watch out behind you, Kenny!' is, I fear, apocryphal, but it is certainly true that Dalglish is the only British footballer I know who was regularly referred to in television commentaries by his Christian name, as in: 'Kenny hits it left' or 'Kenny's back looking for the ball'. This is a measure of just how Dalglish – the last great 'traditional Scottish player' paralleling Bobby Charlton's particular status in England – is idolized in his own country. However, just occasionally in commentary, 'Charlie' was (and is) treated with just the same, inclusive, affection. 'Champagne' and 'cheeky', were the easily applied adjectives, and for a while it looked as if he would be the next truly great Scottish player. When he seemed likely to move in 1983 it was regarded as a great loss to the Scottish game, and various journalists and managers appealed for him to stay; 'to give it one more year'. However, it was also thought that some of the interested English clubs – Manchester United or Liverpool (where he could be tutored by Dalglish) – would be most appropriate if the golden boy *had* to go. When he eventually signed for Arsenal there was a general feeling that he had made a bad choice, not simply because their rather dour style did not seem likely to provide a context in which his ball skills would flourish, but also because it was felt that London might provide just too many temptations for the Glasgow lad. Soon enough, Nicholas was 'writing' his own 'Birds, Booze and Me' article in the *News of the World* in an effort to shake off the 'bad boy' label: 'Perhaps they'll stop calling me the second George Best'. It was true he had just got a three-year ban for drink-driving offences, had a mirrored ceiling in his bedroom and had gained a 'playboy' image for being out on the town every night, but this did not validate all the gossip: 'On a boys' night out after a game the most I'll have is seven or eight pints of lager. That, to me, isn't being drunk'. However, he did admit to being 'fit and healthy, with all the normal appetites' and that 'plenty of girls come up and make propositions. I know that's because I'm a sort of celebrity and I don't like that. But it can be quite handy for a night'. As the front page of the same paper carried the story: 'I Gave the Boot to Cheating Charlie' by 'sexy TV star Suzanne Dando', this admission was just as well (*News of the World*, 25 November 1984).

Back in Scotland he is still regarded as a 'special' player but, for whatever reason, Nicholas' early promise was never quite fulfilled. He's a bit of a sad case, regarded as a tiring veteran at 29 years of age, looking to leave Celtic and get a move, perhaps, 'to the Continent' where his skill might be appreciated. To Scots he represents the living embodiment of a great talent laid to waste by a combination of readily available distractions and over-regimented tactics, easily found in England, which can quickly stifle the spontaneous genius of the Scottish ball-player.

National identity

One cultural problem which the migration of Scottish football talent underlines is that of the complexities of a national identity: what it is to be 'a Scot' and how that is to be maintained, or not, in the face of the economic riches of England. One of the bricks that can become dislodged in stepping across the Wall can be the one that makes you a Scot. For a time 'Anglos' were not chosen for the national team and they are still regarded with suspicion. To take a recent example, Alan Hansen (who left Partick for Liverpool when aged 21) is felt to have been less than whole-hearted in his desire to play for Scotland. There were a number of unofficial bans on further selection, recalls, 'clear-the-air talks', etc., but he did not seem over-concerned to represent his 'nation'.

It is not a simple matter of individual motivation here but of structures of power. When Scots go south they move out of the control of their national federation and fall under the sway of English clubs and English rules. However, one of the peculiarities of the British situation is that many of the managers of top English clubs are Scots. In the last few years, Liverpool players have become notorious for regular 'injuries' which have caused them to withdraw from international duty but have healed sufficiently to allow them to play for the club soon after. Just as bad was Alex Ferguson (once national manager and severe critic of the spirit of the Anglo but now managing Manchester United) withdrawing his players from international duty to take part in a lucrative club friendly abroad. Scots are quick to note that for many years the English manager had rights to players in the English League which the other national teams did not and, even yet, they are the beneficiaries of much more co-operation – English League matches postponed before important English international matches and so on. The club versus country clash is a staple part of the football tradition in Britain, but in 'northern Britain' its edge gets particularly sharp when the club is elsewhere and the manager is, apparently, a Scot. For the question often posed through the routines of football migration is: What exactly is a Scot?

Scot or not?
Football (and the migration of footballing talent) has always meant a lot to Scots and meant different things for them than for the English (Moorhouse, 1984). But material forces, structural relations and, so, cultural representations do change. They do not alter quickly but, in Scotland, what soccer denotes is changing. Simply put, it is moving under the push of unbridled economic power. Many of the forces that have structured Scottish football are changing; there are new issues for Scottish football and Scotland to contend with. One of these is that the pattern of the migration of talent has altered and there has been more of a movement of European and English players (especially top-class ones) to Scotland. Not many years ago Scottish newspaper quizzes could ask: 'Name the four players who have played in the premier league this year who could not play for Scotland'; now Rangers alone

could often field a side of non-Scots. Some papers wryly declared that the sensation, when the 'Protestant' Rangers signed Maurice Johnson, was not that the manager had signed a Catholic but that he had signed a Scotsman. The national manager complained in 1990 that the number of 'foreigners' now playing in the premier division meant that chances for young Scots were being drastically curtailed and that, in the long term, this could sap the strength of the Scots side. More recently fears were expressed that the 22 overseas players and many English now available for teams in the premier division alone meant that contemporary Scottish football had become 'full of foreigners' mostly of quite average ability. It was argued that the £6 million paid for the overseas men had affected the routines of the internal transfer market and was adding to the great financial problems of Scottish football (*The Scotsman*, 22 February 1993).

Sometimes the newcomers are not held to understand the special features of the Scottish game. They are thought to be unaware of the volcanic intensities which are said to underlie the clash of the Old Firm, for example, and so engage in (unconciously) provocative behaviour. Generally, though, the imports have been welcomed. They are quickly pictured in all the tartan attire of 'Scottishness'. They all declare how different the country is from English myth, as with Mrs Terry Butcher: 'This isn't what we expected of Scotland from the TV in England. You just hear about going into a bar in Glasgow and having a bottle pushed in your face. It just isn't true. Everywhere I go people are helpful' (*Sunday Mail* 14 September 1986).

The Scots media has taken on the entirely new role of arguing the case of these 'imports' for selection as English internationalists. It is a reiterated belief in Scotland that the English players who have come to play in Scotland are not given the same chance to represent their country as Englishmen playing in England and, moreover, that there is a conspiracy, 'in the London media', to influence the English manager to pick players from the English League in preference to Scottish-based players, as with the dropping of Woods of Rangers as England goalkeeper to be replaced by Seaman of Arsenal in 1991. There has been criticism of the fact that the English team manager rarely, if ever, attends a Scottish League game and so can hardly be said to be giving the English 'exiles' a close scrutiny. In other words, the Scottish perception that the English have always slighted the standard of play in the Scottish League and assumed that the Scottish game is not really 'first class' is now given a new twist and is said to operate to the detriment of English players who have reversed that century-long flow across the border. Scottish commentary now takes up its cudgels on behalf of English players, and the non-recognition of Rangers winger Walters was a long-running issue. Now, some of these players, including Woods and Walters, have moved south again, perhaps in the belief that they would stand a better chance of gaining international caps.

Discussion of the English lack of interest in Walters was often couched in terms of 'if only he were Scottish . . .', but in fact Scots have used very, very few players in the international team who were born outside their boundaries. Passing quickly over Lord Kinnaird (Cheam, Eton and Trinity Cambridge) and his cap in 1873, up to 1986 only six players played for Scotland who were born in England. Four were introduced into the Scottish squad in 1972 when the rule changed to allow those born 'abroad' of Scottish parents to play. Three of the six were goalkeepers (a position at which Scots tend not to excel). The present first-choice keeper, Goram (son of a goalie transferred from from Third Lanark to Bury), has a Lancashire accent, and was greeted at his first game at Hampden Park with triumphant crowd chants of: 'You're no English any more!' However, selection of non-territorials has been circumspect. Joe Baker had lived most of his life in Scotland, played for a Scottish club, spoke with a thick Lanarkshire accent, and was regarded as 'Scottish' by most Scots, but he played as centre-forward for England because of his place of birth. Now ever-developing patterns of labour migration are throwing up more complicated issues of national identity.

A recent interesting case is that of Stuart McCall, born in Yorkshire of Scottish parents, and, as a youngster, sought by both England and Scotland. Indeed as a 20-year-old he was picked for the under-21 sides of Scotland and England on the same day, and had just half an hour to choose his 'nationality'. His father, a Scottish footballer with three English clubs, wanted him to choose the old country but he opted for England in November 1984. However, by 1988 he was turning out for Scotland against England in an under-21 UEFA match and is now a regular member of the full Scottish squad. In 1984 he had joined the English team in Turkey but: 'I felt it was a mistake almost from the start. I was put on the bench and they tried to bring me on with a minute to go. But I took my time re-tying my boots and generally warming up and luckily didn't get on, otherwise that would have been that' (*Glasgow Herald*, 22 March 1988). He had avoided the terrible fate of becoming 'English' by being canny and by a matter of minutes for: 'My heart simply wasn't in it and I opted out of being classified as English for international purposes' (*The Scotsman*, 22 March 1988). He informed the Scottish authorities that if he was given the opportunity to become a 'Scot' he would not need to be asked again, but he had to wait for three years before being chosen for another Scottish squad.

In January 1991 another player miraculously seemed to have made a much easier transition. One of the Rangers' English imports, Spackman, was a surprise choice for the Scottish team against the USSR and qualified because of his ancestry. His grandfather had been born in Prestonpans. It appeared that Roxborough, the Scottish national manager, had long been an admirer of 'MacSpackman' (as the player was immediately dubbed) and then had discovered he was qualified to play for the country:

> It was some months ago that our committee in discussion clarified the position of eligibility for Scottish players that if they were eligible under FIFA rules but, very importantly, had a Scottish bloodline, then we could consider them. And it was only after that that I decided to look very closely at Nigel Spackman in our context (STV local news, 28 January, 1991).

Roxborough added that the player had a dual possibility of international honours but had chosen Scotland and was very enthusiastic about playing for the country: 'And you've got to remember now that he's adopted here anyway, because he plays here and lives here and therefore he was more than delighted to be involved'.

The local sports broadcast on BBC TV also began with the paradox that: 'Rangers' English midfielder Nigel Spackman looks set to pull on the dark-blue jersey of Scotland', but quickly followed up with another reference to the mysterious concept of a 'bloodline'. Spackman himself offered a somewhat opaque justification:

> I think it's the first time that any player has played for Scotland because of their grandparents and this is a one off. But I think as I'm playing in Scotland, as I'm living in Scotland and I've been up here for 14 months now, I think that's going to help me. I don't think if I was still playing at maybe Liverpool or QPR or Chelsea or something I would have been picked because I wasn't actually playing in Scotland.

On the BBC local news programme Roxburgh emphasized again the player's commitment to the cause and added:

> There's a bonus for us because he lives and works here now as well which is a help. And if you ask me that question then are you

going to question John Barnes? I mean John Barnes has no English blood in him. He plays for England. Are you going to question half the Irish team? I mean where does it end? So what we're saying here is that if someone is eligible to you and in this case, very important for us, that they have a bloodline . . . that must be emphasized, we will not take [just] anybody under the standard FIFA rules. We have our own interpretation of it. And therefore the fact is that he has Scottish blood in him and he feels a commitment to Scotland and that's good enough for us.

Swathed in a tartan scarf Spackman made the same points in the Scottish papers the next morning, and added further proof of his national credentials: 'If I'm picked to play there will be a little lion roaring in my heart. My grandfather died about 20 years ago, but I remember sitting on his knee when he was wearing a Stewart tartan blanket – sorry, I mean kilt' (*Daily Record*, 29 January 1991). In *The Scotsman* he was pictured looking at the First World War medal his Scottish granddad had won, while the journalist added a few more wrinkles to the story:

> Scotland, unlike the other home countries and the Republic of Ireland, has always spurned the idea of adopting players purely on the basis they hold a British passport and express a willingness to play under a flag of convenience . . . Roxburgh saw the matter as having been 'clarified' by the case of the youth player Shaun Rouse who is, coincidentally, on Rangers' staff. Rouse was wanted by Scotland but claimed by England on the basis that he had been born in Great Yarmouth, though the teenager lived in England for only one week before his family moved to Aberdeen. Under FIFA regulations, England were acting within their rights and now the SFA is accepting that what is good enough for Graham Taylor is also good enough for Andy Roxburgh.

There were more references to 'bloodlines', the numerical advantage England enjoyed anyway, and the laughable practices of Eire.

Actually, the question of Spackman's eligibility had been raised exactly one year before but his claim had been quickly dismissed:

> Under FIFA rules Spackman's British passport is enough to entitle him to play for any of the home nations, but apart from the Irish, they observe a code of ethics, which means that at least one of Spackman's parents would have had to be Scottish . . .

There is another reason why his desire to win recognition will not be satisfied in Scotland. We don't play people called Nigel. If we made allowances for Spackman . . . we might be opening the international door to any Theodore, Dirk or Cyril (*Glasgow Herald*, 22 January 1990).

The newspaper protestations of, among other 'colonials', Zimbabwe-born Bruce Grobbelaar that they 'wouldn't mind turning out for Scotland', like Brian Clough's yearning to manage the national team, had been similarly pooh-poohed. But by 1991 it seemed things were not quite so clear-cut. It appeared Roxburgh had other players in the same position in mind: 'Perhaps the Scots eventually might adhere strictly, like some other nations, to FIFA's ruling that a player who holds a British passport is eligible to play for any of the home nations. Scotland is too small to hamper international prospects further by imposing its own restrictions' (*Glasgow Herald*, 29 January 1991). The national manager, it was said, had had many players recommended to him but could not pick them because of SFA's past policy.

Dissent was certainly expressed: 'Spackman was an Englishman last week, is still an Englishman today and will remain an Englishman when he pulls on a Scottish jersey' (*Evening Times*, 29 January 1991), but generally the Scottish media thought this selection could just about pass but that this was where the line had to be drawn. Scotland did not want to get like the Irish who, some thought, took a close look at anyone who had ever drunk a Guinness. It was argued that 'players will surely always have a drop or two of Scots blood' (*Daily Record*, 29 January 1991). A fairly lengthy and rather unpleasant semiotic reading could be provided about what is going on in some of these quotes. The idea of 'Scotland' being carried in the blood as opposed to the head is preposterous, and starts to steer 'nationality' into stormy waters. There has not yet, I think, been a modern 'Scot' good enough to play for his country while born of English parents (though plenty have of Irish parents) but this will surely occur eventually, and I doubt the Scottish authorities and media will be so keen on corpuscle-counting then.

The first English-Scots international of recent times – Wilson – soon intervened in the dispute. Noting that his parents' place of birth meant that *he* had certainly felt Scottish (though this had not stopped him gaining schoolboy honours for England and, before his first cap, he had played only two games – both friendlies – on his 'native' soil), he did think that claiming nationality through one grandparent was stretching matters too far and would just lead to increased media interrogation of the motives and spirit of Spackman. 'Like me, I am sure he would find that initial meeting with the squad awkward to say the least. An English accent in the midst of a gathering of the clans goes down like roast beef and Yorkshire pudding on Burns Night' (*Sunday Times* (Scotland), 3 February 1991). Actually if Spackman had been allowed to join the 1991 Scottish squad he would have been able to lend his ear to at least two others with English accents, and another dappled with the inflexions of southern Africa.

However circuitous all the reasoning, we can see how the Scottish authorities were trying to negotiate some of the problems that arise about 'nationality' when labour generally, and football talent in particular, crosses frontiers. They were trying to distinguish this somewhat odd choice of player from what Eire now routinely does and, of course, from perfidious Albion (the English beast is never far away in Scottish demonology). The next day Spackman was pulled out of the Scottish squad when the English FA objected, or at least it seemed that they had told the SFA that they were about to write and point out that the SFA had contravened a 1988 agreement between the home associations about eligibility which contained no mention of grandparents (or 'bloodlines' for that matter).

In effect the home associations *have* to adopt different rules from FIFA. Its rules on eligibility say that players can play for any country whose passport they hold but, since Britain has one passport but four footballing 'countries', adhering to this would allow players to choose whichever home 'country' took their fancy (and Joe Baker probably would have played for Scotland!). So the home associations have their own code and stick at either 'country' of birth or 'country' of natural parents. A player with parents born outside the UK, but with a passport, can elect for whichever 'country' he wants – thus Barnes and England despite his Caribbean 'blood'. Spackman is 30 and has never figured in English plans, so it seems likely it was the precedent rather than the player that the FA was concerned about. Both the Northern Irish FA and Welsh FA also complained (considered particularly rich in Scotland as it was quickly pointed out that Wales at present play a Belgian-born cockney in their team) and there was talk about 'breaches of gentlemen's agreements', and about 'floodgates opening'. The Secretary of the SFA said they would be pursuing the matter and hinted that, if they had to, they would be going to FIFA's Player Status Committee for a ruling: 'Does a domestic agreement supersede a FIFA ruling? . . . it is my view that there is a basic unfairness in any system which apparently restricts the ability of anyone to represent the country of his choice' (*Glasgow Herald*, 31 January 1991), but soon after the matter was dropped, probably because the home associations have no wish to broadcast the various oddities which occur because of their unique position in world football (Moorhouse, 1989). However, for reasons I will sketch in a moment, similar cases may become pertinent soon enough.

While there was some routine English-bashing at this outcome there was a feeling that the SFA should never have got into such a position, should have done their research better, and it provoked a deal of discussion about just who was eligible to be a 'Scot' in various sports. It became plain that there are different rules for almost all sports. Via his grandfather Spackman would have been perfectly qualified to play rugby for Scotland (as is the New Zealander Lineen) and even Walters could have turned out for the land of the mountain and the flood at cricket, basketball or athletics through a two- or three-year residency qualification (*Glasgow Herald*, 16 January 1991). It emerged that there was some disagreement about quite what this football rule was intended to do, with the Secretary of the SFA stating: 'This agreement was never intended to stop senior players playing at international level. It was designed to stop the poaching of younger players' (*Daily Record*, 30 January 1991).

DISCUSSION

We can now see the kind of issues I think are raised by the migration of footballers within the British Isles. Some are old, some are new. Some are of general applicability, some are particular to the odd circumstances of a 'United Kingdom' which for football purposes consists of four countries and three major leagues (Moorhouse, 1989).

First of all there are the effects on the feelings between countries. Behind migration lie patterns of economics and power. It is these that breed migration and generate the cultural preoccupations that attend on the movement and gain symbolic display through it. These are complex. In Scotland there is a profound duality. A fatalistic sense of loss mingles with the pride that the English simply cannot get by without taking Scottish talent. Then the lack of comprehension, and failure to grasp what all the fuss is about, in the country that takes the talent simply fuels irritation at a superiority achieved, or at least claimed, by nothing more worthy than callous cash payment.

Then there are all those 'personal dangers' for the players that move. The structural forces which compel migration get displaced into failings of character, weakness in personality and the frailty of 'human nature'. Structures remain relatively unexamined as some Scots are thought to 'sell out', an old simplistic phrase for all manner of rather complicated phenomena in modern life. People in the old country are constantly disappointed, but live in hope that the rising generation will prove more immune to blandishments.

Thirdly there are all the official limitations and competing definitions about who is or is not one of the 'nation'. This may well become more pertinent. It was not lost on opinion in Scotland that Spackman was a Ranger and that it was very convenient for the club to have him defined as a 'Scot'. For new UEFA restrictions on the number of 'non-indigenous' players who can be in a team, designed to defend the integrity of 'national competitions', seem set to affect the selection of nationality. Will British managers be quite so keen for some of their players to become 'Irish' at the international level, for example? In 1993 the manager of the Scottish team was trying to pick a Liverpool player, Don Hutchison, whose father had been born in Scotland, for the under-21 squad. The manager of Liverpool, Souness, a former captain of Scotland, was reluctant to agree to this as this would make the footballer a 'foreigner' in UEFA club competitions. In effect, a Scot was denying the right of another man to become one. At the moment UEFA rules that 'England is a foreign country' (which, of course, in many respects Scots like to believe it is) but this makes Rangers (and their ideas of competing with the very best in Europe) very dependent on finding a lot of big fish in the rather small Scottish pool, a handicap on rivalry with major foreign clubs which seems unfair. However, if English sides are not allowed to play many 'foreign' Scots (and it should be remembered that there is still a routine flow of players to England), then one traditional and staple source of income for almost all Scottish club will be curtailed to some degree (Moorhouse, 1991). Of course, one possibility of the new Europe is much greater migration of labour, and it might well be that more Scots will move to continental clubs, but this would not involve Scots in the same bitter-sweet relation as that much shorter trip to the south. Anti-Englishness, the essence which defines 'Scottishness', would not be renewed through the routines of the market for soccer talent in quite the same way.

Lurking here, though, is a deeper issue about what it is to be a 'Scot' (or Catalan or Basque) in a period which is likely to see a much greater migration of labour, and whether that really matters. Indeed, the issue really is what is 'national identity' going to become in a Europe which seeks to encourage mobility? Put another way, what is the most appropriate basis for football competition in the future? Nationality always has been a dubious (and violent) basis. Talk of 'bloodlines' makes me, at least, uneasy. Partly hidden here is the relative salience of European club competition versus country, but if a lot more players start to move hither and thither then perhaps we should ask what their real claim to represent 'their' country is? Maybe residence is a rather more reasonable basis for selection than birth. However, in the particular case I am considering, to worry away about who is a Scot is to worry away at what is 'Scotland'. Not only how long its (and England's, Wales's and Northern Ireland's) peculiar place in world football competition can survive, but how long claims of 'nationhood' can continue without sounding totally irrelevant. In recent years Eire seems to have shown that a team, most of whom don't know the words of the national anthem, can easily 'represent' a nation, but for Scotland the issue is rather more fraught because it doesn't have an anthem. As one journalist put it obliquely about the Spackman affair: 'Because Scotland is not, in the strictest sense a country at all, these are murky waters' (*Evening Times*, 29 January 1991). Scots sneer at the Republic of Ireland and its 'Guinness-drinking' qualification but Eire has a recognized flag and is a nation-state; it has a place. Scotland really only has sport with which to strut its independent existence on the world stage. Otherwise symbols are all, there is only tartan, Nessie, stags, crags, glens and blazing beacons. A small country, subject both to a deal of out-migration and the oppression of well-meaning general rules, maybe Scotland will have to forget birth and turn to the heart. Who *wants* to be a Scot may be more important than any 'blood'. Alex Cropley, another of the English-born internationals, put it this way in 1971: 'I have always thought it ridiculous that just because I spent the first three years of my life in England, I was considered English'. More pithily: 'I am, in everything, bar birth, Scottish' (*The Scotsman* 5 October 1971). The ramifications of such a declaration of independence may well need to be pondered more generally for sporting contests in the new Europe which is steadily emerging.

REFERENCES

Cosgrove, S. (1991) *Hampden Babylon: Sex and Scandal in Scottish Football* (Edinburgh: Cannongate).
Commission on Industrial Relations (1974) *Professional Football*, Report No. 87 (London: HMSO).
Evans, R. (1824) 'Blue bonnets over the border: a celebrated Scots air' (London: R. Evans).
Lamming, D. (1987) A Scottish Internationalists' Who's Who 1872–1986 (Beverley: Hutton Press).

Lay, D. (1984) 'The Migration of Scottish Footballers to the English Football League' (Southampton University: unpublished undergraduate dissertation).

MacLennan, S. (1974) *Leaders in Attack* (Lossiemouth: Lossiemouth Printers).

Moorhouse, H.F. (1984) 'Professional Football and Working Class Culture: English Theories and Scottish Evidence', *Sociological Review*, 32, 285–315.

(1989) 'One State, Several Countries: Soccer and Identities in a "United" Kingdom', Colloquium Paper, (Florence: European University Institute), pp. 1–14.

(1990) 'Scottish Shooting Stars: Footballers as Working Class Symbols in Twentieth Century Scotland' in Holt, R. (ed.), *Sport and the Working Class in Modern Britain* (Manchester: Manchester University Press) pp. 179–97.

(1991) 'On the Periphery: Scotland, Scottish Football and the New Europe' in Williams, J. and Wagg, S. (eds), *British Football and Social Change* (London: Leicester University Press) pp. 201–19.

Munro, G. (1947) *Gold in His Boots* (typescript in Glasgow University library).

Taylor, H. (1970) *Scottish Football Book No. 16* (London: Stanley Paul).

Part Two:

Comparative Trends:
Contemporary Case Studies

7

Dimensions of International Talent Migration in Latin American Sports

Joseph L. Arbena

The international migration of sports talent into, out of, and within Latin America has been for some time and remains today a significant phenomenon. Unfortunately, with minor exceptions (cited below), no studies, especially of a quantitative or geographical nature, have been done to document and evaluate the nature and impact of these movements. Therefore, my intention here is to sketch out those areas over the last century where I believe the most migration has occurred and in so doing to highlight various intra- and extra-regional forms of such migration. I likewise suggest some future research topics and raise a few questions about the theoretical implications of the sport talent migration theme in Latin American history.

In doing this, I indicate the types of sources I have so far explored which offer insights into the sport migration process in Latin America and comment on other materials which might aid further researchers (Arbena, 1989). Throughout I have chosen to assume the role of *Latin* Americanist in the traditional sense; thus I will not be dealing directly with West Indian cricket, nor with the extensive literature which exists on that subject.

IN-MIGRATION

If we examine international sports talent migration in Latin America in terms of the three spatial dimensions mentioned above (into, out of and within), we will conclude that the least activity, in terms of both quantity and organization, has been in the first category, that is from the outside in, though by no means should this suggest that such movement has been absent and thus unavailable for study. A historical example is to be found in the visits to Mexico of Spanish bull-fighters (*toreros*) beginning in the late nineteenth century after the re-establishment of the *fiesta brava* following several decades of liberal suppression of this 'violent' Hispanic festival. Mexicans were anxious to bring the revived activity up to the highest performance standards and Spain offered the best models both to watch and to emulate (Guarner, 1979). A few Mexican *toreros* have also sought experience and recognition in Iberia, though this has rarely involved more than isolated and temporary individual visits (Maria y Campos, 1943). Within Latin America the country that rivals Mexico as a centre of classical bullfighting (*toreo*), and is thus also a site for interchange with Spain, is Peru; after Mexico and Peru, only Colombia and Venezuela maintain traditional *toreo* and ongoing contacts with the former mother country. What this may say about the Hispanic context of the broader culture of these societies is potentially quite revealing, even if the activity itself is increasingly marginal to the practice of sport and the migration of sports talent (Calmell L., 1936; Luna, 1967; Salas, 1980–81).

Also, for almost a century Basques from areas of both Spain and France have carried their unique culture, including their diverse ball games of which jai-alai is only one, to different regions of Latin America, either as professional players (in this case, jai-alai is the major sport) or as part of the larger European migration process. Perhaps this has been most conspicuous in Cuba, Mexico, Florida, and other circum-Caribbean areas, as well as in the Southern Cone, though some evidence of this transfer is also observed in Ecuador and various Andean regions (Llanes, 1981; Tufiño, 1928).

This larger European migration has made other limited (one might even say superficial) yet notable contributions to Latin American sport. For example, Silvia Poll, born in Nicaragua of German parents but now a Costa Rican citizen, became an international swimming star and a celebrity in her new land after she set two records and won eight medals at the 10th Pan American Games at Indianapolis in 1987 (Kenny, 1988). Also, throughout the 1970s, virtually the only hope Colombia had of winning Olympic medals lay in the hands of a talented pistol marksman likewise of recent German origin. Although the achievements of these athletes do not reflect general improvements in local sports facilities and training, they have provided their adopted homelands with moments, however fleeting, of celebration and pride. They also result obviously from migrations which took place for other primary reasons, with sports merely an incidental, however important, consequence.

Migration of sports talent from the United States to Latin America has been relatively rare. Perhaps the most important example involves baseball players. From the 1930s until at least the 1960s, many North

American professionals supplemented their incomes and kept in shape by playing winter ball in the Caribbean, especially Cuba and the Dominican Republic. Before the racial integration of the American national pastime, many black stars followed whites to the islands, a process which probably did as much to facilitate better race relations back in the States as it did to improve baseball in the Caribbean or to promote trans-culturation among English-speaking and Hispanic athletes and their communities (Rogosin, 1985). Since the 1970s, higher salaries in the majors have reduced North American participation in Latin winter ball, though a few younger players still use the opportunity to work on their game and potential managers seek to develop and demonstrate their leadership capabilities. In addition to filling spots on Caribbean winter teams, several American players have made or extended their careers in the Mexican leagues, though never in the numbers envisioned by the Mexican owners who tried unsuccessfully to attract players from across the border in the 1940s (Agundis, 1956; Wulf, 1980). But, except in the special and limited Mexican case, this baseball migration has been seasonal at best, in either or both directions.

More recently a few basketball players from the United States, insufficiently skilled to play even in Europe or the North American minor leagues, have found brief employment in Brazil and the River Plate countries where they may aid the locals in honing their skills. That baseball, though of much less significance, is also played in the Southern Cone – for example, Argentina, Paraguay, parts of Brazil – is no doubt due mainly to Japanese immigrants rather than those from North America or the Caribbean (Pastrian, 1977; Zelada Silva, 1988).

OUT-MIGRATION

More common, or at least more visible over the years, has been the migration of Latin American sports talent out of the region, mostly to North American or Europe. Before 1959, many Cubans took pride in the number of their countrymen who became successful professional athletes, mainly boxers and baseball players and mainly in the United States. After 1959, the anti-Castro community cited those heroes of their youth as evidence that the old Cuba was a source of champions (Ferreiro Mora, 1978; Torres, 1976). Not surprisingly, since 1959, the backers of the Cuban revolution have cited that same evidence to support their contention that capitalist/neo-colonial Cuba had an elitist sports system which gave opportunities to few people and then exploited, through foreign export, those few (usually black) athletes from the lower classes who did reach the top. For example, Ferreiro Mora (1978) mainly recounts the triumphs and fame of the legendary Kid Chocolate (Eligio Sardiñas) in his prime, while Fernádez (1981) focuses more on the difficulties facing the Kid after his career ended and on the contrasting economic security and respect he later enjoyed in Cuba under Castro.

Whatever the merits of the debate, it is clear that before 1959 for Cuban athletes to succeed as professionals they usually had to leave their island republic (Arbena, 1990). Perhaps an extreme case is that of boxer Evelio Mustelier (Kid Tunero), who during the 1930s and 1940s fought principally in Europe, as well as the United States and Latin America, marrying a Frenchwoman and eventually settling in Spain (Mustelier, 1985). Certainly a valuable study waits to be done on those Cuban athletes and their children who for professional or political reasons chose to remain and play outside Cuba after Castro's victory over Batista (Sheer, 1971; Gammons, 1986; Senzel, 1977). The Sandinista triumph in Nicaragua in 1979, which likewise triggered a change in sports policy, did not provoke as serious a disruption in sports talent migration because the number of talented athletes affected was much lower, though Alexis Argüello, winner of world titles in three weight divisions, lost his property to the government and chose to settle in Miami until the Sandinistas left office (Anon., 1992).

Following the Cuban revolution, the supply of fresh Cuban athletes for North American markets dried up (Figueredo, 1984). In the case of baseball, at least, new sources were found in other areas of the circum-Caribbean. The most prominent of these has been the Dominican Republic, though baseball players in smaller numbers have also reached the major leagues from Mexico, Panama, Nicaragua, Colombia, Venezuela and Puerto Rico. Mexico is surely underrepresented in North American organized baseball for the size of its population and the talent of its athletes, a function of Mexican contract law which makes transfer to foreign teams more difficult and expensive than elsewhere; there were only eight Mexicans in the major leagues in September 1991 (Banks, 1985; Jamail, 1991; Estrada, 1991). Those same countries have also provided many of the championship boxers of the last two decades, as well as a few jockeys and American football players.

Despite periodic sketches offered in *Sports Illustrated* and occasional popular biographies – most in Spanish unless dealing with exceptional Latin baseball players such as Roberto Clemente – very little is known about these 'migrant workers', their backgrounds, their experiences, and the impact of their careers on their homelands and their host societies. Useful as a starting point should be the recent volume by the Oleksaks (1991) which, in addition to a narrative overview of baseball history in the circum-Caribbean realm, provides a tabular, statistical summary of the careers of over 500 Latins known to have played in the major leagues.

Preliminary evidence from various sources suggests that the departure of these Latin players to pursue their baseball careers elsewhere has a mixed impact on the lands and peoples they leave behind. Certainly there is a sense of pride in the athletic and economic accomplishments of the exported players, including satisfaction in beating the Americans, often considered imperialists, at their own game. The regional press appropriately devotes special coverage to the achievements of all Latins in the big leagues. Simultaneously, there is a sense of loss, a feeling that the home country is being robbed of its own human and recreational resources. Similarly, the gratitude felt because the *gringos* have recognized the skills of their countrymen is somewhat offset by a perception that Latins are neither always understood nor treated fairly by the anglophone whites who dominate professional baseball (Klein, 1990 and 1991; LaFrance, 1985; Krich, 1989).

For the individual athletes, more severe surely are the problems they encounter in the North American environment. Virtually every biography and autobiography of Latin ballplayers I have read (Arbena, 1989; Cepeda, 1983) cites the obstacles they face in adapting to their new homes: language; differing cultural forms and norms; isolation from team-mates, fans and the press; and, since most Latin players, whether of African or Amerindian roots, are darker-skinned, racism, more before the civil rights movement but to some degree even into the 1990s, a problem Afro-Caribbeans appear to face in Europe as well (Maguire, 1991). Some clubs are trying to help players adapt by offering English language instruction and guidance in basic social behaviour, but time and resources are limited and the impact so far is minimal (Klein, 1990; Banks, 1991).

Interestingly, there are signs that the Japanese intend to follow the North American pattern of recruiting and importing young Dominican baseball talent. The psycho-cultural problems which could arise from an expansion of this migration can only be imagined, but the experiences of US players in Japan suggest that the adjustment for Dominicans there could be even more difficult than in the United States and Canada.

Much to the dismay of soccer fans in the far south, a similar relationship has developed between various South American countries and wealthy European professional clubs, principally in Spain and

Italy, secondarily in England and France. In the words of Argentine journalist Osvaldo Bayer (1990): 'The central countries, in the same manner as they carry away the riches of the Third World, likewise carry off their best soccer players.' The result for Uruguay, laments long-time player and coach, José 'Pepe' Sasía, is that 'now the best Uruguayan players play here as little boys, when they are just beginning, and as veterans when they are finishing. Their [whole] youth and their peak athletic years are spent abroad'. It is a problem, argues Sasía, rooted in the region's social and economic conditions (Sasía, 1989).

Those clubs with players to sell make money up front, and the families of those who play in Europe may gain from the inflated salaries. For example, Boca Juniors of Buenos Aires bought the contract of Diego Maradona from Argentinos Juniors for the equivalent of 24 million French francs and resold it shortly thereafter for about 60 million. The transfer of Brazilian stars Cerezo and Zico to Italian clubs earned their former owners 25 and 30 million French francs respectively (Bourg, 1986). All of this seems to support on the global level Bale's assertions that 'in professional sport, clubs at the economic margin and geographical periphery are often forced to sell their best young players in order to survive' (Bale, 1989).

Meanwhile back home, say critics, the quality of play on the field drops markedly, as do attendances and gate receipts (Sebreli, 1981). Likewise, the geographical dispersal of the best players from the Southern Cone countries allegedly makes it more difficult for the coaches of their national teams to put together consistently an experienced, winning combination for international competition (Minotti, 1978; Bilardo, 1986).

North America has not been the destination of many professional soccer players from Latin America. Although the recruitment of Pelé (by the New York Cosmos to help inaugurate the North American Soccer League in the 1970s) made big headlines world-wide, more Europeans than Latins seem to have followed the dollars in that ultimately failed venture. And only a handful of Latin Americans are apparently interested in the chance to play indoor soccer up north (Bodo and Hirshey, 1977; Diaz, 1987).

Not all Latin Americans involved in soccer consider the export of their best performers such a bad thing. In 1987 the president of Chile's National Association of Professional Soccer bragged of the fact that recent years had seen his country's star players attract the attention of the world's soccer powers, a number of them transferring to foreign teams. This he cited as evidence that the quality of Chilean soccer was improving dramatically (Nasur Allel, 1987). José Dosal Estrada (1990), former player and now a well-known sports journalist, in discussing the career of Mexican soccer hero Hugo Sánchez, proclaimed that for both the athlete and his country being successful in Spain was the greatest goal and honour.

Less significant economically, at least on the surface, but of possible cultural importance, is the increased recruitment by North American colleges and universities of Latin American scholarship athletes. Thus far I sense that the major sports where this has occurred are tennis, track and field, soccer and basketball, the last especially in relation to Puerto Rico, though the future, I suspect, could see other countries helping to stock NCAA and NAIA roundball squads. (Even the NBA has evaluated and signed a few Latin players of international quality.) The University of Oregon, for example, enjoyed the services of Joaquim Cruz, Brazilian Olympic gold medallist at 800 metres in 1984; Clemson University laid the foundations of its championship soccer programme in part on recruits from Jamaica and Guyana; and schools like Southern California and Miami of Florida have strengthened their tennis traditions with Latin students. Baseball is obviously not a factor here because Latin baseball players are usually of poor economic and educational backgrounds; few are prepared for college and most prefer to sign professional contracts as soon as they can. Other sports in which colleges field teams do not offer as many professional alternatives, particularly for young people who are good enough to play in the United States but lack the talent to turn professional in Latin America (Bale, 1991).

INTRA-LATIN AMERICAN MIGRATION

This out-migration of athletic talent is not exactly a new phenomenon even in South America. For a variety of reasons, athletes, especially professional and semi-professional soccer players, have been crossing international borders, even oceans, for several generations. In particular, there has long been easy movement among the neighbouring countries of Argentina, Paraguay and Uruguay, while a few Latin stars were testing the European fields of Italy and Spain. Following the Argentine soccer players' strike of 1948, there was an even greater exodus from the pampas, both to Europe and to other South American countries such as Chile and Colombia which were struggling to catch up athletically with their more powerful continental competitors. Vacant positions in Buenos Aires were filled in turn by players imported from weaker South American economies (for example,

Peru, Bolivia and, as before, Paraguay), intensifying a process which in a sense still continues (Ramírez, 1990; Ramos Ruis, 1973; Meza Vera, 1978).

The reactions in the recipient countries to these types of migration has varied, depending on circumstances. On the one hand, after a plane crash killed most of the famous Alianza Lima soccer team in December 1987, Peruvian fans were grateful that several players from Santiago's Colo Colo club came to fill the gap, despite the fact that historically Peruvians have looked on Chileans as a source of aggression and pain (Burgos and Del Mastro, 1991). In another context, the Colombian coach who took his national team to the 1990 World Cup in Italy felt that the tradition of importing Argentine and other foreign players to stock local clubs had hindered the development of Colombian talent and of a true Colombian style of play (Maturana, 1990). In recent years, Colombia has not only improved its international performance but has begun to export to Europe its own top performers, such as Carlos Valderrama, as well as that same national coach, the result of a new focus on exploiting domestic resources.

International migration of Latin American soccer talent has not been confined to players. After their playing days have ended, many athletes pursue a career in coaching, a career which is often inaugurated along the sidelines of foreign fields. On balance, Argentines seem to be the most in demand. The coaches of both their World Cup championship teams (Menotti and Bilardo) have extensive experience away from the River Plate, Menotti as late as 1991 being named to direct the Mexican national team after several years working in Brazil and Spain (Hartley, 1992); and before them such figures as Carlos Desiderio Peucelle and Julio Tocker travelled widely across Latin America as ambassadors of gaucho soccer (Peucelle, 1975; Tocker, 1984; Bayer, 1990). Of course in some instances successful, or at least colourful European coaches have taken turns leading Latin American club and national teams.

Although in the introduction I indicated my intention to ignore the British Caribbean, at least as it pertains to cricket, I close this section on intra-Latin American migration by looking at two aspects of emigration from the anglophone Antilles. During the mid-nineteenth century and again in the early twentieth century, thousands of English-speaking blacks and mulattos moved to the isthmus of Panama to work first on the railway and later on the inter-oceanic canal. As a consequence, more recently some of Panama's most prominent athletes have come from (usually black or brown) anglophone families. These include the phenomenal Alfonso Teófilo ('Panama' Al) Brown

(1902–51) who, like many of his Cuban contemporaries, lived his life, built his career and ultimately died abroad and alone – in this case in New York of tuberculosis. Less tragic is the story of exceptional baseball batter Rodney Carew, while less well known are the successful anglophone-Panamanians Oscar Layne (cyclist) and Lloyd La Beach (Olympic sprinter). (Salsa and film star Ruben Blades is an example from another area of popular culture.) And there have been more, all of which suggests a potential study of the role of the British community in isthmian sports (Morales, T., 1989), though not just in Panama, since anglophone-Caribbeans probably aided the introduction of baseball to Costa Rica as well (González Villavicencio, 1954). (Undeniably, Cubans, to return to the Latin sphere, were influential in spreading baseball all over the Caribbean basin rimland).

Secondly, in his recent study of Dominican baseball, Ruck (1991) discusses the Cocolos, British West Indians who migrated to labour in Dominican sugar-cane fields. Hard workers, they carried a sense of discipline and community, and a love of cricket. 'Without these English-speaking, cricket-playing sojourners, Dominican baseball would never have become the best in the Caribbean', for it was the Cocolos' sons and grandsons who transferred their skills, their sense of teamwork and their ambitions to the baseball diamond.

CONCLUSION

Throughout this chapter I have been suggesting subjects which strike me as offering fruitful areas for future research. In dealing with those and perhaps other examples, I wish also to propose that scholars consider two issues which I find intriguing. First, in analysing the nature of this international migration, I think it important to study the dynamics from both sides, that is, both the forces which push sports figures out of their home country and those complementary factors which pull them to other lands. In both cases I insist on including cultural and historical factors, not just economic or political ones (to an extent, this perspective is addressed in other chapters in this volume). Simultaneously, we should not ignore those factors which impede such migrations on either side: contract restrictions, emigration laws, family ties, public pressures, etc., in the exporting countries; quotas, cultural barriers, nationalistic sentiments, etc., in the importing countries (Jamail, 1991).

Second, and obviously related, is the question of whether these migrant players ultimately settle down and reside in the recipient countries or whether they eventually return home. If the former, it would be interesting to know what influenced their decision and how they adjusted to their new residence. Personal observation suggests, for example, that a good number of those Argentines who migrated to Colombia following the 1948 strike chose to remain, several gaining post-athletic fame as owners of popular Argentine-style steak houses. If, however, they went home, it would seem worthwhile to learn further if the players' prior fame, fortune, and international travels affected their relations with family, former neighbours and old team-mates who had more limited experiences. Most of the Latin baseball players from Caribbean countries who reach the North American big leagues appear to follow the second path, building larger houses back home where they reside during the off-season while still active and where they end up after retirement, apparently more comfortable culturally and linguistically with their old (extended) families and friends.

One additional theoretical question derives logically from the entire process of international labour migration, whether specifically related to sports or not. In a sense, what I am asking, at least indirectly, is whether certain international sporting relationships actually exacerbate underdevelopment or if these patterns of muscle drain are merely reflections of deeper, more pervasive structural problems that affect sports but are not caused or markedly worsened by them. By bringing income into the labour-exporting country, via player sales or the return flow of salary earnings, are these out-migrations of players really benefiting the country economically, or are they robbing the country of important economic and cultural resources and in turn damaging the quality of play and the psyche of frustrated fans? Klein, in his work on American baseball recruitment in the Dominican Republic, has suggested that the penetration of a 'foreign' sport and its institutions can be, for the recipient country (whose athletes then emigrate, if only temporarily), at one and the same time a source of exploitation and development, of cultural colonialism and nationalism, of domination and creativity, of humiliation and pride, of hegemony and resistance, though my sense is that for Klein the bottom line is that the exporters of talent, however resilient, lose more than they gain (Klein, 1988 and 1991).

To summarize: multi-directional international talent migration in the Latin American sports world is a significant process. Unfortunately, except for recent studies of the movement of circum-Caribbean baseball players to North America, virtually no part of the phenomenon, historical or contemporary, has received systematic, let alone quantitative study. These preliminary remarks are based mainly on isolated anecdotal evidence: memoirs, autobiographies and biographies; superficial histories, journalistic accounts; and my own personal impressions. No doubt, the further exploration of periodicals and club rosters and extensive interviews, among other sources, will generate more hard data. Especially in Spanish and Portuguese there exists sufficient literature to initiate such projects. And for Latin migrations to either North America or Europe, even English language sources should be adequate to support early analyses at least within the recipient countries.

In the meantime, I tentatively offer the proposition that the weaker Latin American economies have lost talent, resources, and long-term support for national identity to stronger societies either within Latin America or in North America and Europe. Reciprocal flows, while not culturally or economically unimportant for some Latin American countries, have not over the long term benefited the peripheral countries as much as those closer to the metropolitan centre. These sports migration patterns, I perceive, follow roughly the same lines or steps of power/dependency which characterize other dimensions of international relations in this corner of the third world. But the final word, if there is such a thing, awaits much more extensive research and interpretation, especially in the highly subjective area of popular satisfaction versus disillusionment, of development versus under-development, and of freedom of action versus dependency.

REFERENCES

Agundis, T.M. (1956) *El verdadero Jorge Pasquel. Ensayo biográfico sobre un carácter* (México, DF: Gráfica Atenea).
Anon. (1992) 'Argüello fights for his property', *Times of the Americas*, 36,2 (22 January), 19.
Arbena, J.L. (1989) (comp.), *An Annotated Bibliography of Latin American Sport: Pre-Conquest to the Present* (New York: Greenwood).
(1990) 'Sport and Revolution: The Continuing Cuban Experience', *Studies in Latin American Popular Culture*, 9, 319–28.
Arroyo, E.A. (1982) *Panama Al Brown* (Paris: Lattes).
Bale, J. (1989) *Sports Geography* (London: Spon).
(1991) *The Brawn Drain: Foreign Student-Athletes in American Universities* (Urbana, IL: University of Illinois).
Banks, L.W. (1985) 'Babe Ruth of Mexico', *Sport*, 76, 2, 66–74.
(1991) 'Béisbol, Si; Inglés, Coming Along', *Sports Illustrated*, 74,18, 6–8.
Bayer, O. (1990) *Fútbol argentino* (Buenos Aires: Editorial Sudamericana).
Bilardo, C.S. (1986) *Así ganamos: La verdadera lucha por la Copa* (Buenos Aires: Sudamericana/Planeta).
Bodo, P. and Hirshey, D. (1977) *Pelé's New World* (New York: Norton).
Bourg, J.F. (1986) *Football Business* (Paris: Olivier Orban).

Burgos, H. and Del Mastro, M. (1991) 'Muerto el gol, nace el vandalismo', *Quehacer*, 71, 68–87.

Calmell L., J.E.A. (1936) *Historia taurina del Perú, 1535–1935* (Lima: Taller Tipográfico de 'Perú Taurino' y 'De Perla y Oro').

Cepeda, O. with Markus, B. (1983) *High and Inside: Orlando Cepeda's Story* (South Bend: Icarus Press).

Diaz, J. (1987) 'The Shirtless Wonder', *Sports Illustrated*, 66,10, 68–9.

Dosal Estrada, J. (1990) *Hugo, mi amigo* (México, DF: Editorial Pax México).

Estrada, L. (1991) 'Mexican Major Leaguers Enter Final Stretch', *Times of the Americas* 35,19 (18 September), 22.

Fernández, U. (1981) 'La leyenda vivente du Chocolate', *Cuba Internacional*, 13,139, 48–51.

Ferreiro, Mora J. (1978) *Historia del boxeo cubano* (Miami: Selecta Enterprises).

Figueredo, J. (1984) 'Baseball Has Lost Its Cuban Connection', *The Sporting News*, 17 December, 52.

González Villavicencio, S. (1954) *Cinco ases del beisbol de antaño: Los hermanos Masís Mora* (San José: Imprenta Nacional).

Gammons, P. (1986) 'Cuba's Next Generation Arrives in Full Force', *The Sporting News*, 3 February, 39.

Guarner, E. (1979) *Historia del toreo en México* (México, DF: Editorial Diana).

Hartley, R. (1992) 'Argentine Presence in Mexican Soccer Starts at the Top', *Times of the Americas*, 36,1 (8 January), 19.

Jamail, M. (1991) 'Put Baseball on the Free-Trade Agenda', *The Washington Post*, 114,325 (26 October), A13.

Kenny, M. (1988) 'Costa Rica's Golden Girl Makes a Splash', *Américas*, 40,4, 53–4.

Klein, A. (1988) 'American Hegemony, Dominican Resistance, and Baseball', *Dialectical Anthropology*, 13, 301–12.

    (1990) 'Headcase, Headstrong, and Head-of-the-Class: Resocialization and Labeling in Dominican Baseball', *Arena Review*, 14,1, 33–46.

    (1991) *Sugarball: The American Game, the Dominican Dream* (New Haven, CT: Yale University Press).

Krich, J. (1989) *El Béisbol: Travels Through the Pan-American Pastime* (New York: Atlantic Monthly Press).

LaFrance, D.G. (1985) 'A Mexican Popular Image of the United States Through the Baseball Hero, Fernando Valenzuela', *Studies in Latin American Popular Culture*, 4, 14–23.

Llanes, R.M. (1981) *Canchas de pelotas y reñideros de antaño* (Buenos Aires: Municipalidad de la Ciudad).

Luna, P. (1967) *La fiesta brava en Colombia* (Cali: Editorial América).

Maguire, J.A. (1991) 'Sport, Racism and British Society: A Sociological Study of England's Elite Male Afro/Caribbean Soccer and Rugby Players' in Jarvie, G. (ed.), *Sport, Racism and Ethnicity* (London: Falmer) pp. 94–123.

María y Campos, A. de (1943) *Ponciano: El torero con bigotes* (Mexico, DF: Ediciones Xochitl).

Maturana, F., with Clopatofsky Londoño, J. (1990) *Maturana* (Bogotá: Intermedio Editores).

Menotti, C.L. (1978) *Como ganamos la Copa del Mundo* (Buenos Aires: El Gráfico).

Meza Vera, R. (1978) *Arsenio Erico, el paraguayo de oro* (Asunción: Imprenta Comuneros).

Morales, T., E.A. (1989) 'Historia del deporte en Panamá' in Ueberhorst, H. (ed.), *Geschichte der Leibesübungen, Vol. 6: Perspektiven des Weltsports* (Berlin: Bartles & Wernitz) pp. 1026–30.

Mustelier, E. (1985) *Kid Tunero; veinte años de ring . . . y fuera* (Madrid: Editorial Playor).

Nasur Allel, M. (1987) *Fútbol chileno, 1985–1987* (Santiago: Asociación Nacional de Fútbol Profesional).

Oleksak, M.M. and M.A. (1991) *Béisbol: Latin Americans and the Grand Old Game* (Grand Rapids, MI: Masters Press).

Pastrian, H. (1977) *Béisbol: reseña histórica internacional y argentina* (Buenos Aires: Federación Argentina de Béisbol).

Peucelle, C.D. (1975) *Fútbol todo tiempo e historia de 'La Máquina* (Buenos Aires: Editorial Axioma).

Ramírez, P.A. (1990) 'Alzas y bajas en el fervor por el fútbol', *Todo Es Historia*, 23,272, 88–96.

Ramos Ruiz, A. (1973) *Nuestro fútbol, grandeza y decadencia* (Buenos Aires: L V Producciones).

Rogosin, D. (1985) *Invisible Men: Life in Baseball's Negro Leagues* (New York: Atheneum).

Ruck. R. (1991) *The Tropic of Baseball: Baseball in the Dominican Republic* (Westport, CT: Meckler).

Salas, C. (1980; 1981) *Los toros en Venezuela*, 2 vols (Caracas: Imprenta Nacional).

Sasía, J.F. (1989) *Al fondo de la red* (Montevideo: Signos).

Sebreli, J.J. (1981) *Fútbol y masas* (Buenos Aires: Editorial Galerna).

Senzel, H. (1977) *Baseball and the Cold War* (New York: Harcourt Brace Jovanovich).

Sheer, H. (1971) 'Cuban Ball Players in the Major Leagues', *Baseball Digest*, 30,11, 72.

Tocker, J. (1984) *Mi Fútbol* (Cali: Editorial Londir).

Torres, A. (1976) *La historia del béisbol cubano, 1878–1976* (Los Angeles: privately printed).

Tufiño, L.G. (1928) *El juego de pelota en la República del Ecuador* (Quito: Talleres Tipogaráficos Nacionales).

Wulf, S. (1980) 'Béisbol Is in His Blood', *Sports Illustrated*, 53,8, 24–9.

Zelada Silva, P.J. (1988) *Deporte en el Paraguay: origen, evolución, práctica, legislación, autoridades* (Asunción: Edipar).

8

Skating on Thin Ice? The International Migration of Canadian Ice Hockey Players

Simon Genest

Migration is an essentially *geographical* phenomenon. Like other migrants, those who ply their sporting talents move from place to place, often between different cultural and physical environments and collectively form migratory flows at a variety of geographical scales (Bale, 1991; Rooney, 1980). Canada is the home of ice hockey (Kidd, 1970; Ojala and Kureth, 1979) but in recent decades the out-migration of Canadian ice hockey players has been a characteristic feature of the sport's geography. While the recruitment of Canadians by US college hockey squads and professional teams in the National Hockey League (NHL) has been commonplace for many years, the migration of Canadian players to Europe (and Japan and Australia) has been a much more recent phenomenon. The purpose of this chapter is to chart the extent of such migration, focusing especially on the regional (Canadian) origins of such migrants and their national destinations in Europe.

The sources and destinations of such migrants are far from randomly distributed over the respective continents which form the context of this study and there is a clear pattern, hence encouraging a geographical analysis of the 'hockey drain'. In doing so, the richness of the data, which are invariably available for the examination of sports talent migration, is clearly exemplified, as is the nature of the potential mapping techniques which so graphically summarize the dominant spatial flows.

Before 1970 the recruitment of Canadian ice hockey players was strictly the affair of North American hockey clubs. Migration was on an intra-continental, not an inter-continental scale. The extent of movement from Canada to the south can be revealed by the fact that of players recruited to the NHL in 1970, for example, almost 80 per cent came from major junior leagues in Canada; none was recruited from Europe. By 1975 Canada continued to dominate the sources of NHL talent and just under 3 per cent were European imports. While by the late 1980s this figure had risen to around 15 per cent it remained dwarfed by a much larger migration of Canadians to the USA (Genest, 1991: 95). With *perestroika* the migration of European talent to the NHL has increased, but what is arguably more dramatic is that the traditional pattern has changed to one where the flow of Canadian talent has become global rather than continental.

The NHL continues to exercise a monopoly over professional hockey and refuses expansion despite the interest in many cities in obtaining a franchise. This situation creates a saturation of the labour market for top-flight players. The development of European ice hockey, on the other hand, has accelerated since the late 1970s. As a result, European teams recruit more and more Canadian players who are either without adequate employment or willing to live the adventure of Europe at the twilight stage of their careers. These are the factors which explain, in large measure, the rapid increase in the number of Canadian players being recruited by European teams since 1970 (Figure 8.1). It can be seen that the numbers of such migrants rose from around 70 in 1970 to almost eight times that number by the late 1980s. If, in addition to these official transfers, the naturalized players whose names are not on the list and the non-registered transfers were taken into account, we would observe that more than 1,500 Canadians migrate each hockey season to Europe to earn their living and to promote Canada's national sport. This figure is even

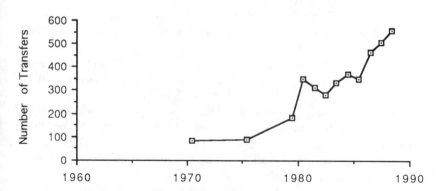

Figure 8.1   The number of international transfers registered: Canadian ice hockey, 1970–89

Table 8.1   Canadian Amateur Hockey Association:
CAHA Branches and Regions

Branches		Regions
British-Columbia Amateur Hockey Association*	BCAHA	Pacific Region
Alberta Amateur Hockey Association**	AAHA	
Saskatchewan Amateur Hockey Association	SAHA	West Region
Manitoba Amateur Hockey Association	MAHA	
Ottawa District Hockey Association	ODHA	Ontario Region
Thunder Bay Amateur Hockey Association	TBAHA	
Ontario Hockey Association	OHA	
Quebec Ice Hockey Federation	QIHF	Quebec Region
New Brunswick Amateur Hockey Association	NBAHA	Atlantic Region
Prince Edward Island Hockey Association	PEIHA	
Nova Scotia Amateur Hockey Association	NSAHA	
Newfoundland Amateur Hockey Association	NAHA	

*   Yukon is with BCAHA
** North West Territories are with AAHA
Source: CAHA

more impressive when it is realized that it represents twice the number
of Canadian players currently in the NHL.

The study of migration patterns of Canadian hockey players to
Europe and beyond over recent decades requires an analysis of
athletic, economic and cultural criteria. It would be inadequate to
consider Canada as a single cultural unit and an oversimplification to
study migration with respect to a single national point of origin.
Instead, we will seek to identify directional flows and preferences as
they relate to the cultural and regional origins of Canadian migrants
and their eventual destinations in Europe.

The Canadian Amateur Hockey Association (CAHA) is an organization which controls and directs amateur hockey and provides for its
promotion and development everywhere in the country through its
various provincial, inter-collegiate and inter-university affiliates. The
CAHA is comprised of 12 branches which have jurisdiction over
Canada's provinces and territories (Table 8.1 and Figure 8.2).

Each year the Association notes the total number of licensed
Canadians as well as the inter-branch and international transfers
involving Canadian players. This information is compiled in annual
reports which are distributed to affiliated members. Transfers are
inscribed on small cards and are not computerized. Sifting through

Figure 5.2 Canadian Amateur Hockey Association, Branches and Regions

Canadian Amateur Hockey Association
Branches and Regions

Regional Limit
Provincial Limit

Pacific Region

BCAHA

AAHA

West Region

SAHA

MAHA

TBAHA

OHA

Ontario Region

ODHA

QJHF

Quebec Region

NAHA

PEIHA

NBAHA

NSAHA

Atlantic Region

1000 km

0

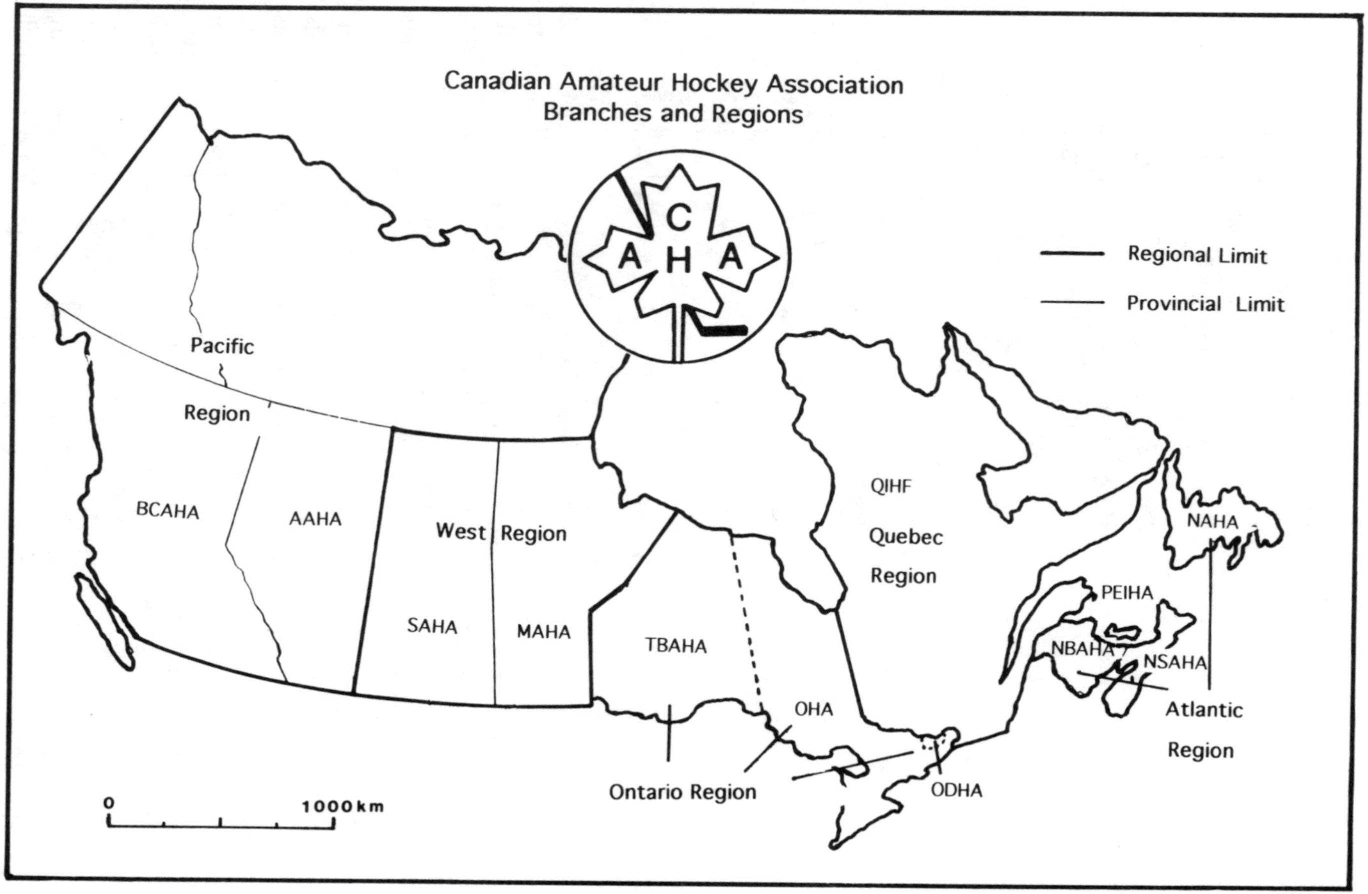

Source: Canadian Amateur Hockey Association

Table 8.2 International Transfers of Canadian Hockey Players; 1979–80 to 1988–89

From Canada To	Austria	Belgium	Britain	Denmark	Finland	France	Holland	Italy	Norway	Spain	Sweden	Switzerland	West Germany	Yugoslavia	Australia	Japan	Total
1979–80	15	0	0	4	5	12	33	6	2	0	5	7	70	0	0	2	161
1980–81	16	8	8	3	5	25	58	17	2	4	5	38	133	0	6	3	331
1981–82	20	3	5	6	4	12	31	17	1	1	8	46	120	1	17	0	292
1982–83	21	4	8	5	9	23	37	22	4	0	8	48	71	2	1	0	263
1983–84	18	0	38	7	3	18	28	22	3	0	12	52	85	3	21	5	312
1984–85	14	6	35	0	4	21	26	41	2	0	17	64	98	3	16	0	348
1985–86	14	5	31	1	7	18	27	30	1	0	17	41	118	9	12	0	331
1986–87	17	8	95	2	14	18	44	18	4	0	24	57	127	9	9	0	446
1987–88	22	14	108	2	16	22	22	44	4	0	20	51	149	2	9	0	485
1988–89	29	6	106	4	26	45	32	32	3	0	27	52	168	7	2	0	539
Total	186	54	435	34	93	214	338	249	26	5	143	456	1139	33	93	10	3508

Source: CAHA

these files makes it possible to follow the career patterns of players throughout Canada and outside the country.

Given on each card is the name of player, his association of origin, successive destinations and dates of transfer. Obviously, using this information, detailed analysis of migration patterns is possible. The present study is limited to international transfers. The players leave Canada for a European destination in the autumn and usually return home in April or May, spend the summer, then leave again the following autumn. The process can thus be conceptualized as a seasonal international migration. In many instances, the players return to the same team and city year after year.

Many players are also involved in a naturalization process. This is more and more frequent as European authorities institute rules regulating the number of foreigners permitted in each team. Naturalization may result in the permanent settling of the player in Europe, but this is not a normal practice. The acquisition of permanent-resident status is desired purely for practical and not political reasons. A team can include one or two foreign players and up to five naturalized players in some divisions, but players having dual nationality do not often settle permanently in the land where they practise their sport. The majority of these players continue to migrate seasonally. However, their names no longer appear on the transfer lists once they have obtained dual nationality. This explains why the figures from the CAHA reveal only 539 official transfers in 1988–89 (Table 8.2). If the number of Canadians with dual nationality was included the figure would rise to 1,500.

A FLOURISHING MIGRATION

These lists of registered transfers in the CAHA reports are the only official information on the migration of Canadian players abroad. First, each report enables us to calculate the annual transfers from a single origin (Canada) and several overseas destinations (Europe, Japan and Australia). Table 8.2 contains data on all transfers registered since 1979–80, in all 3,508. This does not necessarily reflect the total number of individual migrants because several players renew their transfer each season by requesting an extension of their permit. The data reflect the total number of transfers, not the total number of migrants.

In 1988–89, 537 players migrated to Europe compared with 159 in 1979–80. It is in the 1980–81 season that the increase is the greatest, 331 compared with 161 the year before. In 1982–83 there was a slight slowing when the number of migrants dropped to 263. Thereafter, the annual migration of players increased each year until 1988–89. When data from earlier periods are examined for comparative purposes (1970–71 and 1975–76), it becomes clear that the close of the 1970s marked a period of rapid increase in migration. Thereafter, most European countries established some form of regularity in their annual recruiting. This was especially the case for Austria, France, Holland, Italy, Norway and Switzerland. Britain was an exception. According to available data, no Canadian hockey players migrated to Britain until the 1979–80 season. The number of migrants here went from 38 in 1983–84 to 108 in 1988–89, making it the second most important destination for this period. The Scandinavian countries, whose hockey development is well ahead of that of western European countries, still make use of a small number of Canadians. Sweden is the largest Scandinavian importer of Canadian hockey talent. Outside Europe, Australia and Japan hire Canadian players and coaches. No fewer than 93 Canadian players headed for Oceania during this period and 10 to Japan. Japan forbade the arrival of foreign players after the 1983–84 season.

The former German Federal Republic (GFR), without a doubt, was the most important European employment market for Canadian players (Figure 8.3). In the 10 years 1979–89, 1,139 transfers to this country were recorded. Switzerland and Britain come in second and third with 456 and 435 respectively. The absence of hockey migrants to eastern Europe testifies to the importance of economic and political barriers. Yet, *perestroika* made it possible for the first Soviet players to play in the National Hockey League in 1989. The recent opening of eastern Europe does not for the moment, however, constitute an attractive labour market for Canadian players whose salary demands would go unmet in the East.

Thus, the migration of Canadian hockey players to Europe can be conceived of as two vectors, the most important of which is Anglo-German including the former GFR, Holland, Austria and German Switzerland. This vector accounted for about 70 per cent of all official transfers over the past decade. The second vector links the Latin countries of western Europe which have within their bounds the Alpine regions: France, Italy, and Switzerland. Since 1979, these three countries have shared 15 per cent of all official migrations. Switzerland, it can be observed, sits astride both vectors. This cartographic model illustrates a primary cultural and regional distinction between the preferred destination zones of Canadian hockey migrants (Figure 8.4).

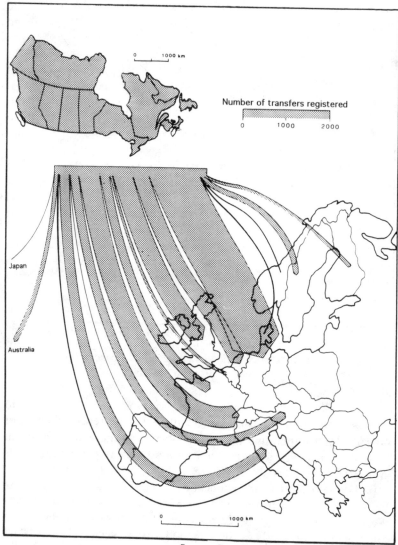

Source: Canadian Amateur Hockey Association

Figure 8.3 International transfers of Canadian ice hockey players, 1979–80 to 1988–89.

REGIONAL DIFFERENCES IN THE SOURCE REGIONS

The lists provided by the CAHA facilitated the identification of migrants to a particular European destination, but what of the regions

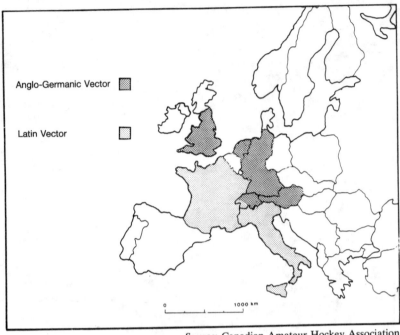

Anglo-Germanic Vector

Latin Vector

0   1000 km

Source: Canadian Amateur Hockey Association

Figure 8.4 The migration of Canadian ice hockey players
conceived as two vectors

of origin? The same files were consulted once again. Two seasons were selected for comparative purposes: 1980–81 because it marked the period of greatest increase, and the most recent period for which information was available, 1987–88.

In 1980–81 322 Canadian hockey players officially transferred to Europe. Ontario contributed 153 or 47 per cent, followed by the Far West or Pacific region with 22 per cent. Ontarians were playing in 14 countries, but primarily in the Anglo-Germanic vector. The Western and Pacific regions followed the same tendency. In 1980–81, the former GFR included 85 per cent of the players from Manitoba and Saskatchewan. With respect to Alberta and British Columbia, 85 per cent could be found in the Anglo-Germanic vector (Table 8.3). The Québec patterns are significantly different. In 1980–81, France, Switzerland and Italy employed the services of 42 of the 61 Québec hockey migrants (69 per cent). Only eight transfers are recorded for West Germany and none for Britain.

Table 8.3 International Transfers of Canadian Hockey Players 1980–81

From \ To	Austria	Belgium	Britain	Denmark	Finland	France	Holland	Italy	Norway	Spain	Sweden	Switzerland	West Germany	Australia	Japan	Total
Pacific Region BCAHA, AAHA	1	0	0	0	1	1	18	2	0	0	2	5	42	0	1	72
West Region SAHA, MAHA	1	0	0	0	0	0	1	0	0	2	0	1	33	1	0	39
Ontario Region ODHA, TBAHA, OHA	11	6	8	3	3	4	35	11	2	2	3	13	50	2	0	153
Quebec Region QIHF	3	2	0	0	1	20	3	4	0	0	0	18	8	0	2	61
Atlantic Region NBAHA, PEIHA, NSAHA, NAHA	0	0	0	0	0	0	1	0	0	0	0	1	0	3	0	5
Total: Canada	16	8	8	3	5	25	58	17	2	4	5	38	133	6	3	331

Source: CAHA

In 1987–88 485 transfers were recorded (Table 8.4). The Far West (Pacific) and West showed the strongest increases. During that season, 133 hockey players from Alberta and British Columbia went to Europe compared with 72 in 1980–81. From Saskatchewan and Manitoba, 68 went compared with 38 in the previous period. Despite some minor changes in destination patterns, the vast majority of hockey migrants from every province except Québec flowed into the Anglo-Germanic vector.

As noted above, the past decade has seen the development of a new market, that of Britain. Only eight transfers were recorded for Britain in the earlier period compared with 108 in 1987–88. At the same time, the flows towards other countries within the Anglo-Germanic vector remained unchanged. Thus, it seems that between 1981 and 1987 Britain accounted for the increase in the number of migrants from Ontario, the West and the Far West and channelled their flow.

The opening of the British market appears to have been as advantageous for Québecois players as for the others. In 1987–88, the former GFR and Britain shared 36 per cent of the Québecois transfers compared with 13 per cent in 1980–81. Despite an important increase in the number of annual migrants (108 versus 61 in 1980–81), the recruitment by Latin countries seems stable. The Anglo-Germanic vector would seem to have opened up for players from Québec. On the other hand, it would seem that the Latin vector holds no more interest than before for players from Canada's other regions. Flows to France have diminished from Ontario, the West and the Far West. English-speaking hockey players tend to find work within the Anglo-Germanic vector, whereas French-speaking players, who in the earlier period headed for the Latin countries, seem to have diversified their destinations in order to take advantage of both the expanding Germanic market and, more importantly, that of Britain.

POSSIBLE EXPLANATIONS

The creation of migration chains does not depend solely upon the interest that a player may have in performing in a specific setting, nor upon the clubs for which they play. A third party is frequently responsible for forging links between market areas and regions of production. Indeed, the role of the 'agent' is extremely important. English-speaking agents from Ontario, and the western provinces are largely responsible for the network of relations established with teams in Germany, Britain, Austria and Holland. Their contacts appear less fruitful in the Latin countries. There is obviously a linguistic barrier.

Table 8.4 International Transfers of Canadian Hockey Players, 1987–88

From / To	Austria	Belgium	Britain	Denmark	Finland	France	Holland	Italy	Norway	Sweden	Switzerland	West Germany	Yugoslavia	Australia	Total
Pacific Region BCAHA, AAHA	4	1	25	1	1	0	7	11	0	8	7	61	2	5	133
West Region SAHA, MAHA	7	1	17	1	2	0	4	5	1	1	3	24	0	2	68
Ontario Region ODHA, TBAHA, OHA	7	1	43	0	9	0	9	18	2	7	20	42	0	2	160
Quebec Region QIHF	1	11	17	0	1	21	2	9	1	4	19	19	0	0	105
Atlantic Region NBAHA, PEIHA, NSAHA, NAHA	3	0	6	0	3	1	0	1	0	0	2	3	0	0	19
Total: Canada	22	14	108	2	16	22	22	44	4	20	51	149	2	9	485

Source: CAHA

Few anglophone-Canadians are hired by French clubs who prefer French-speaking Québecois. But how does one explain the increased Québec presence within the Anglo-Germanic vector? First of all, it must be remembered that there are players from Québec whose mother tongue is English and others who speak English, both having English-speaking agents. It is obvious that the bilingual competence of Québec players and agents gives them a major advantage when seeking employment in Europe. At some time or other in their career, top flight Québecois players have no choice but to come in contact with anglophones whether on national teams or in the leagues. As with other aspects of French Canadian culture, Québecois hockey must adapt, protect itself and take advantage of every situation which presents itself in anglophone North America.

The cultural explanation refers to recruiting practices and contract negotiations between Canadians and European team directors. Indeed, it is in English that most contracts with Germans and Austrians are negotiated. However, with respect to the day-to-day functioning of the clubs, whether German, Austrian, French or Italian, it is the official language of the country which is used by players, coaches and management no matter what their nationality. Thus, Canadian players in Germany have no choice but to learn German if they wish to adapt in the long run to their new team and their host country.

Culture is a powerful explanatory variable in analysing sports migration towards Europe. But it should be stated that the economic power of professional sports has begun to modify this situation. High calibre European clubs, those of the first division, have shown greater flexibility in their selection of recruiting basins. These teams call upon professional players from the NHL or its minor league system. These star players demand large salaries. Swiss and German clubs of the first division now have the means to hire such players. It is no longer the traditional relational network cultivated by agents working in specific regions with cultural affinities which influences recruitment as much as the professional antecedents and personal reputation of the player. These clubs bid for the best players available, no matter the salary demanded. This procedure is entirely independent of the traditional networks established previously.

CONCLUSION

This chapter has indicated how the geographic flows of migratory sports talent can be explored, quantitatively and cartographically, by using the readily available data contained in one of the many rich statistical sources so readily available to scholars of sports. It has highlighted a fundamental geographic change in the migration patterns of Canadian ice hockey players, from one dominated by migration south to the bulk of the NHL teams, to one characterized by migration to the growing hockey regions of Europe and to the increasingly 'hockeyized' areas of Asia and Australasia. The chapter has also highlighted the fact that national and continental patterns of migration have superimposed on them subtle but important regional dimensions. In the present case this is illustrated by the significance of French-speaking *hockeyeurs* moving to the Latin regions of Europe and the English-speaking Canadians elsewhere.

Ice hockey exemplifies an expanding sport at the global scale. The kinds of pattern identified in this chapter might form a sort of preface to all such studies in talent migration; indeed, such an approach might inform studies concerned with more interpretive accounts of the trade in athletic labour by identifying the source and destination *regions* (as well as nations) and the precise extent of such trade.

REFERENCES

Bale, J. (1991) *The Brawn Drain; Foreign Student-Athletes in American Universities* (Urbana, IL: University of Illinois Press).

Genest, S. (1991) 'Etude Géographique du Processus de Diffusion du Hockey sur Glace dans le Monde' (Laval University: unpublished MA dissertation).

Kidd, B. (1970) 'Canada's National Sport' in Lumsden, I. (ed.), *The Americanization of Canada* (Toronto: University of Toronto Press), pp. 257–74.

Ojala, C. and Kureth, E. (1979) 'From Saskatoon to Parry Sound: A Geography of Skates and Sticks in North America', *The Geographical Survey*, 4,4, 22–34.

Rooney, J. (1980) *The Recruiting Game* (Lincoln, NE: University of Nebraska Press).

9

Professional Sports Migration to Finland during the 1980s

Kalevi Olin and Matti Penttilä

Migration is regarded as a symptom of basic social change. Its importance as a social phenomenon currently seems to be growing. Therefore, questions have been raised as to why people move from one country to another. Furthermore, what kind of people are more prone to migrate? And what are the motives of the migrants who make this kind of decision? It is known that migration varies during different times. It is also known that it has changed greatly during the last decades. Because of the improved physical and technical circumstances today, it seems to be easier now to make a decision to migrate, particularly, if a migrant has financial inducements to make a move. Also the development of modern society in more professionalized task areas has created new opportunities for people to migrate.

Professional sports as an institution, and sports migration, are areas of modern society of growing interest to sociological researchers. Professionalization of sport has, however, reached different stages in different societies. For example, in Scandinavian countries like Finland professionalization is still a quite new phenomenon even in the most advanced sports like ice hockey, soccer, basketball and volleyball. There are grounds for stating that these sports could be better described as semi-professionalized, because work outside sport still plays a significant role in their make-up.

Professional sport seems to create favourable opportunities for migration. It is international by nature: there is a well-established network with the same kind of social norms and rules for both international and national competitions and leagues. Therefore, the easier it is to migrate in an institution like sport, the easier is the decision to move from one country to another and to start a career as a professional athlete.

As a concept, migration indicates a movement of individuals and social groups between two societies. Opportunities offered are compared by individuals involved in the migration process (Jackson, 1986: 14). From this point of view sports migration does not seem to differ to a great degree from that of non-sports migration. According to Söderling (1988: 11) the personal decision to migrate is dependent on the social values the individual has decided to live by. The migrant assesses the potential benefits of the decision (Straubhaar, 1986: 845–50). Rose (1969: 146–7) has emphasized the role of economic factors as the main motives to migrate. They certainly play an important role. In another category there are factors that make the need for exodus so strong that the economic considerations fade into the background (Georg, 1970: 39–48). These factors can be religious, political or racial in nature.

There are studies which show that a great variety exists in the size and direction of migration (Ravenstein, 1885: 167–235; 1889: 245–305; Thomas, 1958: 125–30). Most people move only a short distance. Furthermore, there are theories looking at movements of migrants, not only in terms of distance, but also in terms of opportunities (see Jansen, 1970) as referred to above. For example, in 1940 Stouffer presented his theory of intervening opportunities:

> the number of persons going a given distance is directly proportional to the number of opportunities at that distance and inversely proportional to the number of intervening opportunities.

Results of the study by Rose (1970: 85–92) proved that in this theory the social class as an independent variable plays an important role, because the lower classes experienced more intervening opportunities in a given distance than did the upper classes. Thus it could be hypothesized that the better educated the sports migrant has been, the fewer intervening factors he or she experiences in terms of migration and vice versa.

Furthermore, a special type of selectivity plays a role in migration. This is often connected with the so-called 'push and pull theory' in the literature. Its basic functions are presented by Bogue (1961):

> Migration that has a very strong 'push' stimulus tends to be much less selective with respect to the community of origin than migration which has a very strong 'pull' stimulus. Where there is a condition of very strong 'push' but no strong 'pull' origin selectivity is at a minimum. In other words, selectivity of

outmigrants from any community tends to vary directly with the strength of attractive 'pulls' from other communities and inversely with expulsive 'pushes' from the community itself (quoted in Jansen, 1970: 13).

It is evident that both push and pull factors function in every case where the sports migrant is making the decision to move from one country to another. If there is no chance to start or continue their sports career as a professional player in their native country the push factors could be assumed to facilitate the decision to move. The situation may be in relation to the playing skills or age of the player. As far as age is concerned, some earlier studies indicate that people in the age range 20–34 are more inclined toward migration than other age groups (Daniel, 1939: 290–308; Pourcher, 1964; Buechler, 1987). Family and friends as well as changes to these, certainly play their part as well.

Over the past 30 years, the number of professional athletes migrating to a foreign country has escalated. At the beginning of the 1980s there were at least 600 Americans in western Europe playing professional basketball (Dryansky, 1982: 112–17). In Finland, this specific form of migration started as far back as 1939 when a Hungarian ice hockey player moved to Finland to play for the Helsinki club Kiffen (Honkavaara, 1991). Already at the beginning of the 1930s several Russian immigrants played ice hockey for the Helsinki club Unitas. Furthermore, still referring to Honkavaara (1991), we know that four Tartarian brothers who were Turkish citizens played ice hockey for the Tampere club Ilves from 1939 to 1945. These men had, however, also lived in Finland before. In addition, according to Honkavaara (1991) one Swede played ice hockey for the Helsinki club HSK in 1941 and another Swede for the Tampere club TPK between 1943 and 1949. (The second one took Finnish citizenship in 1944.) The first mentioned Hungarian player in 1939 is regarded as the first foreign professional to enter Finnish ice hockey.

Finnish basketball received its first foreign players in 1972 when two Americans moved to play in the Finnish championship league. One played basketball in the Turku club TNMKY (Turku Young Men's Christian Association) and the other in the Helsinki club HNMKY (Helsinki Young Men's Christian Association) (Finnish Basketball Federation, 1979). During the 1973/74 season there were already six American professional basketball players in the Finnish championship league. Three of them played in three Helsinki clubs (HNMKY, Pantterit and Playboys) and the others in TNMKY, the Espoo club

Honka and the Kotka club KTP (Finnish Basketball Federation, 1979). From then until 1989 about 250 foreign professionals, mainly from the United States, played in the Finnish basketball leagues. This trend of using foreign aid has also spread to other sports like soccer and volleyball (Aulio, 1989).

The channels of international migration are likely to be active in the future, as well. The commercialization of sport is prone to change its nature, but it can be recognized also that the change in the nature of sport and the rise in the required level of achievement will cause increasing commercialization which will gradually dominate the sports world. Equipment contracts, buying and selling of athletes and transfer fees are phenomena of today's sport (Puronaho, 1988: 184–7). Furthermore, the changing needs – increase in leisure time, for example – of the wide audience will facilitate the process of professionalization and if superior athletes can be obtained elsewhere, it is in the interests of both club and coach to recruit them (Maguire, 1988; Bale, 1987). Other factors likely to facilitate the migration of professional athletes are according to Heinonen and Lahtinen (1990) the new opportunities for eastern European athletes to move to a country where they can earn significantly more than in their home country, and the opening of EC borders in 1993.

This comparative study focuses on the change in sports migration during the 1980s in Finland. The perspective selected raised the question how did the athletes, who migrated mainly from the United States to Finland, differ at the beginning, middle and end of the 1980s by age, marital status, education, ethnicity, social status of their parents, and their most important reasons for moving to a new country, all of which functioned as variables.

The data were collected from three studies that concerned the migration to Finland of professional athletes in team sports. Subjects of the first study by Olin (1984) consisted of all the foreign players (N=30) in the Finnish basketball leagues during the season 1981/82 and 1982/3. They were sent a questionnaire or in 15 cases of non-returns, personally interviewed. In addition, 11 coaches of those teams with a foreign player gave the researchers information about players who were unavailable.

In the second study by Brooks and Penttilä (1988) a total of 14 American basketball players, four of whom had become naturalized Finnish citizens and participated in the top league of the Finnish basketball series during the 1986/87 season, were mailed a demographic data sheet and the Sports Participation Questionnaire. Five questionnaires were returned. Personal interviews were conducted in

Finland with three basketball players who did not return the question-naire, and the director of the Finnish Basketball Federation.

The subjects of the latest study consisted of all the foreign players in the Finnish basketball, volleyball and ice hockey leagues (N=61) during the playing season 1988/89 (Olin, Lahtinen and Heinonen, 1990; Heinonen and Lahtinen 1990). Subjects included 20 basketball players, 13 volleyball players and 28 ice hockey players, 66 per cent (N=40) of whom returned a completed questionnaire.

After all the data from the three studies above were gathered together, they were analysed by comparing the studies in a longitudi-nal manner by examining the percentage differences that had occurred in the variables over the three periods. In regard to the most important motives of the sports migrants, the percentages were converted to rank order, which enable proper comparison between the studies. The data was presented in cross-tabulation format.

Table 9.1 shows that most of the sports migrants had moved to Finland at the age of 25 or less. In Olin's (1984) study this age group accounted for 48 per cent and in Olin et al's (1990) study 51 per cent. It was not possible to make comparisons with the study of Brooks and Penttilä (1988), because age was not included in that questionnaire. In considering the results by Olin et al. (1990), it is necessary to remember that, in addition to basketball players, ice hockey and volleyball players were included in the study.

The percentage of sports migrants belonging to the 26–32 age group was clearly larger (48) at the beginning than at the end (36) of the 1980s. There were grounds to argue that migration had begun to appeal to more professionals from the higher age group at the end of the 1980s since the number of players over the age of 32 had increased from 4 per cent to 13 per cent (Olin, 1984; Olin et al., 1990). However, if this interpretation is not correct then the results may reflect the differences between the sports and sports migrants involved, since in the 1990 study, it will be recalled, basketball, volleyball and ice hockey players were included. In general, the results by age seem to follow those of the general migration studies (cf. Daniel, 1939: 281–308; Pourcher, 1964; Buechler, 1987: 1–9).

The results suggest that sports migration now attracts more athletes from the older age groups than before. It could be argued, of course, that the interpretation in terms of attraction is not correct. This is true if, for example, the players in the over-32 group have not found any way to get work outside sport other than by migration, when planning to end their careers as professional athletes. Another explanation could be that in the United States the chances of basketball players

Table 9.1 Age of the sports migrants (%,N)

Age	Olin 1984	Olin et al. 1990
Under 26 years	48	51
26–31 years	48	36
Over 31 years	4	13
Total	100 (N = 25)	100 (N = 38)

Table 9.2 Marital status of the sports migrants (%,N)

Marital status	Olin 1984	Brooks & Penttilä 1988	Olin et al. 1990
Single	73	75	50
Married	22	25	50
Total	100 (N = 26)	100 (N = 8)	100 (N = 38)

aged 32 or more being offered a professional contract or continuing their professional careers are lower than for the younger players. This is due to the higher level of prowess required to play in US basketball than in the Finnish league.

When examining the results by marital status, we found (Table 9.2) that a clear majority (73–75 per cent) of foreign players in Olin's (1984), as well as Brooks and Penttilä's (1988) studies were not married. Figures were high compared with those of Olin et al. (1990): in this study 50 per cent of the players were married. The lower figure could be explained by the inclusion in the Olin et al. study of ice hockey and volleyball players, as stated earlier. Thus basketball players seem to differ from ice hockey and volleyball players.

Some reasons for the differences might be found in the fact that those prepared to migrate in the sport of basketball had probably just finished their university or college careers, a fact probably also compatible with the results by age and educational background of the players (see Tables 9.1 and 9.3). It is true to say that basketball is strongly regarded as a university game in the United States. On the contrary, in ice hockey the players probably had greater experience of professional sport before moving to Finland.

Table 9.3   Educational background of the sports migrants (%,N)

Educational background	Olin 1984	Brooks & Penttilä 1988	Olin et al. 1990
University graduate	92	88	68
No university education	8	12	32
Total	100 (N = 25)	100 (N = 8)	100 (N = 38)

Results in Table 9.3 indicate that sports migrants had a reasonably good educational background. Around 90 per cent of the players according to Olin's (1984) and Brooks and Penttilä's (1988) studies had taken a university degree before moving to Finland. In this regard, no significant change was found among basketball professionals. Even according to Olin et al.'s (1990) results, two-thirds of the players had a university-level degree.

A comparison of sporting and non-sporting migrants showed that they differed to a great degree (cf. Buechler, 1987: 1–9). Normally, non-sporting migrants did not have as good an educational background as found in the data presented here. However, there were grounds for believing that the level of education of the general migrant might correlate with the fact that he or she was affected by the push or pull factors in terms of migration (Bogue, 1961; Jansen, 1970: 13). It could be argued that the pull factors attract more people with a better educational background, if the labour force of the area was lacking in that kind of personnel. However, this explanation did not fit well here, because playing in Finland as a professional player is not a matter of university education but simply a matter of being a skilful athlete and, at least in the United States, many skilful athletes can be found in universities and colleges studying or just finishing their studies.

Basketball belongs to that group of sports in which black athletes predominate. This is shown in Table 9.4 which shows the figures for the ethnic background of the sport migrants. At the beginning of the 1980s 69 per cent of the basketball players were black (Olin, 1984), while in the mid-1980s the figure was 62 per cent (Brooks and Penttilä, 1988). At the end of the decade the figure was only 18 per cent (Olin et al., 1990). (The latest study was affected by the fact that its data included players from ice hockey and volleyball, sports that are dominated by white athletes. The fact that 82 per cent of the basketball, volleyball and ice hockey players who migrated to Finland at the end of the 1980s were white supported the interpretation.)

Table 9.4   Ethnicity of the sports migrants (%,N)

Ethnicity	Olin 1984	Brooks & Penttilä 1988	Olin *et al.* 1990
White	31	38	82
Black	69	62	18
Total	100 (N = 26)	100 (N = 8)	100 (N = 38)

Table 9.5   Social status of the sports migrants' parents (%,N)

Social status of the parents	Olin 1984	Olin *et al.* 1991
Upper social class	7	8
Middle social class	86	89
Lower social class	7	3
Total	100 (N = 15)	100 (N = 36)

One purpose of the study was to find out from what kind of families the sports migrants came and what changes, if any, could be found in this regard during the 1980s. Results in Table 9.5 show that no particular change had occurred: 86 per cent of sports migrants came from the families of middle-class social status at the beginning of the 1980s (Olin, 1984), and the figure at the end of the decade was practically the same at 89 per cent (Olin *et al.*, 1990). One explanation for the results might be that Americans are prone to classify themselves as 'middle-class' but it is quite difficult to define precisely what 'middle-class' means. However, it seems that there is something special in middle-class families in terms of social values, ideals and dreams, which encourages children to migrate.

It is often asked why athletes move to a foreign country and whether this follows the more general reasons relating to migration as a social phenomenon. It is known that sports migration is not as long-lasting as migration in general because playing careers in sport are limited. As Söderling (1988: 11) among others has shown, every migrant makes a personal decision when moving to another place, having considered and assessed the potential benefits of the decision (Straubhaar, 1986).

Table 9.6   Most important motives of sports migrants to move to Finland
(ranking order)

Motive to move	Olin 1984	Brooks & Penttilä 1988	Olin et al. 1990
Becoming familiar with new country	1	–	4
New life experiences	2	–	3
Improvement as a player	3	3	2
Better status as a player	4	–	5
Better earnings	5	3	1
To play as a professional	6	–	9
Friends in Finland	7	–	10
Opportunity to change the club	7	–	6
Unemployment in native country	9	–	10
Becoming familiar with new people	10	2	8
Finland a good country to live	11	–	7
Opportunity to continue as a player	–	1	–
Opportunity to fulfil university studies	–	3	–
Recognition of the American recruiter	–	3	–
Wife or husband in Finland	–	–	8

1 If the figure indicating the ranking order of the variable is the same with two or more variables then they have had the same percentage figure.

It is interesting to compare whether there were any changes in the motives to move to Finland during the 1980s.

Table 9.6 shows such similarities and differences. It was found that motives seem to be the same at the beginning and at the end of the 1980s (Olin, 1984; Olin et al., 1990). However, an interesting change was found: the ranking order of the most important motives had totally changed. At the beginning of the 1980s the most important motive to move to Finland was to become familiar with a new country and the second most important motive the opportunity for new life experiences. The former reason dropped to fourth most important at the end of the 1980s and the latter dropped to third. Furthermore, it was found that the sporting motive, that is the motive to improve oneself as a player, had retained its importance (1984=3rd/1990=2nd) during the decade. The same seemed to be the case in regard to gaining better status as a player (1984=4th/1990=5th). Regarding the opportunity for greater earnings, the results indicate that the pull factors relating to the migrant's economy had started to play a much more important role (1984=5th/1990=1st) by the end of the 1980s.

In terms of the results by Brooks and Penttilä (1988) which were not totally comparable with the earlier studies due to the differences in the questionnaires, it was found that the most important motive to move to Finland was expressed as the opportunity to continue playing. The second most important motive was found to be the opportunity of becoming familiar with new people. In this regard Brooks and Penttilä's (1988) results, however, followed those of Olin (1984) and Olin et al, (1990), because these variables were found among the five most important motives for migration. Other motives that were ranked in Brooks and Penttilä's (1988) study from third to first were improvement as a player, better earnings, opportunity to use their education and the role of an American recruiter. For the players emphasizing the last variable mentioned, migration to Finland was probably expected to provide career opportunities that were unobtainable in their native countries.

For some players the decision to migrate was driven by an opportunity to change clubs (1984=7th/1990=6th), but for others the motive to play as a professional was no longer as important at the end of the period (1990=9th), as at the beginning (1984=6th). Results indicated that 'Finland as a good country to live in' (1984=11th/1990=7th) had gained in importance as a motive towards the end of the decade.

The basic problem that was posed at the beginning of this chapter was to describe the changes relating to sports migration to Finland during the 1980s. The specific areas of interest were age, marital status, education, ethnicity, social status of the players' parents and motives for the decision to migrate.

In regard to age, earlier studies of general migration indicated that persons in the age group 20 to 34 were more inclined toward migration than other age groups (Buechler, 1987: 1–9). In this study it was found that most of the sports migrants had moved to Finland at the age of 25 years or less both at the beginning and end of the 1980s. The figures in the Olin (1984) and the Olin et al. (1990) studies were 38 and 51 per cent, respectively. However, in the older age groups, 26–31 years and over 31 years, some significant changes were observed. Since the beginning of the 1980s, the number of players in the over 31 age group had increased from 4 per cent to 13 per cent.

The results suggested that the oldest age group had become more involved in professional sport in Finland toward the end of the decade. The reason for this change can be deduced from the fact that the Olin et al. study included ice hockey and volleyball players in addition to the basketball players – sports that typically employ white, eastern

European and non-college background players. On the other hand, the Olin study included only basketball players who were predominantly black, American and ex-college players. Based on this background, it could be argued that the black basketball players had entered Finnish professional sport straight from college and were integrated with their teams in Finland for a shorter period of time than their white, predominantly eastern European counterparts. However, the duration of stay was not an objective of this chapter. As stated above, in general the results by age seemed to follow the findings of the general migration studies.

As far as the marital status of the players was concerned, it was noted that between the Olin (1984), Brooks and Penttilä (1988) studies and the Olin *et al.* (1990) study, the amount of married players had increased from 25 to 50 per cent. This finding seems to correlate with the background of the players with regard to their age, education and ethnicity. In the Olin *et al.* study (which included ice hockey and volleyball players) the migrants were typically older, less educated and white, in contrast to the earlier studies where the subjects were younger and black ex-college players, who had entered professional sport in Finland straight from college or a short duration of professional play in some other country.

In terms of educational background, it was found that the Olin and the Brooks and Penttilä studies were significantly similar in their results. About 90 per cent had a university-level degree, whereas in the Olin *et al.* study the proportion of players with degrees had decreased to 68 per cent. Again, this may be explained by the difference in the background of the basketball players on the one hand and the ice hockey and volleyball players on the other. When the educational background of the players was compared with the corresponding figures for general migration (cf. Rose, 1970: 85–92), it was found that the players were much more highly educated than general migrants. This difference can be explained by the fact that sport is traditionally a central element of college life, especially in the United States. Therefore, athletes who are employed in professional sports are obliged to maintain a certain level of educational standards in order to play in a college team. Moreover, it should be pointed out that the career of a professional athlete is of relatively short duration, and the realization of this fact may have caused the players to educate themselves in preparation for the time after their career in professional sports was over.

The results regarding ethnicity showed that the subjects in the Olin and in the Brooks and Penttilä studies were predominantly black – 69 and 62 per cent, respectively. The subjects in these studies were basketball players, a sport that is traditionally dominated by blacks. In the latest study by Olin *et al.* the subjects were 82 per cent white. Once again, this difference is due to its inclusion of players of ice hockey and volleyball from white European countries.

The study of changes in the social status of the players' parents during the 1980s was another objective. No such a change is observable. Most players' parents both at the beginning and end of the 1980s were of middle-class status (just under 90 per cent).

One explanation for this might be that there is something unique to the families of middle-class social status in terms of social values, and even ideals and dreams, that encourage children to migrate if such an opportunity exists. A further explanation may be found in the study on migration by Rose (1970: 85–92): the lower classes experience more intervening opportunities which discourage migration.

Turning to the motives of sports migrants for moving to a new country, the Olin (1984) study found that the five most important ones were (1) becoming familiar with a new country, (2) new life experiences, (3) improvement as a player, (4) better status as a player and (5) better earnings. When compared with the Olin *et al.* study made at the end of the 1980s it was found that the ranking order was completely changed. The number one motive from the beginning of the 1980s, becoming familiar with a new country, had fallen to fourth place by the end of the decade. New life experiences had switched from second to third position, improvement as a player from third to second, better status as a player from fourth to fifth and, perhaps most significant of all, better earnings had become the most important motive at the end of the eighties from fifth place at the beginning of the decade, probably due to increased materialism of players and commercialization of sport.

Thus by the end of the 1980s the same kind of factors had begun to apply to sports migration as already applied to general migration: the decision to migrate depended on an assessment of the potential benefits of migration (Straubhaar 1986). Among these the economic factors were, according to Rose (1969), regarded as being of primary importance.

Moreover, the study by Olin *et al.* may have accentuated the economic motives and new opportunities for migration (cf. Jansen 1970; Jackson 1986) by inclusion of athletes from the poor eastern European countries. Players seem to have become more like itinerant labourers than crusaders in a strange land looking for new life experiences, which may have been the case at the end of the 1970s and at the beginning of the 1980s, when professional sport in Finland was a relatively new phenomenon. The results seem to support this interpretation, since the motive of becoming familiar with a new country fell from first position to fourth.

One of the major limitations to the comparison of the studies was the fact that Olin *et al.* used a slightly different set of subjects. As has been noted, the study included, in addition to basketball players, ice hockey and volleyball players, unlike the earlier studies that used only basketball players. Significant differences were found between this study and the previous ones in terms of age, marital status, educational background, ethnicity and the most important motives of the players to move to a new country, but one must bear in mind the subject groups when interpreting the results.

In comparing the Olin (1984) and the Brooks and Penttilä (1988) studies, it can be said that the results were almost identical with regard to the marital status, educational background and ethnicity of the sports migrants. The findings suggest that no change had occurred in these areas of study between the beginning and the end of the 1980s. When the Olin (1984) and the Olin *et al.* (1990) studies were compared, some significant changes were observed in all the study areas except in the social class of the players' parents. However, some of the variance in the data may be due to the differences in the subject groups and therefore the study is not totally reliable in reflecting any changes during the 1980s in age, marital status, educational background and ethnicity of players, the social status of players' parents or their motives for moving to Finland.

In spite of this slight limitation, the study has given some insights into the world of professional sport during the 1980s and lays down a challenge to extend this branch of study to the 1990s when some major changes are expected to occur, both in the world of sport and in the world in general.

NOTE

The data in this study were collected as a part of the larger study on 'Sport and International Exchange' initiated and conducted by Dr Kalevi Olin.

REFERENCES

Aulio, E. (1989) 'Koriskentillä 18. "jenkkikausi" ' (The 18th 'jenkki' period in Finnish Basketball), *Daily News Helsingin Sanomat*, 17 September 1990.
Bale, J. (1987) 'Alien Student-athlete in American Higher Education: loca-

tional Decision-making and the Sojourn Abroad', *Physical Education Review*, 10, 81–93.

Bogue, D.J. (1961) *Techniques and Hypotheses for the Study of Differential Migration*. International Population Conference, unpublished.

Brooks, D. and Penttilä, M. (1988) 'The Socialization of American Basketball Players in Finland', Paper presented at the annual meeting of the North Central Sociological Association, 15 April 1988 (Pittsburgh, PA).

Buechler, H.C. (1987) 'Introduction', in Buechler, H.C. and Buechler, J.-M. (eds), *Migrants in Europe: The Role of Family, Labor, and Politics* (Westport, CT: Greenwood Press) pp.1–9.

Daniel, G.H. (1939) 'Labour Migration and Age Composition', *Sociological Review*, 3, 281–308.

Dryansky, G. (1982) 'American Jump Shots in Europe', *New York Times and Magazine*, 28 November, 112–17.

Finnish Basketball Federation (1979) *Statistical Yearbook in Basketball* (Helsinki: Finnish Basketball Federation).

Georg, P. (1970) 'Types of Migration of the Population According to the Professional and Social Composition of Migrant' in Jansen, C.J. (ed.), *Readings in the Sociology of Migration* (Oxford: Oxford University Press) pp.39–48.

Heinonen, O. and Lahtinen, J. (1990) 'Foreign Professional Athletes as Migrants in Finland', unpublished MSc thesis, University of Jyväskylä.

Honkavaara, A. (1991) 'Ice Hockey Players' Migration to Finland' Telephone interview with K. Olin, 13 April 1991. University of Jyväskylä. Department of Social Sciences of Sport. Unpublished report.

Jackson, J.A. (1986) *Migration: Aspects of Modern Sociology* (New York: Longman).

Jansen, C.J. (1970) *Readings in Sociology of Migration* (Oxford: Oxford University Press).

Maguire, J. (1988) 'The Commercialization of English Elite Basketball 1972–1988: a Figurational Perspective', *International Review for the Sociology of Sport*, 23, 305–23.

Olin, K. (1984) 'Foreign Star-recruit Players as Immigrants: Finnish Basketball as an Illuminative Example', University of Jyväskylä, Department of Sociology and Planning for Physical Culture, Research Report No. 31.

Olin, K., Lahtinen, J. and Heinonen, O. (1990) 'Social Integration of Foreign Professional Players into Sport and Society: A Migration Perspective', Paper presented at the International Sociological Association 12th World Congress on Sociology for One World: Unity and Diversity, Research Committee 27 Sociology of Sport, 9–13 July 1990 (Madrid).

Pourcher, G. (1964) *Le Peuplement de Paris* (The Peopling of Paris) (Paris: Cahier Presses Universitaires).

Puronaho, K. (1988) 'Raha ratkaisee urheilussa' (Money Decides in Sport), *Liikunta ja tiede* (*Journal of Sport and Science*), 25, 184–7.

Ravenstein, E. (1885, 1889) 'The Laws of Migration', *Journal of the Royal Statistical Society* 48, 167–235; 52, 241–305.

Rose, A. (1969) *Migrants in Europe: Problems of Acceptance and Adjustment*, (Minneapolis: University of Minneapolis Press).

(1970) 'Distance of Migration and Socio-economic Status of Migrants' in

Jansen, C.J. (ed.), *Readings in the Sociology of Migration*, (Oxford: Oxford University Press), pp.85–92.

Straubhaar, T. (1986) 'The Cases of International Labour Migrations: A Demand-determined Approach', *International Migration Review* 4,20, 835–55.

Söderling, I. (1988) 'Maassamuuton ulottuvuudet: Yksilö, alue ja yhteiskunta-tason tarkastelu Suomessa vuosina 1977–1978 maassamuuttaneista' (Dimensions of Population Movement: Individual, Regional and Social Level Consideration in Finland in 1977–1978), University of Turku. Series C, Part 65.

Thomas, D.S. (1958) 'Age and Economic Differentials in Inter-state Migration', *Population Index* 2, 125–30.

10

Do Markets Make Footballers Free?

Fiona Miller and Steve Redhead

There are two conflicting moves in labour market freedom of movement in Europe. First, there is the European Community's declared intention to move to a free market in labour (especially as a result of the Single European Act, 1986), among member states by 1993, and the decision of the European Union of Football Associations (representing a far wider constituency than merely the European Community states) to limit the free movement by, for instance, restricting the number of foreign footballers to four per squad for European competition matches from season 1991–92 (and to classify, for example, Scots, Welsh and Irish as 'foreigners' in England). This UEFA rule has recently been described by the Member of the European Parliament (MEP) for Cheshire East as 'illegal under the Treaty of Rome as it restricts the freedom of movement of labour and goes against the concept of an open market'. In any event it seems that a decision on free movement in football's case has already been postponed until at least 1995.

The second aspect of 'freedom' here involves the transfer system which MEPs have described as 'a slave trade', much to the chagrin of bodies like the Football League and, to some extent, the Professional Footballers' Association which has campaigned to replace transfers with a European-style compensation system.

There are those on the new right in the vanguard of the 'new Europe' who might however argue for a different interpretation altogether. They regard a 'free market' as one based on free competition, where competition can only be free when all participants start with the same advantages and disadvantages. On this analysis, a free market requires not only uniformity of certain basic ground-rules and standards, but also the 'harmonization' of certain rights and freedoms. This would include organizations and individuals alike. This removal of the restrictions, seen by many not on the new right as unnecessary barriers to trade and social welfare, has of course not been without opposition.

Consequently, within the new European Economic Area (EEA)[1] the deadline of 1 January 1993 was agreed (under the Single European Act, 1986) for the major obstacles to a single, open market to be overcome – if not by co-operation then by intervention.

The European football industry however, has been subjected to persuasion and negotiation, offered compromises, and given ultimatums to change its regulations since 1974. As this chapter points out, the stage of direct intervention may finally have been reached as the balance of forces between new right free marketeers and labour market protectionists continues to shift to the right.

THE LAW AND THE MARKET

Jimmy Hill, formerly Players' Union Chairman and now a prominent TV personality, said in his 1961 publication, *Striking For Soccer*, which details his time in charge of the union, 'it is difficult to treat professional footballers as one does ordinary employees' (Hill, 1961). In the intervening years, Hill's own personal political trajectory – he was a vocal and active supporter of 'rebel' tours of professional sports players to South Africa in the 1980s for instance – has followed the well-trodden path to the right. Along with many other commentators on the modern player's rights, Hill's contemporary view is still (as it was in the 1960s battle to abolish the old transfer system and the maximum wage) *against* 'restraint of trade', but is now in favour of extinguishing any difference between a professional sports player and any other worker. As he said in 1961 it may be 'difficult'; but in the 1990s, that is exactly what the European Community expects the footballing authorities to do.

Since the 1970s numerous representatives have expressed concern at the employment practices used in the football industry. Reports have been written and threats and ultimatums issued but, nearly 20 years on, no real changes have been made. The dispute between the European Community (EC) and European Free Trade Association (EFTA) and the various European football authorities actually centres around two issues: (a) the use of a 'quota' system on the number of foreign employees permissible and (b) the payment of compensation to an employer when an employee leaves service – that is, the transfer fee.

Quota systems have been in sporadic operation in various countries since professional football began, significantly affecting player mobility. Each national association currently (1991–92 season) sets its own quotas, but the usual choice among European football organizations is two or three foreigners permitted to play for a club at any one time. Spain for instance allows four foreigners to be employed in first division clubs, providing no more than three are on the pitch at once; Greece allows three foreigners, as does the English Football League (the English Premier League saw no reason to change this rule), and (after much experimentation) the Italian first division. The Scottish Football League sets no quotas at all on European Community (and presumably now also EFTA) players, but will only allow ten non-EC players to participate in its League at any one time (work permits are required for those non-EC players).

In the Netherlands in the 1991–92 season, clubs could play only two foreigners at a time, and the quota has been enforced: on 10 March 1991, for example, in a match between Feyenoord and Willem II Tilburg, Feyenoord started the game with two foreigners – Griga (Czech) and Kiprich (Hungarian), but in a 67th-minute substitution a third foreigner, Mark Farrington (English) joined the Feyenoord players. When the referee realized this he ordered one of the three to leave the pitch. Feyenoord were not allowed to play another substitute, and subsequently lost the match. In fact, the Dutch football rules on nationality are fairly flexible, and residency will qualify a player as a non-foreigner. Similarly, the English, Welsh and Scottish Football Associations do not regard each other as foreign at all; rather, they have a long tradition of cross-pollination.[2] However this is where the situation starts to get difficult. European clubs are also members of UEFA, a supra-national co-ordinating body which organizes and disciplines them, and UEFA sets its own quotas for its own competitions. As qualification for these is based on a team's domestic league and cup performances, these quotas tend to be respected in national association rules.

UEFA quotas for the 1991–92 season were four foreigners permitted per squad; under renewed pressure from the European Commission a change was made as from 1 July 1992. In a 'gentleman's agreement' – the legal enforceability of which is questionable – UEFA has agreed that its national associations will be allowed to *employ* as many foreign players in their first divisions as they like. Any restrictions on the number of such players being *fielded* by a club in a particular match would seem to be left to the discretion of each national association, with one proviso as expressed in a European Commission document on 'Professional Footballers' published in 1991:

From the 1992–93 football season, the national associations

coming under UEFA (Union of European Football Associations) will have to allow at least three non-national players plus
two non-national players who have, by that date, been playing
uninterrupted in the country concerned for five years, including
three years spent in youth teams, to be in the line-up for domestic
first division championship matches.

The national associations or federations will also be able to apply
more favourable systems if they so wish (as is already the case, for
example, in England, Scotland and Belgium). As a general rule, clubs
will be allowed to take on as many non-national players as they like,
and the national associations which operate a licensing system will be
required to issue licences to all those players.

These are the essential results of the negotiations which Martin
Bangemann, Vice President of the Commission, has been pursuing
with representatives of UEFA and the professional footballers' associations. The Commission had given Mr Bangemann a mandate to do
so in April 1991 in the hope that improvements might be made to the
initial position adopted by UEFA at its Stockholm meeting of 31
January 1990, and the new system, based on an amicable arrangement,
entered into force on 1 July 1992 rather than 1 January 1993 as UEFA
had wanted. Moreover, the system will be extended by the end of the
1996–97 season to the other divisions in which professional footballers
play. The Commission and UEFA will hold consultations every four
years to verify that the system is operating properly.

A first step has also been taken in another area: Mr Bangemann had
suggested that the terms of a future standard contract specifying the
general principles governing some aspects of the contractual links
between clubs and professional players should be negotiated with
UEFA. He had sent out an exhaustive questionnaire on this subject to
the associations of the Community's members states and to UEFA
thereby complying with the wish expressed by the Commission in April
1991 concerning the concept of the professional player who is also a
Community national.

An agreement of principle has been reached on one specific aspect
of professional football–the question of transfers – which had attracted
the attention of both the Commission and the European Parliament.
Thus the principle has been accepted that any professional footballer
will be free to play for another club at the end of his contract with his
former club irrespective of the usual negotiations between clubs
concerning compensation, in particular for real and demonstrable
costs incurred in training young players. Although this first step has

now been accomplished, it is clear that the standard contract will require more detailed discussion with all the parties concerned.[3]

This document may at first sight seem like a concession by UEFA towards a free market in labour, but it must be remembered that national associations are still at liberty to impose their own quotas, and have so far shown little willingness to throw open their doors to what many regard as an 'alien' workforce. Add to this the decision by UEFA that Scots, Welsh, Irish and English are now supposed to regard each other officially as foreigners, and the labour market begins to contract again. If we turn to the transfer system, used throughout Europe, (despite a modified compensation system on the Continent) further serious restraints on player mobility are encountered. Although each national association currently uses its own version of the system, attempts have been made to standardize the restrictions. The basic concept involves an employee (the professional footballer) being registered with his national association by his employer, any change of employer involving a transfer of the registration. An employee can only work for someone who holds his registration. Furthermore, when an employee leaves, his former employer must be paid a fee by his new employer. This fee is to be paid even when the employee is no longer under contract to work for his former employer.[4]

The UEFA rules are actually close to the current UK position on dealing with transfers, where it is at least made clear that a player's consent is necessary for a transfer to take place.[5] Until 1991, in contrast to many other continental European countries, the local Belgian rules took little or no account of the player's position: if at the end of his contract of employment no other club wished to employ him on the transfer fee specified, and the player did not wish to re-sign with his former employer, the player would be suspended and could play for no one at all. In 1991 this was challenged in the Belgian courts by a professional footballer, Jean-Marc Bosman, in the case of *Bosman* v *FC Liege and URBSFA*, as a result of which the Belgian FA has complied, at least, with UEFA's rules on the subject. Bosman however, was subsequently unable to find work as a professional footballer and would appear to have been unofficially 'blacklisted' for his legal action.

On the other hand, the French football authorities operate with the advanced idea that a transfer fee should be paid to an employer only when an employee leaves *during* an existing contract; at the end of his contract a player may go and work for whoever he wishes. If no one wants to employ him, then he can follow the example of Gabriel

Calderon who, immediately after failing to be taken on by any other club, drove to an unemployment office in Paris and registered for state benefit.

The current situation, then, in the European football industry contains restraints of trade, restrictions on movement, elements of racial discrimination, and other practices which limit freedom of movement in the labour market. With the pressures to harmonize for 1993 conflicting with the football industry's efforts to stall further change until 1997, the European Commission appears to be losing its patience and may well pursue positive legal action against the football authorities in Europe. The *legal* grounds for such a challenge are clear, even in translation.

First, Article 7 of the Treaty of Rome makes discrimination on the grounds of nationality unlawful and Article 48 guarantees the free movement of European Community (and now EFTA) workers between member states of the Community. Paid sports players have been classified as workers, and football as an economic activity,[6] so that this law applies directly to national sports associations and clubs alike, and it is irrelevant that the association makes no profit, or that the club may be going bankrupt.[7] Nor is it any argument to claim that, based as it is in Switzerland, UEFA need take no account of European Community laws. Apart from the fact that European Community law has been taken to apply to organizations based outside the EC if that enterprise trades directly or indirectly within the Community,[8] Switzerland as a member of EFTA is now directly subject to all the basic laws of the EC – EFTA having joined the European Economic Area. Individual players or clubs can bring a case in their national courts against the rules of their own national football association. Where necessary, a national court can refer to the European Court of Justice for an interpretation of the finer points of the European Community law concerned, the national court then implementing that law to obtain a result.

This strategy has not been particularly successful to date. When the Italian Football Federation was instructed to change its rules in 1976,[9] it simply ignored the judgment. Individual players (and even clubs) are not keen on instigating legal action against their employers (the Bosman case would graphically illustrate why this is so) and each national association would have to be challenged in its own national court. As far as UK players are concerned, the situation would appear to be even worse, as the European Community regards Scotland, Wales, England and Northern Ireland as one member state. Therefore restrictions on movement imposed by UEFA or by their domestic football associations do not involve 'freedom of movement between member states', and as such are not subject to Article 48 and unlikely to fall within Article 7.[10] Nor do local UK laws on racial discrimination apply.[11] The second line of attack under the Treaty is therefore to use Articles 85 and 86 which prohibit the prevention, restriction or distortion of competition within the European Community. Under *these* provisions, the Commission itself is empowered to investigate situations, amend the rules of an organization, and punish by use of heavy fines any breach of the Treaty in this area. It is these powers which the Commission would use to investigate the effects of the European football industry, and the Commission then finds itself once more faced with the diverse interpretations of 'free competition'. The unbridled free market view of the new right in Europe is increasingly being transformed from rhetoric into reality.

THE LAW OF THE MARKET

This latter interpretation of market forces is the sports labour market protectionists' greatest fear, and representatives of UEFA, the national associations, and even the various players' unions forecast terrible consequences of removing the restrictions. In Britain, for example, football industry protectionism has been rife in the last decade. Gordon Taylor, the Professional Footballers' Association Chief Executive in England and Wales argued in an interview in the mid-1980s that 'our biggest worry if the restrictions are lifted is that our best players will be snapped up abroad and be replaced by cheaper inferior foreign players'. This is underlined by a more exact statement by David H. Will, formerly of UEFA and currently a FIFA representative, in *Ninety Minutes* magazine in 1991 that 'it's better to protect the development of young footballers in each country than to have our clubs overstaffed by foreign players'.

If the European Commission is successful and both the quota and transfer fee systems are removed, at least for European Community players in European Community countries, the consequences could certainly be traumatic in an industry which is already feeling the effects of economic recession. So how are the football clubs of Europe reacting to the challenge? As long ago as 1968 Arthur Hopcraft in his book on 1960s football culture was complaining about Britain's non-thinking, old-fashioned clubs 'stuffing money under the mattress' (Hopcraft, 1968). In the meantime, the elite rich clubs have become much richer and the rest *much* poorer in relative terms. Some have gone bankrupt, or ended up in non-league divisions, effectively as part-time enterprises. Super leagues are seen by the elite as the 'final solution' to a long-term problem. However, there are those in the football world who have expressed a concern about this kind of future for European soccer. Various representatives of the football authorities, both at local and UEFA level, have argued strongly for retention of the present restrictive transfer and quota systems. What is perhaps more surprising is the attitude adopted by the union representatives of the players themselves; they emphasize not the potential opportunities but only the potential drawbacks in the 'freeing up' of the professional footballers' labour market. In other fields of European business this would be instantly condemned as blatant and unlawful discrimination, and in the present free market competitive climate, as protectionism: a label used as a 'four-letter word' by the new right in the 1980s.

The football industry protectionists' argument on the quota issue is, in summary:

1 Remove the quota system and the distribution of talent will suffer – the top European football clubs will buy up and hoard the best players, thus completely dominating the football leagues of Europe.

2 Talented players will be drawn away from their home countries by the promise of riches abroad, and there will be a resultant fall in the standards of domestic soccer.

3 Foreign replacements would be a cheap and easy alternative, but then clubs would rely too heavily on these imports and relinquish their expensive youth policies and their interest in home grown young talent.

4 This would lead not only to a fall in interest in soccer as a career, but more widely to a fall in interest in soccer as a spectator sport. Why should people support a side staffed only with foreigners and with no local talent involved?

5 Remove the quota system and there will be a fall in the standards of the national football team. Too many foreigners in the League and it resembles the Italy of the 1960s; too many nationals playing abroad the result is the Brazil of the 1990s. 'Globalization' here means a sameness and negativity of play characterized by much of Italia '90.

6 Overall, player mobility would lead to the ruination of the football industry as it has been organized since, at least, the 1950s.

The same argument about economic ruin and cultural change has been made by football protectionists who wish to defend the transfer system as well as the system of quotas. Again the protectionist postition can be elaborated as:

1   Remove the transfer fee, the protectionists argue, and it will be bad for business. Smaller clubs stay solvent by selling players, and the resulting loss of revenue would mean clubs closing down, players being made redundant or at best having to accept wage cuts.
2   The protectionists also insist that the transfer system exists to compensate clubs for money invested in training players. Especially players who then leave, to bring success to another team. Why, they argue, should clubs continue to spend money on developing youngsters, if they are to be literally 'free' at the end of their contract term?

The balance of forces between the new right and the protectionist positions has massively shifted over the 1980s. For the protectionists the policies of the new right (in governments such as those of Margaret Thatcher and John Major in the UK) have been precisely the *cause* of the economic and social hard times which have affected working conditions and pay in the professional sports labour market over the last decade.

Protectionist positions, however unsatisfactory in terms of developing civil liberties of professional sports players, remain a defence against the onslaught of the new right in social and economic policy. They do, however, in Britain's case when practised over many decades, create a deferential football culture which reinforces a conservatism already instilled in working-class life in England over two centuries. 'Modernization' policies (for example all-seater stadia as recommended by the report of Lord Justice Taylor after the Hillsborough disaster in 1989) become targets for defending players and their traditional football culture *against*, just as (more successfully and more justifiably) with government plans to introduce identity cards for all fans in England and Wales under the Football Spectators Bill of 1989. A culture of 'defence' is continually reproduced. This is manifestly *not* a culture of resistance or modernization and its echoes resound in 'the new sports writing' – the otherwise laudable efforts of the football fanzine movement, situated mainly in the UK.

FOOTBALLERS WITH ATTITUDE?

In 1986 one of the present authors wrote an essay title, 'You've Really got a Hold on Me: Footballers in the Market' (Redhead, 1986). This chapter has revisited the terrain of the earlier study, and today it could be argued that the statement (derived from a 1960s pop song) should now read, after many years of new right ascendancy, 'You've *Still Really Got a Hold on Me*'. One approach to the continuing dilemma for player associations such as the PFA is to concentrate on the disciplined yet 'free' image of British football culture and ask why is it that footballers in the UK have so infrequently asserted their employment rights compared with their European counterparts, a situation highlighted by Jean-Marc Bosman's court case against Liege, his former employer, which is in effect a modern day re-run of George Eastman's High Court victory in 1963 for the European stage. The answers to this question are to be found in the historical and contemporary development of professional football in Britain as a 'man's man's man's game' (to mis-sample another song) where difference is routinely scrutinized, policed and in some cases, ultimately, extinguished. We would emphasize, in consequence, that changes in youth culture and football spectatorship, linked to changes in football's place as a modern cultural industry along with popular music, might offer a fruitful area for study and development of policy (Redhead, 1991). Whether footballers – or other professional sports players – can change their historically conservative 'attitude' to fit neatly alongside a developing participatory, democratic fan culture is, however, a more difficult field of enquiry. Footballers are notoriously models of working-class Toryism and the problem for the protectionists in the industry (including unions) is to arrest the tide of rights discourse becoming more and more right-wing. The notion of professional footballers having rights to freedom has taken on a distinctly radical-right inflexion in recent years and any attempt to hold back the 'facts' of the market are regarded as politically suspect. The problem for the protectionists remains how to continue the defence of hard-won historical rights of players in the wake of the rise of neo-liberalism, and yet not resort to a 'Little Englander', nationalist approach themselves.

Bankowski (1974) developed an anarchistic theory of law, elevated to a general theory of law (Mungham and Bankowski, 1978) which, essentially, counterposed law to freedom. From the perspective of the market, on the other hand, the notion that markets *create* freedom for workers in general and footballers in particular was taken to task in Redhead's (1986) paper. During the 1980s, however, such an argument was transformed into official government policy in both the UK and the USA. That it remains a rampant market debate in Europe is confirmed by the comments of a Euro MP arguing that there is no reason why footballers should be exceptions to the total freedom of movement of labour across the national boundaries of the ever growing European economic community (Larive, 1990). This free-market ideology may be contrasted with protectionist views such as: 'total individual freedom may be achieved at an overall loss to the industry' (Taylor, 1990: 2) and 'restrictions on the number of players of other nationalities who may play in any match on any day are for the specific good of football' (Will, 1990: 3). What appears certain, therefore, is that neither law or the market, in themselves, can make footballers free.

NOTES

1   EEA is made up of European Community and European Free Trade Association states, using common principles. East European states now express interest in joining the programme.
2   As far back as the 1880s clubs in northern England were fielding vast numbers of Scottish players – nine in the 1888–89 record-breaking Preston North End side; and when Tottenham Hotspur became the first southern team to win the FA Cup they used four Scots, an Irishman and two Welshmen (and three northerners). It could be argued that, for example, Liverpool's continually successful sides from the 1960s on contained only a handful of *English* players.
3   Press release from the European Commission, 18 April 1991.
4   Arguments over fees should not concern the employee, and if a contract has actually ended, his transfer should be facilitated and money be of secondary importance, according to UEFA policy.
5   This consent may be bought; see *Shilton* v *Wilmshurst* (*Inspector of Taxes*) HL 7 February 1991, reported in the *Independent* newspaper.
6   Case 36/74 *Walrave & Koch* v *Union Cycliste Internationale* (1974) ECR 1405, 1 CMLR 320 Case 13/76; *Dona* v *Mantero* (1976) ECR 133.
7   Case 53/83 *Levin* v *Staatssecretaris van Justitie* (1982) 1035, 2 CMLR 544.
8   Case 85/76 *Hoffman–La Roche* v *Commission* (1979) ECR 461, 3 CMLR 211.
9   *Dona*, n. 6 above.
10   Cases 35 and 36/82 *Morson & Jhanjan* (1982) ECR 3723, 2 CLMR 221.
11   Race Relations Act 1976, s.36.

REFERENCES

Bankowski, Z. (1974) 'Does Law make Footballers Free?', unpublished paper.
Hill, J. (1961) *Striking for Soccer* (London: Peter Davies).
Hopcraft, A. (1968) *The Football Man* (Harmondsworth: Penguin).
Larive, J. (1990) 'Political, Legal and Economic Aspects of Football in the Light of 1992's Europe', unpublished paper given at conference on 'Le football et l'Europe' (Florence: European University Institute).
Mungham, G. and Bankowski, Z. (1978) *Images of Law* (London: Routledge).

Redhead, S. (1986) 'You've Really got a Hold on Me: Footballers in the Market' in Tomlinson, A. and Whannel, G. (eds), *Off the Ball* (London: Pluto).

(1991) *Football with Attitude* (Manchester: Wordsmith).

Taylor, G. 1990, 'Respect of the Sovereignty of European Nations' Football Talent', Colloquium Paper no. 155/90 (Florence: European University Institute).

Will, D. (1990) 'Football and Europe', Colloquium Paper no. 97/90 (Florence: European University Institute).

11

The Flood from the East? *Perestroika* and the Migration of Sports Talent from Eastern Europe

Vic Duke

The initial inspiration for this title came from Gordon Taylor, chief executive of the Professional Footballers' Association. Speaking at the launch of *Rothman's Football Yearbook 1990–91* in August 1990, he warned of the danger of a flood of eastern European footballers entering English football now that transfers to the West were no longer officially restricted and also because transfer fees were relatively low in European terms.

Given my previous work on Czechoslovak[1] sport (Duke, 1990a) and my impending visits to both Prague and Budapest in autumn 1990, the statement seemed worthy of further systematic investigation. The data in this chapter are restricted therefore to Czechoslovakia and Hungary, but the scenario of liberalization – in sport as well as society as a whole – is a familiar one throughout much of eastern Europe.

The next section will summarize the politico-economic context of the changes in Czechoslovakia and Hungary, which is important with respect to both the similarities and differences between the two countries. More specific consideration of the changes in eastern European football follows in the third section, which highlights the financial crisis facing football clubs (and sports clubs in general) in the 1990s. The fourth section examines data for both countries on the migration abroad of professional footballers as of December 1990 in the case of Hungary and for the period 1989–91 in the case of Czechoslovakia.

THE POLITICO-ECONOMIC CONTEXT OF *PERESTROIKA*

Economic, political and social change has been pronounced in eastern Europe, particularly since the 'year of revolutions' in 1989. The whole process of change can be traced back to the new leadership and new direction in the then existing Soviet Union established by Mikhail Gorbachev. His call for radical reform in the Soviet Union was interpreted as a green light by would-be eastern European reformers to press forward with demands for a transformation of the system. To Gorbachev *perestroika* was not confined to economic change but was a major programme of planned change in all aspects of social organization (see Gorbachev, 1987). Football is no exception and was therefore bound to alter, as is discussed later.

There were obvious similarities between Czechoslovakia and Hungary (and other eastern European countries) in their adherence to some form of state socialist society (Giddens, 1981). Among the main ingredients of such a society were: a system of central planning of all aspects of the economy (including facilities for sport and the wages of full-time sports players); a meshing of the ruling communist party and the state such that all manner of appointments were subject to political influence (including officials in sports organizations and football clubs); an official ideology espousing the historical role of the pro-letariat; and the predominant position of working-class organizations (including the linking of football clubs and sports clubs in general to party and worker organizations).

Another more recent connection between the two countries is their non-violent transition from one-party state socialism to a form of pluralist democratic capitalism. The 'velvet revolution' consisted of a series of massive peaceful demonstrations which led to the ending of the Communist Party monopoly of power in Czechoslovakia (see Schermer, 1990). In Hungary the party (actually the Hungarian Socialist Workers' Party) took the leading role in the 'negotiated revolution', which resulted in their defeat in the ensuing election (Bruszt, 1990). Whereas the 'velvet revolution' was instigated from below, the 'negotiated revolution' came from above. In order to understand the different behaviour of the ruling party in each country, it is necessary to highlight important differences in the earlier history of the two countries (which ultimately came to influence the pace of change in football).

The year 1968 represents the peak of the earlier wave of communist reformism in eastern Europe. During the brief months of the Prague Spring, Alexander Dubcek introduced both economic reform (market-ization) and political reform (democratization). It was the latter which particularly incurred the wrath of the Soviet hierarchy and resulted in the Warsaw Pact invasion and the ensuing years of purges and 'normalization'. For almost 20 years following the invasion, change of any sort was not on the party agenda in Czechoslovakia.

By contrast, Hungary opted for economic reform only (remembering all too well their own invasion in 1956 by Soviet tanks). January 1968 witnessed the beginning of the New Economic Mechanism, which introduced some aspects of marketization into economic activity. Hungary's initially limited economic reform was tolerated by the Soviet leadership and flourished to become Kadar's successful hybrid of 'goulash communism'. The gradual intensification of economic reform, which provided an examplar for some of Gorbachev's reforms under *perestroika*, led to changes in many aspects of society including sport/football. Changes to the organization of football thus began in Hungary but have since spread to (most of) the rest of eastern Europe.

CHANGES IN EASTERN EUROPEAN FOOTBALL

The major organizational changes in eastern European football towards the end of the 1980s were professionalization of the players, independence for the football authorities and football clubs, the switch from traditional 'socialist' sponsorship to more commercial forms and the lifting of restrictions on transfer to the West. Taken together this package of reforms provided both new opportunities and new problems for football clubs and players. Successful players at successful clubs were likely to benefit but ordinary players at ordinary clubs could be facing a bleak future in the 1990s.

The traditional view in the socialist republics of eastern Europe was that top-level football players were not professionals. They were registered as employees of the factory/enterprise/ministry who sponsored their club. In practice they trained and performed as full-time 'professional' sportsmen. The Union of European Football Associations (UEFA) classified eastern European players in a hybrid category as neither professionals (in the commercial sense) not amateurs (in the part-time sense). Not until 1988 did UEFA alter the status of footballers in Czechoslovakia and Hungary to that of full-time professionals.

The changes in Czechoslovakia took place in two separate stages, the first before the 'velvet revolution' of November 1989 and the second after it. The first stage was largely a response to pressure for change from within but also partly influenced by the general context of *perestroika* (see Duke, 1990a). The second stage completed the transition to an independent and professional football industry.

Starting from the 1988–89 season, Czechoslovak first-division footballers were recognized officially as professional sportsmen. They became contract players with their club and received a salary from the state according to the terms of their contract, which varied according to status and experience. The professionalization of players represented a marked increase in status for the sportsmen involved. None the less, at this first stage the salaries paid to the players were from the state and not from the club as a private concern. The pay scales were determined by the state bureaucracy rather than the market.

The need to introduce professionalization was highlighted by a financial scandal at first-division Bohemians Prague. The president, secretary, treasurer and 20 present or past players of the club stood trial on charges of corruption and embezzlement. Several officials were imprisoned but then released as part of the general amnesty following the 'velvet revolution'. This case highlighted the use of unofficial payments to top up wages.

After the 'velvet revolution' the pace of change in all aspects of Czechoslovak society intensified. The second stage in spring 1990 gave players freedom of contract and on 2 May 1990 the football association became independent of the state. A switch from total state finance to independent status and the accompanying need to be self-financing cannot be achieved overnight. Hence the Czechoslovak FA went through a transition period with state finance progressively reduced until the summer of 1991. From that point on, the FA and the clubs were totally independent private enterprises and the players possessed real professional contracts in the western sense.

Hungarian football has undergone more gradual changes over a longer period, but the final stages of the process were completed under the influence of *perestroika*. The first steps towards professionalism were taken in 1979 and official approval was granted in 1983. Open professionalism was introduced in an attempt to overcome match-fixing and corruption scandals. The major scandal of the early 1980s involved 499 players, officials and organizers, some of whom were given prison sentences.

Despite the earlier start in Hungary, the move to an independent professional football structure was completed only about a year ahead of the Czechoslovaks. In January 1989 freedom of contract was granted to the players and the football association became independent of the state in June 1989. As with the Czechoslovak FA there was a transition phase during which the state continued to provide some finance. In 1990 seven per cent of Hungarian FA expenditure was covered by central government.

In terms of sponsorship, the traditional east European model was for sports clubs to be sponsored by a factory, enterprise, ministry or trade union. The players were regarded as employees of the enterprise concerned. Now more commercial sponsorship involving western firms is emerging and *perestroika* was seen as opening more possibilities in the near future.

Many of the clubs continue to be sponsored by heavy industrial enterprises such as chemicals, steel and engineering. For instance, in Czechoslovakia, Banik Ostrava are sponsored by the miners' trade union and Vitkovice by a steelworks; in Hungary, Tatabanya are sponsored by a coal-mining company and Raba Gyor by a locomotive manufacturer. Eastern European leagues also traditionally contained a large number of clubs funded by the army such as Dukla Prague, Honved Budapest, Red Star Belgrade, Steaua Bucharest and CSKA Sofia. The Dynamo clubs were traditionally associated with the secret police, but this connection has been discontinued (officially at least).

Major sponsorship deals with western firms have been restricted thus far to the leading clubs. For example, in Czechoslovakia Sparta Prague, who are the best supported team, were, in August 1990, the first to secure a deal involving shirt advertising in return for sponsorship from Opel. Minolta of Austria followed suit by sponsoring the team from Nitra, now renamed Minolta Nitra. The name change unfortunately deprives us of one of the most evocative names in European football, that of Plastika Nitra. More recently in September 1991, Slavia Prague were taken over by Boris Korbel, an American multi-millionaire of Czech origin.

Only the best supported club in Hungary have so far negotiated substantial foreign sponsorship. In 1990 Ferencvaros received 25 million forints from a French construction company (Bras) along with 5 million forints from a Hungarian firm (Hargita). Hargita's name appears on their shirts. Not surprisingly these firms were involved in plans to convert the club's ground into a 22,000 capacity all-seater stadium by autumn 1991. At present Raba Tyor have the only all-seater stadium in Hungary. Unfortunately for Ferencvaros the deal with Bras ended after only one season.

Ferencvaros are making great strides towards the western model of a football club as a commercial enterprise. To this end the football section became separate from the original multi-sports club in January 1990. Turnover at the football club has increased phenomenally: 16 million forints in 1987–88, 30 million in 1988–89, nearly 50 million in 1989–90 and an expected figure of over 100 million in 1990–91. The club intend to become a limited company by 1994.

The new era of financial independence from the state is, however, taking its toll of the smaller clubs. Between 1988 and 1989 the number of multi-sports clubs in Hungary decreased by 8 per cent and the membership of clubs declined by 19 per cent in the harsh economic climate of democratic capitalism. Similarly in Czechoslovakia, 16 of the 593 registered football clubs closed down in 1990–91 because of financial problems.

In addition to the professionalization of players, there is a greater openness (*glasnost*) to the transfer abroad of football players in return for much needed Western currency. Initially, these transfers operated within strict limits. Footballers could move to the West only after reaching the age of 30 and if they had served the national team with distinction.

More recently younger players have been transferred to the West. This trend started with Alexander Zavarov's transfer from Dynamo Kiev to Juventus at the age of 27 for £3.2 million in the summer of 1988. The flow of transfers to the West from eastern Europe accelerated after the 1990 World Cup finals in Italy. Seventeen of the Czechoslovak squad of 22 are now playing in the West and most of the Romanian squad have been transferred abroad since the finals.

Opportunities for leading players to seek a transfer abroad contribute to the development of greater openness and increased contact with the West. However, the *glasnost* policy of permitting official transfer to the West can be seen as an attempt to stem the flow of unofficial defections. The most notorious case in Czechoslovakia recently was the joint defection of Ivo Knoflicek and Lubos Kubik from Slavia Prague whilst on tour in West Germany. After several months in hiding around Europe and a fruitless attempt to sign for Derby County, both returned eventually to Prague to negotiate compromise deals which took them to St Pauli (West Germany) and Fiorentina (Italy) respectively.

During the initial period of change in both Czechoslovakia and Hungary, control of the transfer process remained bureaucratic despite the involvement of market forces in setting transfer fees. Only when the football associations gained complete independence from the state were transfer fees retained by the individual clubs.

The most significant impact on the rate of transfers would occur if eastern European countries attain associate membership of the European Community and if European Commission rules on the free movement of players prevail (see Duke, 1990b for more details on this). The flow of players to western Europe is then more likely to become a flood.

Although Hungary trod the path of football reform first, Czechoslovakia has moved in the same direction. Independence for the football associations and football clubs provides them with greater freedom but on the other hand this is compensated by loss of the financial security of state support. All the changes – professionalization, sponsorship and transfers – provide opportunities for some clubs and some players but also provide problems for others (probably the majority).

The headlong rush for marketization has led the governments in both Czechoslovakia and Hungary to introduce austerity policies. These involve prices doubling (at the very least) with wages remaining constant. In terms of football, the effect is higher admission charges, and a resultant decline in attendance at matches. The reduced crowds further exacerbate the financial crisis in the game, especially for those clubs without 'new' sponsorship and the players at such clubs.

Professional footballers remain well-off in comparison with other workers in both countries, but the austerity measures are imposing hardship at all levels of society. Hence the solution for the best players is to seek a transfer to the West in order to secure a higher standard of living, not to mention western currency.

THE MIGRATION OF FOOTBALLERS FROM CZECHOSLOVAKIA AND HUNGARY

Tables 11.1 and 11.2 provide data on the movement of footballers from Hungary and Czechoslovakia respectively. The Hungarian data are a cross-section taken in December 1990 of the 56 top professionals playing abroad at that time. In the case of Czechoslovakia, details of top 70 transfers are given based on those playing abroad in 1989 with the addition of subsequent transfers up until summer 1991.

Both Czechoslovakia and Hungary are net exporters of footballers to other countries in (mostly western) Europe. This flow is in large part due to the difficult politico-economic circumstances in eastern Europe in the late 1980s, but it also reflects the fact that both countries possess a substantial pedigree in European football. Czechoslovakia have twice reached the World Cup final and were European champions in 1976. Hungary have also appeared in two World Cup finals and twice reached the semi-finals of the European championship.

In December 1990 there were over 200 Hungarian footballers officially playing abroad. However, around three-quarters of them were playing in the Austrian regional third and fourth divisions. These players are semi-professionals, who live in Hungary and cross the border each weekend to play for Austrian teams in return for match

Table 11.1 Magyars abroad: Location of the main Hungarian professional footballers playing abroad (December 1990)

Austria (1)

Tamas Petres	Voest Linz

Belgium (14)

Jozsef Gaspar	RWD Molenbeek
Emil Lorinc	RWD Molenbeek
Laszlo Distl	Cercle Brugge
Imre Garaba	Charleroi
Karoly Gelei	Antwerp
Laszlo Gyimesi	Winterslag (*)
Ferenc Meszaros	Lokeren
Imre Nagy	RF Borains (*)
Laszlo Szabadi	Eendracht Aalst (*)
Istvan Varga	Waregem
Tibor Balag	Verbroedering Geel (*)
Tamas Manos	Germinal Ekeren
Jozsef Pasztor	Torhout (*)
Gyorgy Bognar	Standard Liege

France (2)

Kalman Kovacs	Auxerre
Zoltan Kanal	Paris FC 83 (*)

Finland (15)

Laszlo Ambrus	Valkeakosken Haka
Attila Heredi	Valkeakosken Haka
Gyorgy Katona	Valkeakosken Haka
Istvan Bodnor	Bollklubben 48 (*)
Mihaly Borostyan	Myllykosen Palloseura (*)
Jozsef Csuhay	Hango IK (*)
Gyorgy Hamori	Hango IK (*)
Endre Kolar	Hango IK (*)
Gabor Dekany	Lovisa Tor (*)
Attila Godo	Farvanpaa (*)
Tibor Gruborovics	Mikkeli Palloilijat
Sandor Kiss	Esbo Bollklubb (*)
Attila Kovacs	Seura Koskenposat (*)
Sandor Kovacs	Laupt FC (*)
Jozsef Varga	Lahden Reipas

Table 11.1 *continued*

Germany (5)

Jozsef Dzurjak	Chemnitzer FC
Peter Distl	RW Erfurt
Gyorgy Fabulya	Energie Cottbus
Gyula Hajszan	Duisburg (*)
Gabor Refi	Regensburg (*)

Greece (2)

Imre Boda	Olympiakos Volos (*)
Imre Katzenbach	Apollon

Italy (1)

Lajos Detari	Bologna

Netherlands (1)

Jozsef Kiprich	Feyenoord

Portugal (1)

Lazar Szentes	Vitoria Setubal

Scotland (1)

Istvan Kozma	Dunfermline Athletic

South Korea (2)

Gera Meszoly	Posko Atomic
Laszlo Pecha	Posko Atomic

Spain (2)

Lajos Schroth	Cadiz
Jozsef Szendrei	Cadiz

Switzerland (9)

Bela Bodonyi	Bulle (*)
Marton Esterhazy	Bulle (*)
Laszlo Dajka	Yverdon (*)
Rezso Kekesi	Yverdon (*)
Antal Nagy	Yverdon (*)
Lajos Kvaszta	Old Boys Basel (*)
Sandor Sollai	Hevron (*)
Istvan Sziggarto	Montreux (*)
Sandor Kincses	Chaux de Fonds (*)

(*) = club not in first division of national league

Table 11.2 Main transfers abroad of Czechoslovak footballers (based on those playing abroad in 1989 and transfers since then up to summer 1991)

Austria (11)

Ivan Cabala	Krems
Jaroslav Zapalka	Krems
Rudolf Bobek	Modling
Vladimir Borovicka	Austria Wien
Vaclav Danek	Swarovski Tirol
Libor Dosek	Stockerau
Vladimir Gombar	Austria Klagenfurt
Stefan Horny	Wiener Sportklub
Miroslav Prilozny	Vorwaerts Steyr
Emil Stranianek	1. Vienna FC
Zdenek Sreiner	St Poelten

Belgium (5)

Peter Fieber	Beerschot
Peter Herda	Charleroi
Werner Licka	Berchem
Marian Takac	RA Louvieroise
Peter Zelensky	RC Heirnis

Costa Rica (1)

Pavel Karoch	Alajuelense

Cyprus (1)

Vladislav Lauda	Limassol

England (4)

Ludek Miklosko	West Ham United
Pavel Srnicek	Newcastle United
Ivo Stas	Aston Villa
Jan Stejskal	Queens Park Rangers

France (12)

Robert Kafka	Bourges
Vladimir Kinier	Bourges
Lubomir Luhovy	Martigues
Stanislav Moravec	Martigues
Jiri Bartl	SC Amiens
Ivan Hasek	RC Strasbourg
Viliam Hyravy	Toulouse
Karel Jarolim	Rouen
Bohouslav Keller	AC Le Havre
Karol Kristof	Clermont Ferrand
Lubomir Moravcik	AS St Etienne
Dusan Tittel	Olympique Nimes

Table 11.2 *continued*

Germany (19)

Zdenek Duris	Schweinfurt
Petr Mrazek	Schweinfurt
Jan Kocian	St Pauli
Ivo Knoflicek	St Pauli
Pavel Chaloupka	Fortuna Dusseldorf
Petr Rada	Fortuna Dusseldorf
Oldrich Machala	Hansa Rostock
Roman Sedlacek	Hansa Rostock
Gunter Bittengel	Bayer Uerdingen
Radek Drulak	Oldenburg
Miroslav Kadlec	Kaiserlautern
Ludek Kovacik	Sachsen Leipzig
Tomas Kriz	SV Darmstadt
Karel Kula	Stuttgarter Kickers
Milos Lejtrich	Munchen 1860
Stanislav Levy	BlauWeiss Berlin
Jozef Marian	VFL Herzlake
Milan Nemec	RotWeiss Erfurt
Frantisek Straka	Borussia Monchengladbach

Hungary (1)

Dusan Fabry	Volan Budapest

Italy (2)

Lubos Kubik	Fiorentina
Tomas Skuhravy	Genoa

Netherlands (2)

Jozef Chovanec	PSV Eindhoven
Stanislav Griga	Feyenoord

Portugal (1)

Lubomir Vlk	FC Porto

Spain (3)

Michal Bilek	Betis Sevilla
Milan Luhovy	Sporting Gijon
Tibor Micinec	Logroñes

Switzerland (7)

Karel Brezik	Chur
Pavel Kloucek	Chur
Jan Berger	FC Zurich
Milan Fryda	Lausanne
Frantisek Jakubec	AC Bellinzona
Vaclav Pechacek	SC Burgdorf
Milan Simunek	Chatel St Denis

Turkey (1)

Stanislav Dostal	Izmir

expenses. Austrian match expenses are very desirable as they are higher than a full-time salary in Hungary.

The leading destinations for Hungarian professional footballers as of December 1990 were Finland, Belgium and Switzerland (see Table 11.1). The Finnish connection highlights the existence of a significant seasonal migration. Hungarian players go to Finland for six months each year to coincide with the summer season there and often return to play in Hungary during the winter months. Language may also play a part in the connection, given the distinctiveness of Hungarian and Finnish as Ugrian languages in contrast to the rest of Europe. The link with Belgium has a long history dating back to the 1960s.

Geographical proximity to Austria does not emerge as a relevant factor in relation to the main Hungarian professionals playing abroad (Table 11.1) – indeed there is only one player in the Austrian first division. This is somewhat surprising, given the large numbers of Hungarian semi-professionals who perform in the Austrian lower divisions.

Only a minority of the Hungarian players are located in Europe's leading footballing nations, which reflects the lack of recent success for the Hungarian national team (particularly in comparison to Czechoslovakia). Of the 56 professionals, 16 are with clubs in the first divisions of Belgium, France, Italy, The Netherlands, Portugal and Spain. Furthermore, only two Hungarians could be said to be playing at major European clubs – Kiprich at Feyenoord and Bognar at Standard Liege.

Another feature which is evident in Table 11.1 is the existence of club cells, where two Hungarians are playing together at a foreign club. This arrangement clearly aids the process of acclimatization into a new culture, and may also reflect a historical link between certain clubs. Hungarian cells exist at Racing White Daring Molenbeek, Valkeakosken Haka, Hango, Bulle, Yverdon, Cadiz and Posko Atomic.

In October 1990 there were 170 Czechoslovak footballers officially playing abroad. Around two-thirds of them were located with lower-division teams near the border in Germany and Austria. As with Hungary, these players are semi-professionals who continue to live in their home country. The flow of footballers out of Czechoslovakia increased markedly in volume immediately after the 1990 World Cup finals in Italy, where Czechoslovakia reached the quarter-final stage before losing to the eventual winners, Germany. During the summer of 1990, 40 first- and second-division players moved to western Europe. In the 1990 Czechoslovak footballer of the year award, the leading nine individuals were all playing abroad.

Table 11.2 documents the 70 main transfers abroad from Czechoslovakia in recent years. The most popular destinations for Czechoslovak footballers are Germany, France and Austria. Geographical proximity is an important factor in transfers to Germany and Austria, which parallel the movement of semi-professionals across the border mentioned above. In contrast to the situation in Hungary, the main patterns of movement for professionals and semi-professionals are similar.

A higher proportion of Czechoslovak footballers have been transferred to leading European footballing nations than was the case with Hungary. This is largely due to the recent success of the Czechoslovak national team in reaching the World Cup quarter-finals. More than half of the main Czechoslovak transfers are to leading nations such as Belgium, England, France, Germany, Italy, The Netherlands, Portugal and Spain. Moreover, more of the Czechoslovak players have been transferred to major European clubs such as Aston Villa, St Etienne, Borussia Monchengladbach, Fiorentina, PSV Eindhoven, Feyenoord and Porto.

The existence of club cells is even more evident in the case of Czechoslovak transfers. Two Czechoslovak footballers moved to Krems, Bourges, Martigues, Schweinfurt, St Pauli, Fortuna Dusseldorf, Hansa Rostock and Chur. A Czech connection emerged briefly at Aston Villa in 1990–91 with Josef Venglos as manager signing Ivo Stas as a player. After an unsuccessful first season Venglos was dismissed and has moved on to Turkey, where he managed Fenerbahce.

CONCLUSION

The movement of Hungarian and Czechoslovak footballers to England in recent years hardly constitutes a flood, although it might be suggested that there has been a flood of Czech goalkeepers! (three of the four Czechoslovak players transferring to England). Substantial movement of eastern European footballers has occurred, but to central and western (mainland) Europe. The faster pace and different style of play in England make it an unlikely venue for large numbers of eastern European outfield players.

Migration rates of footballers from both countries have risen markedly in the aftermath of the political changes in eastern Europe. The increased political freedom to transfer abroad is likely to remain, although some countries (notably Romania) are seeking to reimpose some form of restriction. Economic pressures on leading players to move to the West will also continue in the near future. The austerity policies of the emerging east European democracies involve an unattractive and volatile cocktail of increased unemployment, increased prices and (relatively) static wages.

Only the leading eastern European clubs, who have established substantial western sponsorship deals, will have any chance of persuading leading players to remain in their home country. Even these clubs – such as Sparta Prague and Ferencvaros – cannot compete with offers from Italy or Spain. The debate as to whether leading eastern European clubs can match leading western clubs in footballing terms has been answered by Sparta Prague's qualification for the mini-league stage of the European Champions Cup (two groups of four) in 1991–92 (not to mention the fact that Red Star Belgrade are the current holders!).

The wider pattern of footballer movements in Europe reflects the new international division of labour in football. Italy and Spain stand at the apex of the pyramid as they have the largest attendances, the highest salaries and the best players. By contrast, eastern European countries currently provide a new source of cheap labour. Associate membership status in the EC – if attained – would open the way for a further increase in migration from east to west.

This chapter constitutes a first step in the assessment of the impact of the political and economic changes in eastern Europe on the migration of professional sports labour. There is ample opportunity for further research in extending the time period covered for Hungarian and Czechoslovak football, in expanding the analysis to include other sports, and in widening the comparative framework to other countries. Other contributions to a European database would be most welcome.

ACKNOWLEDGEMENTS

I am grateful to the following for their assistance in the preparation of this paper: Rudolf Bata of the Czechoslovak Football Association, Karoly Csiki of the Hungarian Football Association and Tomas Denes of Nemzeti Sport (Budapest) for the provision of basic data and useful background information; the British Council for funding the flights to Prague and Budapest; Professor Ian Taylor at Salford for allowing me the time to make the visits during term-time; and Zsofia Zsobrax, my interpreter in Budapest, for rendering Hungarian understandable.

NOTE

1   This article was written before the division of the former Czechoslovakian state, but the general analysis remains relevant.

REFERENCES

Bruszt, L. (1990) 'The Negotiated Revolution', *Social Research*, 57, 365–87.

Duke, V. (1990a) 'Perestroika in Progress?: A Case Study of Czechoslovak Spectator Sports', *British Journal of Sociology*, 41, 145–56.

(1990b) 'Football senza frontiere', *Relazione Internazionale*, June, 108–15.

Giddens, A. (1981) *The Class Structure of the Advanced Societies* (2nd edn) (London: Hutchinson).

Gorbachev, M. (1987) *Perestroika* (London: Collins).

Schermer, H. (1990) 'The Velvet Revolution', Staffordshire Polytechnic Department of Sociology Occasional Paper No. 13.

Part Three:

Sports Migration:
Towards A Global Future?

12

Foreign Footballers, Cultural Dreams and Community Identity in some North-western Mediterranean Cities

Christian Bromberger

As an ethnologist, one of my main interests when dealing with football is to catch a glimpse of salient features of local culture as revealed through players' and spectators' behaviour. The interest may seem quite irrelevant here when focusing on the international migration of football players. This kind of migration appears at first to be highly dependent on market laws such as supply and demand or clubs' economic resources, and not on specific features of local culture. Following this formalist economic approach one would assume that the richest clubs will afford the best foreign players whom they choose according exclusively to sports criteria within the limits set up by each national football league. This is partially true: whereas Italian clubs can afford most of the stars on the market, German clubs, which are not so well off, will be less voracious in their recruiting. So, should the only alternative left be to restrain oneself from describing such a rational and mechanical mercantile process draining football stars from the periphery to the richest centres? In that case the ethnological analysis would be much alleviated if not superfluous.

Yet – and fortunately for the ethnologist – the facts are much more complex, intricate, even paradoxical when comparing national and local situations and more precisely clubs benefiting from almost the same financial facilities. Discrepancies affect both the number and the origin of foreign players. For instance, as Bale (1990: 8) stated, 'the number of foreign players in Britain is surprisingly small' (1.9 per cent in the English League in 1987), while it reached 24.5 per cent in the French first division in 1990.[1] In Britain, recruiting foreign talents is 'a relatively recent phenomenon' (Bale, 1990: 7), dating back no earlier than the late 1970s. On the contrary, the tradition of cosmopolitan teams is deeply rooted in French football history: for instance, from 1947 to 1985 France 'imported' 760 players from abroad (plus 90 players from former French African colonies, endowed with a special status). To explain this sharp contrast between France and Britain, one could, tongue in cheek, point out that English players are much better than French footballers, but obviously the difference between the two standards is not so great as to induce such a variation in the respective number of imported players.

Dealing with the origins of those foreign players one may also underline that there is a strong contrast between French and British situations, revealing a complex set of affinities and preferences, more than simple market laws and sports criteria would suggest. British clubs import mostly Dutch, Danish or Norwegian players – all men from the northern states of the continent, plus Yugoslavians (Bale, 1990: 9), while in 1989 and 1990, West Africans (especially Senegalese), Yugoslavs and Argentines are most represented among the foreigners in French football teams.[2] Local situations also differ greatly and cannot be reduced to simplistic explanatory formulae. For instance, if we compare French clubs of a similar standing, some of them appear to be more fond of foreign players than others. Figures show that clubs such as Girondins de Bordeaux and Olympique de Marseille – both anchored in international harbours – and Racing Club de Paris – settled in a cosmopolitan capital – were, on the whole, the ones that hired most foreign talent. During the 1945–74 period they represented up to 20.6 per cent of all players in the Bordeaux team, 18 per cent in Marseilles and 17.8 per cent in the Parisian club. During the same period Rheims and Saint-Etienne – two towns rooted 'deep in France' (*la France profonde*) – used fewer foreign recruits (respectively 12.3 and 7 per cent). Let us not forget that the latter played in the European Cup final.

Beyond the benefit one may expect on the sports field and in business, what does such a hiring practice suggest? It seems to me that the contrasted behaviours we have just evoked rest on different cultural bases and that, clad in the garments of choice seemingly imposed by the search solely for efficiency, profound traits of local identity and citizenship come to the surface. To some extent, then, one may detect obscure imaginary representations at work through mere recruiting decisions always exclusively justified in terms of sports practice and results.

I would like to consider some hypotheses in this direction, by examining the cultural significance of foreign players in three north-western Mediterranean cities: Marseilles, Naples and Turin.[3] The study of these three cases, each seen from a different point of view, will enable us to perceive the complementary faceted process involved in the collective view of the stranger – here foreigners – and the symbolic benefits one may expect.

THE COMPOSITION OF THE TEAM AS A PARABLE OF A COLLECTIVE DESTINY: OLYMPIQUE DE MARSEILLE (OM)

Football's fascination mainly rests on its capacity to link the universal with the particular. On the one hand it symbolizes the prominent values of the modern world: competition, achievement, solidarity, the part played by chance in individual or collective destinies, promotion and demotion, their interdependence on the scale of happiness (it is not enough for my team to win, its rivals must lose too); this also recalls some basic truths, especially that in a world where goods and riches are finite in quantity, happiness for some must mean unhappiness for others. On the other hand, it offers an opportunity to assert one's collective identity, reflected through local playing style[4] and through the composition of the team. Indeed, the team often appears as an ideal representation of the local population and, moreover, reveals the symbolic status of the alien.

To see at a glance what a melting-pot *à la française* can be, how integration works according to republican tradition, one need only consult the composition of the French national team, famous for its 'Champagne football'. For instance, the team that played Yugoslavia on 16 December 1985, was led by Platini, the grandson of an Italian immigrant. Its back line was composed of Battiston (also of Italian descent through his grandfather), Amoros (of gypsy Spanish origin through his father) and Ayache (a Jewish *pied noir* born in Algeria). In the middle, France's 'magic square' starred, besides Platini as the driving force, Giresse (whose mother was Spanish), Tigana (born in Mali, who landed in Marseilles as a child with his family) and Fernandez (who was born in Spain and emigrated with his whole family to France). As for the forwards, they included Touré (son of a Malian immigrant) and Stopyra (whose grandfather was a Pole). On the bench sat Bellone and Ferreri, both of Italian descent (see Beaud and Noiriel, 1990: 83). As a counterpoint to that team of mixed origins, a true caricature of a nation founded on a contract acknowledging the *jus soli* (the right to the soil),[5] were the German teams which took part, with varying success, in the World Cup finals of 1982, 1986 and 1990, the quasi-perfect illustrations of a nation founded on a community of blood.

Now, in that light, let us consider in detail the case of Marseilles, a town strongly characterized by immigration and a substantial foreign mixed population (20 per cent were foreigners in 1936, about 10 per cent are today). The OM team well reflects the cosmopolitan *ideal* of the city. From its start in 1898, but mainly from the beginnings of professionalism in 1932, OM carried out a policy based on the recruiting of foreign stars, associating footballers from central Europe to north Africa to form a single spectacular team. Later on, after the Second World War, Swedish, Yugoslav, Brazilian, West African, and more recently English stars took over and made a deep impression on the image and memory of the club. This inclination for foreign flavour shows in the supporters' favourites among the champions of yore. It is striking that French-born players who performed a leading part in the glory of their club (Crut Boyer before the war, Dard, Scotti, after the war, Bonnel, Bosquier in the intervening years) are not so easily recalled as foreign stars whose feats live on in the spectators' memories: in the 1930s and 1940s Kohut, a Hungarian forward, nicknamed 'Storm Lightning', Vasconcellos, a Brazilian goalkeeper, nicknamed 'Jaguar', Ben Barek, 'the Black Pearl of Morocco', a fantastic dribbler; nearer to our time those twirling and fusing forwards such as Andersson and Magnusson the Swedes, Skoblar, the Yugoslav, Jairzinho and Paulo Cezar, the Brazilians. One could argue that, most of the time, the foreign stars were the pick of the attack and that this contributed greatly to their fame and popularity in a city devoted to spectacular football. But this does not account for it all: on the one hand one can find many 'forgotten' French players who counted amongst the leading goalscorers of the club (Zavelli, Dard, Pironti, Robin etc.); on the other hand, it was a goalkeeper – a foreign one, the Cameroonian Bell, nicknamed 'the Black Panther' – who was the supporters' favourite in 1985–86.[6] In fact, it appears that, all qualities being equal, foreign players are invariably granted a magnified aura compared with French-born players.

How can this fascination for foreign stars be explained? Would it be the course followed by a great foreign player which sharply reflects the life-story of a successful integration into a harbour-city fashioned, in the nineteenth and twentieth centuries, by successive waves of foreign migrations: Italians, Spanish, Armenians, North Africans, etc? Actually the team, with its foreign stars, gives a completely different picture from the stigmatization of the immigrant community which was a favourite practice in the town. To the xenophobia the newcomer has to face every day, especially if he is poor, responds the long-standing xenophilia when the town indulges in dreams about its past. On the ground such a parable is performed again and again, the mythical story of a collective destiny going back to the very origin of the city, when, according to legend, Massilia was founded by Protis, a seaman from Phocea, who married Gyptis, the daughter of a local king. The medal exhibited by some OM supporters represents this founding couple whose effigy had long adorned the covers of primary state school exercise books issued by the local council. Beyond the founding myth itself, the history of the town tells of the arrivals, encounters and mixing of all these populations so diverse in their origins that had come here to settle and contribute to the making of contemporary Marseilles. The path of foreign football stars offers an expressive and idealized synopsis of that fusion into the city, just as the presence of immigrants in the stadium looks like a rite of passage on the way to integration.[7]

Quite significantly, these talented foreign stars, when they succeed, are said to be 'adopted' in as much as they have given public tokens of their integration in the local society – praising declarations concerning Marseilles, ostensible pilgrimages to Notre Dame de la Garde, the church dominating the city and symbolizing it. A common device to show that the foreign player has been adopted is to nickname him (see examples above), which is a kind of new local baptism. These players soon become socially acceptable, make friends and are often invited as guests. This is different from the situation in Lyons, for example, where they remain isolated and lonely in spite of their fame and renown. 'It's very hard to take root in Lyons', comments R. Domenech, the coach of the local club. 'There exists a kind of exclusion proper to the Lyons people. Most of the stars here, belonged to the region . . . and spectacular foreign stars are not that praised here.'[8]

Furthermore, we may perhaps say that this cult of the foreign adopted player symbolically stresses the *jus soli* as a major way to local citizenship in this part of Europe. One can become a true Marseillais or a genuine Provençal without having a long local lineage. Finally, the Marseilles team appears as the epitome of an inventive form of melting-pot which would be interesting to compare to other cases either regional (the Basque country, for instance) or national (German countries among others) where more rigid conceptions of the sense of belonging prevail. Contrasting with this Marseilles conception, rather heedless of the stars' origins if they ever succeed, is the Scottish paradigm resting on a double exclusion: the exclusion of English players ('Significantly, neither Celtic nor Rangers, despite their wealth, were inclined to buy players from England', Holt, 1989: 258) and the exclusion of Catholics in Protestant clubs and vice versa (see Moorhouse, 1989: 2).

FOREIGN STARS AND LOCAL PRIDE

But this inclination for foreign stars in Marseilles is not only due to the particular history of the settlement of the town. Having one's own identity celebrated by others, in this case by foreign players, is endowed with a symbolic value especially in crisis-stricken towns, sweltering under the heat of a bad reputation. From that point of view, Marseilles and Naples are much alike. Both are wrapped in the nostalgia derived from their grand historical past and are desperately clutching at their own identity as they are jeered at by strangers. Naples, just like Marseilles, has got used to recruiting expensive and attractive foreign stars. Calling on foreign stars is certainly a common practice in Italy, where clubs have considerable financial means at their disposal, but here it also expresses, in a symbolic way, a soft conception of citizenship, emphasizing the *jus soli* and making easy the reinsertion of expatriate members of the community (the so-called *oriundi*).

But the recruiting of foreign stars here bears singular traits. First of all, most of them were South Americans, often *oriundi*, such as those southern Italians that had migrated. Among the most famous, in the 1925–35 season, was Attila Sallustro, nicknamed 'the Football Greyhound', who towards the end of his career married Lucy d'Albert, of Russian descent, who was the star of Teatro Nuovo – what a symbol for Naples! More recently, there have been three South American double wonders: Pesaola–Vinicio in the 1950s, Sivori–Altafini in the 1960s and Maradona–Careca in the 1980s. Secondly, Naples often distinguished itself by its patent challenges and glorious gambles: it was the first club to recruit a black player, La Paz, in 1946; it was the first to purchase a player for over 2 million lire; and in 1953, the Swedish forward Jeppson was transferred for the record amount of 105 million lire. Should we be reminded that the highest transfer ever recorded is by Naples: that of Diego Maradona, in 1984, for the amount of $7.5 million?

Such glorious deeds have a flavour of symbolic revenge. Being able to attract such renowned players, having them proclaiming their true love of the city, is undoubtedly a symbolization of undeniable attraction: the duel of ostentation versus contempt, the acknowledgement, through foreign stars, of the splendours of a town stigmatized within the country. The symbol of this adoption can here again be noticed in the reserved appellations given by Neopolitans to their stars whose public statements and football style are well in keeping with the town they are identified with. Pesaola was nicknamed 'El Petisso',

Vinicio 'ò Lione', Jarbas 'Cané', Sivori 'El Cabezon'. Jeppson, on the contrary, remained Jeppson; this vigorous Swede, who played tennis and practised gymnastics, 'was admired but not loved by the Neapolitan fans', according to Palumbo (Ciuni, 1985: 175).

In the Marseilles and Naples setting, deeply marked by victimization and a thirst for symbolic revenge, people feel particular fondness for foreign players who marry and stay in the city after their career. Isn't this actual proof that the city is definitely attractive? In Naples, the wedding ceremonies of Vinicio, with Achille Lauro, president of the club and mayor of the town, as a witness, and of 'Cané' were major public events. These two foreign players came back and stayed in their adoptive town, just like Sivori, thus continuing to nourish local pride by their presence. In Marseilles, one of the most popular players remains Andersson, a Swede who, after his career, stayed in the city, but where he indulged in drinking pastis so much that he finally died quite drunk at the corner of a street. The same craving for symbolic revenge adds a delectable flavour to transfers of foreign stars recruited from northern clubs, possible through trickery, and people especially appreciate it when a foreign player, who failed in a northern club, blossoms in their town. For instance, Altafini was called a *coniglio*, a rabbit – that is to say a female coward, a terrible slur in Italy – by his coach in Milan but turned out to be a success in Naples. Magnusson, a substitute in Turin, became a star in Marseilles; Maradona failed in Barcelona, but achieved great success in Naples. Could it be said that such a reversal of situation, which benefits the town's image, is most particularly praised in these ill-loved towns?

FOREIGN STARS AND LOCAL STYLE

Those specific traits lead us to consider another variable which plays an important part in the success of a migratory adventure: the capacity of foreign stars to suit local style. From this point of view the case of Maradona should be emphasized: in Spain he was considered a second-class foreigner, as Argentines often are considered in their former mother-country. As a virtuous, facetious, even wily player, a lover of glorious feats, moving about with his family and friends, now a wealthy man but with the culture of the pauper he used to be, Maradona could not properly adapt to the 'geometrical' style of the *Barça*, which had always given its preference to northern European players over South American, or to the Barcelonian cultural dream and ideal, that is to say seriousness and smartness. In Naples, though, his personal style suited the collective style of the city.

With his short legs, his rounded chest sticking out, his cheeky Job's mug and his diamonded ear, Diego had become a true Neapolitan for us all. His love of pretty girls and good food, his mania for racing cars along with his fervent devotion to church and family – his whole family lives and thrives in Naples at the club's expense – his nasty character, his feats, his exuberance, his lack of discipline, all this made him a true and legitimate son of the city.[9]

Such was the identification that some people said that he was of Neapolitan origin because of his name and because of his appearance and his malicious look, reminding them of a Neapolitan *scugnizzo* (small boy). Such unequalled fame was certainly tarnished by the player's rows with his club, his relations with the Giuliano and Russo camorra clans, fathering an illegitimate child, and in 1991, the scanda-lous disclosure of his addiction to cocaine. But, significantly, the myth has not collapsed for all that. After he had been suspended by the Italian football league the *tifosi* went on shouting his name all over the stadium. In May 1991 a group of Neapolitan intellectuals organized a 'Te Diegum' to honour him. Many would see in that downfall another fruit of the continuous plot against their town. Thus a poll published in *La Repubblica* in February 1991 made it clear that 43.2 per cent of the Neapolitans thought Maradona innocent and the victim of a plot, while only 31.2 per cent considered him guilty.

Many other examples taken from the history of OM, Napoli and Juventus would emphasize that necessary correspondence between the personal style of the foreign star and that of the club, so much that the successes or failures of those stars appear as powerful revelations of local specifications. Franz Beckenbauer's unfortunate experience as the coach of OM shows how heavily this game style (traditionally based on panache, virtuosity and dramatic efficiency) weighs on the team. In 1990 the German coach tried to enforce a 'cultural revolution' imposing a resolutely square and strict conception, but failed in his task and was quickly urged to resign.

The style of Juventus of Turin is, so to speak, the inverse of those of Naples and Marseilles. It is the style of an aristocratic 'old lady' (*vecchia signora*), combining the rules of etiquette and the rigorous discipline of the industrial world. Since 1923 the club has been in the hands of the Agnelli dynasty, the Fiat ruling family, that has held power either directly or indirectly. The 'Juventus style', a model invented by E. Agnelli, president of the club from 1923 to 1935, is symbolized by the three Ss, *Simplicità, Serietà, Sobrietà* (Simplicity,

Seriousness, Sobriety), which brings to mind one of the company mottoes. This motto is completed by an adage which it pleased Agnelli to repeat: *Una cosa fatta bene puo essere ancora fatta meglio* (Something done well can be done better). The functioning of the club and its style of play largely reflects this model of rigour. On the ground, it is essential for the players to look like lords in the image of the Agnelli firm and house: fair play, respect of the referee's decision and correctness are the key words here.

In that context the choice of foreign stars must yield to two requirements (besides the sporting demand proper). First of all they must be high-standing international stars, generally from northern Europe (Charles, Platini, Rush, Platt, for instance), able to symbolize the reputation of the firm all over the world. Notice that beyond these universal ambitions the composition of the team reflects the particular history of the firm which has regularly counted in its teams players from southern Italy (for instance, in the last years, Anastasi, Causio, Brio, Caricola, Mauro), as does the company itself which gathers numerous immigrants from Mezzogiorno. Then, in the second place, these high-standing international stars must embody the aristocratic ethic of the 'old lady'. A symbol of the alien conformity with that culture – a culture founded on a seriousness that created a fellowship between Agnelli and Togliatti, the former communist leader who supported Juventus – was the Welsh star of the 1950s, John Charles, whose chivalrous gesture during a famous derby in 1957 has remained engraved on people's memories. After a full back of local rivals Torino hurt his head, Charles helped his injured opponent up and remained with him until the arrival of the physio, although the referee had not stopped the game. The ones who openly depart from these ethical principles are asked, quietly but firmly, to quit the club. Such was the case in 1954 of the extravagant Dane, H. Bromée, of whom the board was suspicious from the start, and who was only given a contract on a match-to-match basis. This awkward situation lasted no more than a year. Such was the case also of Sivori, Agnelli doing nothing to prevent his departure for Naples where, it was said, he was successful and popular and where he stayed after his career. A brilliant but undisciplined attacker, he was fired by Heriberto Herrera, a Paraguayan coach, and former sergeant who had had a career as a player with Atletico Madrid. In the end it seems that the Juventus style could not put up with the repeated pranks of the Italo-Argentine star.

Sivori's story, a perfect revelation of complex extra-sports mechanisms that condition an international career, introduces another variable that may influence these migrations: players may be used as ancillary elements of a commercial strategy. Actually, when Sivori was transferred to Naples, he was undervalued – 40 million lire instead of 130 – because ship owner Achille Lauro contracted Fiat engines for his ships. In reverse order, but with the same background of commercial policy, Juventus hired Boniek who was under 30 years old, the lower transferring age-limit at the time, because Fiat promised the Polish government the construction of a Polski factory (see other examples in Pennachia, 1985).

CONCLUSION

In summary, the above developments underline the plurality of factors involved in the migration of foreign footballers. The importance of market laws and proper sports criteria cannot be denied but one may suggest that this logic based on the maximization of advantages through using foreign players depends, to a large extent, on the local conception of citizenship, on the perceptions of the alien, on implicit or explicit affinities for this or that continent and paradigms of acceptable cultural behaviour. In other words, the transfers of foreign players are not only dependent on a mere economic rationality but on 'a global social rationality'.[10]

The careers of those stars are as informative of their talents as they are of the recruiting communities, and of the ideal image they have of themselves. Discounting those factors would make it hard to understand why northern European clubs should mainly recruit stars from northern Europe, why Juventus of Turin should favour these origins, while Naples should take so much delight in South American stars. The study of international migrations of sportsmen leads us to the heart of one of the major contradictions of our time: the tension between, on the one hand, local loyalties, spatial affiliation, cultural affinities, traditions and history, a world of ascriptions and, on the other hand, personal contracts, market laws, universal rationalism, space without boundaries, a world of achievement.

NOTES

1 I am grateful to Pierre Lanfranchi who provided me with a list of the players involved in the French first-division championship since the 1930s. Most of the figures quoted in the text are based on these data. I am also grateful to Jean-Luc Alberti who performed a crucial part in the translation of this text from French.

2 In 1990 there were 87 foreign players in the 20 French first-division clubs: 29 from western Europe (six English, five Dutch, four German, four

Belgian, three Danish, two Swiss, two Portuguese, one Swedish, one Spanish and one from Luxemburg); 19 from eastern Europe (15 Yugoslavs, two Hungarians, one Pole and one Romanian); 18 from West Africa (eight from Senegal, four from the Ivory Coast, two from Zaire, one from Liberia, one from Ghana, one from Benin and one from Cameroon); 13 from South America (eight Argentines, two Paraguayans, two Uruguayans and one Brazilian); seven from North Africa (four Algerians and three Moroccans) and, finally, one Australian.

3 On football culture in these three towns see Bromberger (1990; 1991); Bromberger *et al*, (1987); Ciuni (1986); Pennachia (1985).

4 Local playing style, as it is perceived by the supporters, does not always correspond to the real practice of the players – who change from year to year and adopt different tactics, depending on the manager, fashion, etc. – but to a stereotyped image, vested in tradition, that the community gives itself and wishes to show to others. Thus style is part of a 'collective imagery' in the sense used by Vovelle (1982).

5 On the French conception of citizenship as opposed to the German one, see Schnapper (1991).

6 According to interviews with 920 spectators in December 1985. Significantly, second place in this 'hit parade' was occupied by a Senegalese winger, Daillo.

7 On the immigrants' attendance in the stadium, see Bromberger (1989).

8 Quoted in *L'Equipe*, 27–28 July 1991, 9.

9 Quoted in *Le Monde*, 24 August 1989.

10 On this comprehensive notion of 'global social rationality' as opposed to 'economic rationality', see Godelier (1971), 205.

REFERENCES

Bale, J. (1990) 'Football Without Frontiers: Some Questions for the 1990s', Colloquium paper, 'Le football et l'Europe', 3–5 May (Florence: European University Institute).

Beaud, S. and Noiriel, G. (1990) 'L;immigration dans le football', *Vingtième siècle*, 26 April–June, 83–96.

Bromberger, C. (1989) 'Le stade de football, une carte de la ville en réduction', *Mappemonde*, 2, 37–40.

  (1990) 'Ciuccio e fuochi d'artificio. L' immaginario di Napoli attraverso il suo football', *Micromega*, 4, 171–81 ('Fireworks and the Ass'), working paper, Unit for law and popular culture, Manchester Polytechnic.

  (1991) 'Lo spettacolo delle partite di calcio. Alcune direzioni di analisi ethnologica' in Lanfranchi, P. (ed.) *Il calcio e il suo pubblico* (Naples: ESI).

Bromberger, C., Hayot, A. and Mariottini, J.M. (1987) 'Allez l'O.M.! Forza Juve! le football à Marseille et Turin', *Terrain*, 8, 8–41 (' "Allez l'O.M.! Forza Juve!" The Passion for Football in Marseille and Turin'), working paper, Unit for law and popular culture, Manchester Polytechnic.

Ciuni, R. (1986) *Il pallone di Napoli* (Milan: Shakespeare).

Godelier, M. (1971) *Rationalité et irrationalité en économie*, Vol. II (Paris: Maspero).

Holt, R. (1989) *Sport and the British. A Modern History* (Oxford: Clarendon).

Moorhouse, H.F. (1989) 'One State, Several Countries. Soccer and Identities in the "United" Kingdom', Colloquium paper 'Le football et ses publics' 19–21 October (Florence: European University Institute).

Pennachia, M. (1985) *Gli Agnelli e la Juventus* (Milan: Rizzoli).

Schnapper, D. (1991) *La France de l'intégration. Sociologie de la nation* (Paris: Gallimard).

Vovelle, M. (1982) *Idéologies et mentalités* (Paris: Maspero).

13

Trans-nationalism, Labour Migration and Latin American Baseball

Alan M. Klein

In many respects, the movement of Latin American baseball players between their native lands and North America deviates from the contemporary profile of trans-national labour migration. The atypical characteristics of Latin American baseball labour are, however, only superficial. In the final analysis, the factors determining this labour migration are the same as those controlling the rest of the social formation (international capital flow and production costs versus labour supply, demand, and demands of labour). The noteworthy component in this study is the articulation between political-economy and culture provided by the study of baseball in the third world. In the continuing attempts to subordinate the sport played by the Dominican Republic and elsewhere to its labour requirements, Major League Baseball Inc. finds itself in a contest. Not only are the Dominicans struggling to retain the sport for their own needs, but baseball has become a primary means of expressing Dominican resentment towards the North Americans. Dominican baseball is shown to be more than a function of labour migration and policy. The Dominican side of this cultural struggle is what political scientist James Scott referred to as 'weapons of the weak'. Field work on baseball in the Dominican Republic was carried out between 1987 and 1989 and covered a complete range of the sport (amateur to professional). Observations were combined with interviews, surveys, and even some direct participation in the Dominican baseball scene (Klein, 1988; 1989; 1990; 1991). What follows is an examination of various Dominican elements and findings within the context of trans-nationalization of North American baseball.

Contemporary scholars in the field of trans-national labour migration no longer view such population shifts as a simple response to impoverished economies and high population density, but rather as a complex of traits, the most important being the international movement of capital independent of the nation-state, production and labour exigencies, and historic policies (Dixon and Jonas, 1982; Sassen, 1988). Clearly, the issues are international, involving both sending and host countries, but, not in a world systems sense in which core and periphery exchange resources and personnel (for example, Wallerstein, 1979 or Frank, 1971). First world–third world relations are much more complex and inverted than ever before (Blim and Rothstein, 1992). For instance, as Sassen (1988, Ch.2) points out, there is a large-scale labour emigration from Latin countries at just the time when these economies are receiving massive infusions of capital to build an industrial base, and at a time when the countries to which these immigrants are fleeing are facing inordinately high unemployment.

These contradictory processes – emigration away from industrializing centres, immigration to areas of high unemployment – are a function of the internationalization of capital, production, and labour. In the case of the United States, which, since the 1960s, has experienced massive immigration from south-east Asia and the Caribbean, there are four trends which have combined to form immigration. First, the flight of traditional manufacturing to foreign areas in response to higher labour costs in the USA. Second, the establishment of key urban centres in the United States as producers of financial and advanced services, creating the need for low-end jobs that reflect the enlarged service sector. The expansion of 'downgraded' manufacturing sectors, especially in the old industrialized north-east of the United States, has resulted in the shift from unionized plants (which have shifted to sending countries) to sweatshop and other non-union facilities. Alongside this form of downgrading we find an increase in dead-end jobs in new industries (electronics for instance). The fourth trend, is that large immigrant communities have themselves become sources for labour and other opportunities (small businesses, informal economic sector etc.).

Studies of these recent immigrants to the USA indicate the following common characteristics: unskilled, low wages, non-European, heavily dominated by women and politically powerless (Sassen, 1988). Finding the conditions more acceptable in the receiving country, most immigrant labourers attempt to stay permanently; they have no intention of going back, except possibly to visit or if they have made enough to retire in the homeland. Unprotected by unions, these immigrants often take hazardous jobs (as with agricultural workers who must endure dangerous pesticides), involving long hours, with almost no legal or social recourse against injustices on or off of the job. While there have been periods in which immigrant labourers to the United States have

)een skilled and highly paid (in the 1950s, for instance), recent
mmigration is made up of unskilled labourers earning low wages
Sassen, 1988). Moreover, the labour migrations of the 1950s were
ieavily made up of European men while current immigration is
)rimarily third-world and heavily female (Dixon and Jonas, 1982;
iassen, 1988).

)ominican migration

\gainst this labour profile, the Dominican case as seen from the work
)f Grasmuck and Pessar (1991) seems to mark a striking contrast,
)rompting further researchers to re-examine some of the aforemen-
ioned conclusions. The Dominican data point to a heavier emphasis
)n extra-economic variables as prompting migration. In particular,
Jrasmuck and Pessar document how post-1960s politics in the Domi-
iican Republic shaped migration to the United States.[1] This does not
leny the powerful impact of economic variables as primary agents in
nigration so much as prompt us to look at a more complete range of
ationales which include political repression in the sending country.

The economic policies of the sending country predictably play a
najor role. Continued Dominican reliance on traditional exports in
he face of declining prices for them as well as rapidly rising costs of
uel offset gains made in the size of the middle class and educational
evels attained in the general population (ibid., pp. 38–44). With raised
:xpectations and shrinking occupational opportunities marking the
980s, Dominicans came to view migration as a desirable alternative to
onditions at home. Importantly, this burgeoning migratory popula-
ion was not, according to Grasmuck and Pessar (65), the most hard-
)ressed rural sectors of society, nor was it overwhelmingly female. The
iuthors showed that the majority – 65.9 per cent – of the urban
nigrants studied were male (65). Similarly, they were able to show
hat educationally, the migrant was better prepared (often more
killed) than the non-migrant (77). In short, the Grasmuck and Pessar
tudy presents a much more complex picture of migration than was
)reviously available.

Against this profile, the picture of the Latin American baseball
)layer is also somewhat contradictory. Following Grasmuck and
'essar, the baseball player from Latin America[2] is male and highly
killed. While most migrants earn more on arriving in the United
itates, baseball players are atypical in that they represent extra-
)rdinary talent in one form of the entertainment industry (sports) and
o are highly paid by any standards. The Latin American player also
liffered from the typical immigrant in that, until the mid-1980s, he

worked in both North America and his homeland in a two-way seasonal labour migration. This is not like the 'return migrant' discussed in Grasmuck and Pessar (80), but rather a unique labour form. Before discussing the actual nature of the immigration, however, I wish to examine the political history of the sport in one of its foreign centres, the Dominican Republic. Following a brief chronicle of how baseball aided late nineteenth- to early twentieth-century American imperial efforts, I will glance at how these same efforts are maturing today. It should be borne in mind that this is a relationship involving conditions and interests in both North America and Latin America, that production and capital accumulation in one area influences the other, and that in its most recent manifestation baseball has finally followed suit in becoming an industry in which international competition among the owners of capital has emerged, altering production and labour processes.

The early phase of baseball imperialism

Poorly organized and minimally functional as baseball was in the late nineteenth century (loose structure, amateur–professional confusion, and the sport's still-evolving cultural place), its role in aiding US efforts at occupying and controlling other countries was clear. No less a personage than A.G. Spalding, one of the game's first great stars and its first significant entrepreneur, boldly proclaimed in 1910 that the function of baseball was to 'follow the flag around the world' (Spalding, 1991: 14). It was through US military and economic presence (including in the early twentieth century a string of Marine invasions in Central America and the Caribbean) that the game spread. Initially, it was in Cuban ports in the 1860s, as well as through returning Cuban students, that Cubans learned the elements of the game which they quickly mastered and exported to other Caribbean islands including, by 1891, the Dominican Republic (Klein, 1991: 16). In Mexico, US employees working for early multinational firms introduced the game in the northern reaches of that country during the 1880s (LaFrance, 1985), while in the Yucatan baseball diffused through the efforts of Cubans fleeing turmoil in their homeland during the last decade of the nineteenth century (Joseph, 1987). Panamanians learnt the game as part of their baptism of fire during the years of the building of the Panama Canal, while Venezuelans were introduced to baseball by returning students and US employees in the petroleum industry (Jamail, personal communication). At roughly the same time but on the other side of the world, US Naval personnel also forcibly introduced the game to the Japanese (Rhoden, 1980).

Having introduced the game to these countries, North Americans uncharacteristically remained somewhat distant in their dealings with baseball in the far reaches. The racially segregated nature of North American professional baseball[3] actively precluded the playing of non-white players, a decision which affected Latin American baseball players as well. Because the game passed quickly into the ranks of the working class and poor, the overwhelming majority of Latin American athletes who were good enough to make a name for themselves were darker-skinned, hence excluded from play in the United States. This is not to say that all Latin Americans were prevented from reaching the major leagues until the breakthrough of Jackie Robinson in 1946. On the contrary, lighter-skinned *beisbolistas* (primarily from Cuba) played throughout the first half of the twentieth century. By the 1930s black and white players from the United States also began playing winter baseball in Latin America (mostly in Cuba, the Dominican Republic and Mexico). This reverse labour migration (USA to Latin America), fostered by racial segregation and economic opportunity, did much to pave the ideological and cultural path for later racial integration in major league baseball (Rogosin, 1985).

Through the first decades of the twentieth century Latin American baseball was perceived by both Latin and North Americans as the game of the gringo, whose playing superiority was universally acknowledged. The periodic visits of North American players (whether they were contingents of Marines or actual groups of players), with their skills, training and, most of all, their money, convinced all concerned of North American domination. Nevertheless, while North Americans viewed Latin baseball as a poor relation, the game, as played 'South of the Border', became steadily better. It also became Latinized, which is to say that baseball was reappropriated by the Latin American cultures that took it on. North Americans, so full of themselves, never really understood that their ethnocentrism and their refusal to allow darker Latin Americans into the game in the United States, was converted by Latinos into a cultural tradition of their own. They excelled at the game in both absolute and relative terms, but more importantly, Latin Americans culturally appropriated the game. The Dominicans, for instance, developed a style of play that was an imprint of life in the cane country of the east, or the Capital city of Santo Domingo (Klein, 1991). The raucous character of players and fans, the music, the interpersonal relations, the flair of the essential movements were all ways in which Dominican culture placed its stamp on the game. Even local traditions of time entered into the game, so that punctuality became unimportant. And, whereas all baseball fans love a display of power, Latin fans prefer to see a flourish of movement and 'hustle'. The preference for artistry over brute force was responsible for Roger Maris (the same who would, in 1961, break Babe Ruth's single season home run record) being dropped from a Dominican team in the late 1950s when he was considered a legitimate power hitter in the United States. One also sees the Latin American signature in the way shortstops 'one-hand' balls they have to field, as opposed to the two-handed style advocated in North America.

LABOUR AND THE PRODUCTION OF BASEBALL

Post-racial integration period
After 1946, American institutions that had previously excluded Blacks (for example, the military as well as baseball) began ponderously and haltingly to integrate. In the case of baseball, this increased the size of the labour pool, and subsequently directly opened the game to the Latin American talent market. By the 1950s, Cubans and Dominicans had made it into the major leagues:

> In the 50s, the breeding ground came from the Havana Sugar Kings, owned by Bobby Maduro. In four years, they sent more than 30 players to the big leagues (Ralph Avila, Los Angeles Dodgers' Director of Latin American Operations in Klein, 1991: 37).
>
> [On Dominican scouting] Trujillo [the Dominican dictator who ruled the country for 30 years] wouldn't let any good players play for anyone but his club, Escogido. He made sure that one of the Capital city teams always won the Dominican championship. I wanted to sign Felipe Alou and Charlie Naranjo, but I was told, 'you'll never sign anyone who Trujillo wants playing for Escogido'. It wasn't until we [the CIA] got rid of him that the doors were opened [to getting Dominican players] (Howie Haak, former Pittsburgh Pirate scout in Klein, 1991: 38).

With the US blockade of Cuba, begun in 1961, the steady Cuban supply of major league talent stopped and major league baseball turned instead to the Dominican Republic and other Latin American countries. What began as a trickle in the 1950s with the appearance in the majors of Dominican Ozzie Virgil, has grown into a torrent, especially from the Dominican Republic and Puerto Rico. In the 1991 season the Dominican Republic and Puerto Rico had the lion's share of players in the major leagues, each with approximately 45 major leaguers. A distant second was Venezuela with 10, followed by Mexico with nine, and one each from Panama, Nicaragua, and Honduras. Not only was there an abundance of talent in these countries, but it was, in comparison with North American players, easy and inexpensive to sign (Klein, 1991). The major league baseball draft, a device used by the cartel of team owners in North American sport to secure players for their teams, is, with the exception of Puerto Rico, not present in the rest of the hemisphere. In the era of free agency and the restrictions of the draft, the openness of the Latin American market was even more appealing.

The free agency period: 1976 onwards
In a series of court cases during the early 1970s, major league ball players broke the chattel-like system known as the 'reserve system' and won the right to sell their labour on an open market. Free agency began in earnest in 1976, and its impact was felt almost immediately. From that point on, salaries, fuelled in large part by mega-dollar media deals[4] have, despite collusion by the owners, risen astronomically. Between 1970 and 1991 the average major league salary increased from $29,500 to $880,000 or by approximately 3,000 per cent; and the increase from 1990 ($597,537) to 1991 is the largest one-year increase ever. Of the 650 players who were on rosters at the onset of the 1991 season, 221 (34 per cent) earned $1 million or more. No other sport has so much of its membership earning these kinds of salaries. One would think that all talented multi-sport athletes would seriously consider the opportunities of professional baseball.

Oddly enough, this unprecedented economic opportunity has been increasingly shunned by African-American athletes in the United States; hence, at a time when young men can earn more from baseball and enjoy greater sport longevity than ever, there has been a muscle drain to more highly visible, yet riskier, lower-paid sports such as basketball and football (*Boston Globe*, 28 July 1991: 52). The 1991 figures on black representation in the top three sports in the United States indicate that, compared with basketball (75 per cent) and football (62 per cent), baseball is a distant third (17 per cent) in the percentage of black athletes playing. Moreover, for baseball, this appears to be an emerging historical trend. Predictably, in the aftermath of the sport's integration following the Second World War, black presence in major league baseball increased when it rose from zero to 11.9 per cent in 1966 (approximating the percentage of blacks in the United States). From 1966 on, the numbers of blacks in the

Table 13.1   White, black and Hispanic presence in Major League Baseball, 1966–91

Year	White	Black	Hispanic
1966	78.1%	11.9%	9.6%
1971	74.3%	14.9%	10.5%
1976	70.8%	17.4%	11.1%
1981	69.8%	18.6%	11.2%
1986	69.1%	18.9%	11.7%
1991	67.2%	17.2%	14.6%

n = 1,037
Source: *Baseball America*, 25 December 1991, p. 12

major leagues increased until 1986 at which point they begin to decline (see Table 13.1).

Even more important is the fact that baseball's minor league system, from which it develops and draws most of its talent, shows an even greater loss of numbers. While 17.2 per cent of major league players are African-American, only 13.1 per cent of minor leaguers are, a trend which reflects an even greater loss of such talent to the seemingly more glamorous National Basketball Association and National Football League.

Within the African-American population in the United States, however, the desirability of football and basketball seems somehow to outweigh the increased opportunities for black players that baseball with its greater longevity, faster rising salaries and expansion offers them. In response to this talent drain, and in part as confirmation that it has reached crisis proportions, the Commissioner of Baseball has lent his support to a programme that will attempt to restimulate interest in baseball among the youth of North America's inner-cities. Using the acronym, RBI (reviving baseball in inner cities), John Young, a former player and scouting director, has attempted to provide facilities, equipment and organized league structure to young children in urban areas. The hope is that by giving youngsters access to the game they will take it up in larger numbers. Baseball's commissioner has also begun to examine a more formal relationship with the National Collegiate Athletic Association (NCAA) to look into the possibility of drafting players out of college. At present, players are drafted out of high school into the minor leagues. They can avoid the draft by going on to college baseball and then sign with whoever they want. Colleges and universities have in essence become free training facilities for major league baseball. If the draft were extended to college baseball, major league baseball would, presumably, have to develop a more formal economic subsidization of collegiate baseball.

Expansion and labour
A second factor that will further shrink the percentage of blacks in major league baseball is the impending inclusion of the cities of Denver and Miami in the National League with two additional teams to follow in the American League. The addition of four new teams will generate approximately 100 new major leaguers and 560 new minor leaguers.[5] Viewed from the perspective of athletes, expansion generates opportunity. Viewed from the entrepreneur's perspective, expansion translates into labour shortages.

The sport's expansion plans are not simply confined to the major leagues. With the advent of baseball as an Olympic sport more and more countries have begun programmes that allow them to compete. Seizing on this historic opportunity to expand, major league baseball has either underwritten or sanctioned the establishment of professional baseball throughout the world. However, in each instance in which baseball as an economic venture seeks to expand, it also generates or expands a local tradition of baseball which can eventually compete for the same labour that major league (which is to say North American) baseball does. The Japanese market, for instance, while limited because of player quotas (two foreigners to a team), has become much more active in being able to draw better players than at any other time (see below). But, it is the establishment of professional baseball leagues in hitherto underdeveloped regions (for example, Taiwan and Korea) that promises real results. The establishment of an Australian Baseball League in 1989 was heralded by major league teams as a major future source of talent, 'Australia is fast becoming American scout's new port of call' boasted one scout (*Baseball America*, 10 December 1991). Players from that country are increasingly being signed to play in North America. However, it is also likely that, if Australian baseball becomes established, it can draw active North American players away as the Japanese professional leagues have.

Latin American baseball labour as a solution to the crisis
These attempts at reviving baseball in North American inner cities and expansion opportunities notwithstanding, North American baseball has had to face a dwindling talent pool within its national boundaries, and has increasingly looked towards Latin America for the calibre of player that is needed. It is not accidental, as Table 13.1 shows, that

Latin American participation in major league baseball has grown in direct proportion to the decline of African-American participation.

Responding to the seemingly unlimited supply of excellent talent in Latin America, by the late 1970s scouts from nearly every major league team could be found scouring the Dominican Republic. Not only was there increasing acknowledgement of the abundance of talent in the country, but it was cheap to sign. Initially, Latin players (other than Puerto Ricans, who are subject to the major league draft), are signed for relatively little. While a legitimate college prospect in the United States typically signs for something in excess of $150,000, his Dominican counterpart will sign for approximately $4,000. Quite simply, a scouting budget goes a lot further in Latin America than it does in the north. However, once the player moves into the organization, and particularly once he plays his way up the ladder, he will be paid the same as any ball player (parenthetically, one problem for Latino players has always been moving through the ranks).

In the headlong rush to grab as many players as possible, scouts would often commit abuses (Brubaker, 1986). For many scouts, the idea that they might be aiding a young, poor Dominican to escape poverty allowed them to rationalize whatever cultural insensitivity and/or greed they might be guilty of. The young men themselves made it easy for scouts to feel this way because they were so openly courting the opportunity. Sylvestre Campusano, Toronto Blue Jays outfielder, typified this relationship when, in answering questions about why he dropped out of school to pursue a scout, he responded by stating, 'We're poor people. When I was growing up, it was hard to even find food sometimes. So, when Epy offered me a $3,500 bonus, I took it. I had to take care of my family.' Hence, cases such as that of one scout who agreed to pay a young signee $4,000 Dominican rather than the $4,000 American that the team he worked for agreed to, pocketing the difference (the exchange rate at the time was $3 Dominican to $1 US), were rationalized by the fact that this pittance was much more than the boy would ever earn on his own. In the 1970s and 1980s cases in which young men were cheated out of their due, or held in camps without their parents' knowledge, abounded until 1984, when President Jorge Blanco placed all Dominican baseball under the government's supervision. From that point on, presidential decree 3450 stipulated that all scouts would be registered with the Dominican government, all minor league contracts signed would be approved by the government, and the academies that had sprung up to train young players would be monitored.

The underdevelopment of Dominican baseball

The impact of racial integration, and later, free agency, has had the overall effect of intensifying North American efforts to 'mine' talent out of the Dominican Republic. This, in turn, has resulted in the underdevelopment of Dominican baseball, a process paralleling the larger North American economic domination of the country (Klein, 1989; 1991).

When major league teams first approached owners of Dominican professional teams about the possibility of collaboration in the 1950s, it appeared mutually beneficial. The 'working relationship', as it was called, would give North Americans access to players. Each team that was able to establish such a relationship would have the players they signed or were interested in protected by the Dominican club to which they signed. In return, the Dominican players would get access to the USA (later Canada also) and the local teams would have US managers and expertise to improve the organization and quality of play. It seemed a balanced form of reciprocity. From 1955 on, Dominican professional baseball stabilized into a six-team league with an organized schedule. Play was confined to the winter so as not to interfere with play in North America, and the presence of North American scouts increased dramatically. For Dominican players the pay off was almost immediate, with a string of Dominican stars coming into the major leagues (beginning with Ozzie Virgil, and continuing through Juan Marichal and the Alou brothers).

Although the search for talented young athletes bore instant fruit, the refinement of that talent and its export abroad was problematic. The US Department of Labor sees no difference between farmhands and athletes as workers; hence, baseball teams must secure work permits (H-2 permits) for their foreign players. At present each team is given 24 visas to be used to import foreign players in their system in North America. Virtually all of these are used for Latin American players, but, given the large numbers of such players signed relative to visas provided, there was a need to ascertain which players were most likely to develop into stars and so provide a return on the team's investment.

Baseball academies as plantations

In the late 1970s two North American organizations (the Toronto Blue Jays and Los Angeles Dodgers) opened academies that would locate, sign, and begin to refine talent within the Dominican Republic, talent to be considered for further development in North America. The development of academies is very reminiscent of the ways in which nearby sugar refineries operate, in that raw materials are obtained cheaply, locally refined (at a reduced cost) and shipped abroad; except that in the case of academies it is young men who are procured and processed rather than sugar cane.

Most baseball academies in the Dominican Republic are little more than moderate-to-poorly equipped operations interested only in the search for raw talent. The Los Angeles Dodger camp (called Campo Las Palmas) is different in that it seeks to develop the young man in his entirety, not just as an athlete. Nevertheless, the primary goal is player development, and having this in common with other academies, a Dominican rookie league has been formed which works to forge skills and foster evaluation.

Each day during that part of the year in which young men are tried out, (scouts are forever roaming the island in search of talented players) dozens of try-outs stand outside the gates of the academies waiting to be examined. By law, these young men are supposed to be at least 17 years of age, but since birth certificates are often non-existent, youngsters can easily lie about their age or borrow another person's birth certificate. Their skills having been honed by years of amateur baseball, these young men seek to impress the personnel at the academy enough to get a 30-day trial or be signed immediately. As in North America, being signed involves a bonus and a change in the player's status from amateur to professional. The Dominican, just like his counterpart in the USA or Canada, is henceforth a 'rookie' and member of the Professional Base Ball Players' Association. What the Dominican needs at this point is a visa to enter the USA or Canada, and to secure this relatively rare permit he must advance his playing skills. Hence there is, at the outset, a labour bottleneck in which the gatekeeping function is performed by the employer (the major league team). This function in conjunction with the entire process of being signed and acculturated in an academy makes for not only a relatively cheaply signed player, but also following Sassen's (1988) assessment of trans-national labour, a docile one.

The academy perceives itself as an extension of the franchise in search of talent, but also as offering young men an opportunity to escape their poverty. Before the advent of academies, young men were expected to move up the ranks of Dominican amateur baseball until they were noticed by professional Dominican teams, and eventually, by major league scouts. By flocking to the academy, by practising their skills year-round as children, and by abandoning and/or de-emphasizing their educations in favour of playing baseball, these young men were, and are, in accord with the ideas of the North American outposts in their country. Overlooked in this mutually beneficial reciprocity is the devastating effect that the academies have on the structure of amateur baseball in the Dominican Republic (Klein, 1989; 1991). By establishing themselves in the country, the academies offered young amateurs an alternative, a way round the traditional amateur system, hence, leading to a severe weakening of that system. A youngster today will move from academy to academy in the hopes of catching on with one before opting for the Dominican amateur leagues.

Only a small fraction of the young men who sign on in the academies ever make it into the major leagues. Three or four times that many may spend their careers in the North American minor leagues, but with limited employment prospects many disappear into major urban centres in North America creating administrative headaches for their employers. Baseball is, for many failed Latin American ball players, a way to get into and remain in North America.

Free agency's impact on Dominican baseball

Through the 1970s, the numbers of Dominicans, Puerto Ricans and Venezuelans playing baseball in North America increased. They played year-round: summers in the USA or Canada and winters in their native countries. There was, in short, a two-way labour migration which included both economic and nationalist factors.

In the late 1960s major league salaries averaged around $27,000, a substantial sum for anyone, but certainly for Dominicans. Nevertheless, Dominican stars, such as Marty Alou, winner of a National League batting title, were earning considerably less than the average in the 1960s. Coming home to play for several thousand dollars more (depending on the player's major league status) was therefore worthwhile (Klein, 1991). The success of Dominican players in North America further fuelled fan interest. While baseball players had commanded adulation throughout the twentieth century, with their increasing numbers and rising success in the USA and Canada, they returned home as national heroes:

> The people were so in love with the game. The way it was: when the ball game is over, the fans wait for us. We go with them. We walk with them. And the people love ballplayers, and we them. It was like a family . . . Then, the hotel was in the middle of the city. So, when you get up in the morning people are waiting for you. And you were talking to them (Klein, 1991: 30).

Because Dominica had one of the lowest standards of living of any country in the hemisphere, any Dominican able to work in the USA was considered successful by his or her friends and family back home. And a man who made a living playing baseball was astoundingly successful: a role model, celebrity and wealthy man all in one. Playing in winter baseball became important for players who wanted to repay their compatriots for support as well as offer hope to the many thousands of young men who were hoping to follow their path out of poverty. It was common for major league stars like Marty Alou (formerly of the San Francisco Giants) to play before his hometown fans in Santo Domingo unflinchingly, in sickness and in health, fatigued or not, 'We [the three Alou brothers] used to play for the same team every year – in the outfield. Yes, I played for Escogido every year for twenty-three years. When I was sick I played, when I won the batting title I played. Didn't miss one [year]' (Klein, 1991: 36).

Free agency resulted, not only in a dramatic rise in salaries of all major leaguers, but also in an increase in the signing of players to multi-year contracts. For Latinos this inadvertently helped to generate a crisis. By signing multi-year contracts worth millions of dollars, Dominicans were, understandably, no longer willing to play winter baseball in which they risked a career-ending injury. The rises in major league salaries had long since outstripped winter salaries, removing dependence on the latter. Hence, by the late 1980s most Latin American stars had stopped playing before their own fans, who showed their disappointment in the form of declining attendance (Klein, 1991: 128).

TRANS-NATIONALISM, LABOUR AND CAPITAL

In keeping with the central idea of dependency theory, the overall impact of free agency and expansion of major league baseball has been to weaken the organization and autonomy of Dominican baseball. For North American baseball interests successfully to address the problem of the shortage of qualified labour at home, they must end up by systematically underdeveloping third world baseball. This is not, however, simply the circulation of goods with the extraction of commodities from the periphery to be processed or consumed in the core; it is more a matter of looking at labour and production.

If baseball, as an industry, constitutes an act of production (the production of an entertainment form), it can be analysed as any other. In this instance, before 1955, Dominicans owned and produced their own, much more modest brand of baseball. They developed their own league structure, owners and talent pool. These players, moreover, spent their careers in their homeland, making the entire cycle of production and consumption a local Dominican one. The opening of North American baseball to people of colour ushered in an era of direct intervention by North American business interests (teams). At first scouts, and later academies, inserted themselves into the fabric of Dominican baseball, in essence usurping control by offering unprecedented opportunities for talented individuals. A brief period of transition ensued in which Dominican players and owners could straddle the fence by fostering Dominican labour exports to North America and hold on to the game by having players perform locally at other times. The labour migration that began in the 1950s grew in direct proportion to the need for skilled labour in North America, but in the era of free agency the ability of these 'workers' to return to their Dominican employers and fans (to remain 'two-way' labour migrants) was short-circuited by astounding salaries and multi-year contracts. Although the two-way labour migration that occurred marked a loss of previous Dominican structural autonomy, it was, nevertheless, essential for the perpetuation of any semblance of Dominican political and economic control over this industry. The elimination of the 'two-way' baseball labour migration and its replacement by straightforward out-migration represents a further underdevelopment of the game. In its most current form, the out-migration is no longer simply confined to one's playing career, but is taking on a permanent status. Whereas athletes might have stopped playing in their homeland during the 1980s, they continued to return to visit in the winter. Now, it is increasingly common to find stars of the calibre of Ruben Sierra (Puerto Rican) or José Rijo (Dominican) wintering in Boca Raton, Florida rather than face worsening economic conditions in their homelands. Clearly, the overall declining ability to produce and run this sport-industry in countries like the Dominican Republic and Puerto Rico as local traditions is linked to North American baseball interests.

The Japanese Compete

The effects of increasing globalization of production, however, have even begun to be felt in the major leagues. It is not simply the case that North American baseball, with its control over legitimacy and capital, marches unimpeded wherever it wants. The flow of economic power and capital, and its consequences, to the Far East has begun to show signs of happening in baseball as well. In 1990, the Japanese opened their own baseball academy in the Dominican Republic (Klein, 1991: 51). Modelled upon the successful Los Angeles Dodgers academy, the Hiroshima Carp (a Japanese professional team) opened their facility nearby. The presence of a foreign competitor on turf that had been the exclusive province of North American baseball is very clearly a harbinger of the changing concentration of global capital. Having come into this virtual colony of the United States, the Japanese show a willingness to compete directly for the same talent pool. Dominican players show some interest because Japanese competition will drive salaries up (Klein, 1991: 52). Others feel that, while they are welcoming the bidding war, the martial style of training and playing in Japan (Whiting, 1979) is just too foreign (Klein, 1991: 52). For the Japanese, who played baseball against Americans as early as the 1890s (Rhoden, 1980), the insistence on competing with or even beating Americans at their own game has now evolved into a strategy that includes using their considerable economic power.

I stressed the impact of the flow of capital from areas of low profitability to areas of high profitability on production and labour processes. Labour migration, most often takes place as a response to lack of economic opportunity (deindustrialization, displacing populations, etc.), as labour-costs (salaries plus the reproduction of labour force) become too high to maintain the expected profit margin, or competing capitalist interests open new labour markets elsewhere. Japan has come to be a source of economic opportunity – albeit on a small scale – for North Americans in a way that portends interesting things for the future. Whereas in the past the only players to play in that country were those at the tail-end of their careers, today players have begun to see playing in Japan as a short-term strategy to re-enter the North American market. Free agency has created a mind-set for North American players in which playing baseball is no longer the goal, but rather the outcome of salary negotiation between themselves (or rather, their agents) and professional franchises. The Japanese have taken advantage of free agency, just as the players have, by joining in the bidding wars for North American players. The case of Cecil Fielder (Detroit Tigers) seems to have ushered in an era in which North American players consider Japanese offers in their negotiations with major league teams. Playing in the shadow of established stars in the Toronto Blue Jays outfield, Fielder opted for a one-year stint in Japan, at the end of which he returned to North America with the Detroit Tigers. A highly successful year (leading the major leagues in home runs) followed, and his success in re-entering the major leagues has spawned similar attempts by other players (*Boston Globe*,

6 June 1990; *Baseball America*, 20 August 1990). This means that Japanese professional teams are now short-term acceptable alternatives to major league baseball, a situation which further internationalizes both the game and labour migration.

The transfiguration of Japanese baseball has also resulted in an increased willingness to come directly into North America. Japanese investors are prohibited from owning controlling shares in major league teams; but that has not precluded their efforts at buying into minor league clubs in North America. Within the past few years there have been efforts by Japanese professional teams and their corporate holders to take over independent teams[6] in the USA and Canada as in the case of the Birmingham Barons of the Double A Southern League (*Baseball America*, 25 August 1990). Financially strapped owners in North America are finding willing investors in Japan. The most widely reported attempt has been that of the takeover of the Salina Spurs in the California League by the Fukuoka Daiei Hawks of the Japan Pacific League. The Japanese investors were further encouraged to buy into the club as a way for them to utilize the North American minor leagues to train their players. What makes the Spurs case completely novel is the presence of a Japanese manager teaching Japanese methods of training. Most recently, the Japanese firm, Japan Sports Systems (which already owns the Double A Southern League's Birmingham Barons) is in the process of purchasing the Vancouver, British Columbia, franchise in the Pacific Coast League. There is an additional effort by one of Japan's largest supermarket chains to buy 9.6 per cent of the New York Yankees from its limited partners (*Boston Globe*, 6 January 1991). There is every reason to think of this as an early Japanese attempt at baseball imperialism, rather than further proof of trans-nationalism of baseball with players moving around the globe in response to capital movements.

CONCLUSION

The growing internationalism of baseball works both to promote and, eventually, to wrest complete hegemony from North American major leagues. This systematic underdevelopment of the third world by the industrial–capital sector is mirrored in baseball. By examining the Latin American case, we see the dismantling of older, locally autonomous baseball industries by North American teams in search of badly needed labour. But competition among industrial powers has also begun to show that the game and its structure will have to withstand competition from at least one other baseball-mad economic stronghold (that is, Japan). This competition occurs in the arenas of searching the globe for talent as well as buying directly into North American professional baseball by foreign interests. In the short run, there is little threat to Major League Baseball Inc. In fact, to the degree that the Japanese are moving into Latin America or investing in North American clubs, one could argue that they are further ensconced in the web of North American baseball and ever more dependent.

The creation of new markets for baseball will flourish in this interaction as is evidenced by the current success of new enterprise launched by major league baseball. The licensing of its products (authentic shirts, hats, etc.) to other countries has spawned a $20 million success in its first year, 1990, primarily in the Japanese market, but moving steadily into other markets. The ideological value of such a marketing strategy is clear. The symbolic power of major league clubs is unquestioned in countries that have a passion for the game, be they in Latin America or the Far East. But as part of a long-term strategy to introduce the game to other countries Major League Baseball International Partners (MLBIP) has global control in mind. Part of its effort is to promote interest by bringing exhibition tours and television transmissions, and developing leagues. MLBIP played an instrumental role in the beginning of the Australian Baseball League, and the beginnings of youth leagues in various countries.

The development of such long-range efforts to expand baseball as a sport-industry involves eventual propagation of a labour force of athletes. For the immediate future, the need for labour will centre on Latin America and North America. Just as the era of mercantilism spawned a period of intense travel and discovery in the service of commerce and primitive capital accumulation among would-be powers in Europe, the present era of baseball has shown that in the face of increased labour shortages and competition from Japan, major league baseball in North America is now determined to expand its horizons first to Latin America, then to the world.

Baseball as political-cultural ideology

Making the leap from sport to political ideology hinges on the placement of the event between what anthropologists refer to as the mundane and sacred. The relationship between politics and economics has been thoroughly examined for over a century (Marx, 1964; Ricardo, 1951, etc.), but mass culture has only recently come under political scrutiny. The sport of baseball is particularly well suited to such an examination because in the Dominican Republic it occupies an inordinately important position situated somewhere between a cottage industry and a cultural icon. With a combined unemployment and underemployment figure of 75 per cent (Black, 1986) there are few economic options available for the men of this country. it is the absence of alternatives, the proud history of the sport and the phenomenal success of those who actually get to play professional baseball that make it easy for young men to view the game as economic salvation. While there are, at present, some 300–400 Dominicans playing in professional baseball in North America, there are hundreds more (in academies) poised to do so, and thousands of amateurs struggling to become professional. Hence, unlike other forms of entertainment in which, while thousands strive for it, few succeed in earning an income, baseball actually affords as many as 1,000 men a relatively large annual salary.

Escape from poverty, however, is not the only way in which the game becomes culturally loaded. Baseball is also a means of culturally confronting North American economic domination (Klein, 1988; 1991). Inter-cultural hegemony, defined as domination by consent of the dominated (Gramsci, 1971; Scott, 1983), is built around two related phenomena. The more obvious of the two is overvaluation of the dominating foreigner and his or her culture. In this desire to emulate foreign culture, Dominicans, like other dominated peoples, often seek, as Bettleheim stated, to 'ape the oppressor'. Despite having a vital tradition of mass culture, Dominicans most often prefer the culture of the foreigner to their own, whether it is American rock music, fashion, or television. There is, for instance, only one Spanish-speaking cinema in Santo Domingo, the capital; all others play North American films with subtitles. It is the same with foreign fashions, which for young Dominicans define upward mobility and provide a further sense of identification with cultural forces outside the Caribbean.

The other side of overvaluation of the foreigner is 'social self-loathing' (Klein, 1991). Both Frantz Fanon (1967) and C.L.R. James (1983) have given powerful examinations of the way in which colonialism promotes the social self-hatred of a people on racial and/or ethnic grounds. Even in contemporary North American society the emphasis on mainstreaming ethnicity and race so as to fit an Anglo-elite model of culture works to foster various forms of group-wide devaluation. Changing names to be more 'American', straightening hair or dyeing it lighter, cosmetic surgery (as in straightening noses or enlarging eyes), are all examples of the ways that members of ethnic and racial minority groups seek to repudiate who they are. In James's work we have a classic study of how the British colonial system used the game of cricket to socialize generation after generation of Trinidadians into accepting their inferiority. More importantly, we see how both social self-loathing and overvaluation of the foreigner are dialectically linked.

For third-world cultures, the antidote to this sort of hegemonic process is to be found in nationalism, which curbs overvaluation of foreign culture and reduces social self-loathing in direct proportion to being able to gain national or cultural pride. That it is nationalistically imbued is verified by a series of findings in my work. A content analysis of the print media in Santo Domingo showed that the sports pages offered the only source of formal expression of mainstream resentment against North American presence in the country. In the pages of *Listin Diario* one would find no attacks against North Americans on the national and international news pages. By contrast, in the baseball-related stories there was ample evidence of gringo-bashing, whether in the outrage expressed at major league teams who were tampering with Dominican teams or broadsides against North Americans who had signed to play winter ball, but were leaving prematurely (Klein, 1991: 119–37). During the summer months the pages of the sports section would be full of stories boasting of Dominican exploits. Little concern for the individual games' outcomes was evident, as headlines would lump the Dominican successes of the previous night's games irrespective of team or league.

Similarly, in a survey conducted in Santo Domingo (Klein, 1988; 1991), when questions were posed that sought to determine cultural-symbolic preferences (for example, which baseball hats one preferred, that of their favourite Dominican team or their favourite North American team), 78 per cent reversed their cultural-consumer preferences for things American by choosing the Dominican hat. When asked to explain their choice, there was an overwhelming recourse to nationalism. Examples of resistance to North American presence also included examination of concrete behaviour (Klein, 1991: 134–7).

What is significant in all this is that resentment and resistance centre on the sport of baseball as opposed to other institutions. As an industry, the political economy of baseball suggests that structurally North Americans are destroying the local tradition by making it completely dependent. Ideologically, however, there is evidence to suggest that Dominicans are trying to contest this course of events. In looking at mass culture in the inter-cultural relations between North America and the Dominican Republic we can see both hegemony and resistance as ongoing, and the need to examine the widest range of societal institutions possible. In moving beyond a simple focus on North America and the Dominican Republic, we have also seen that the flow of capital and production based on factors such as labour costs, etc., also have dramatic impacts on the sport, most notably in the initials stage of competition for labour, and between Japan and major league baseball. As the game becomes more international such competition is bound to intensify, giving even greater meaning to Spalding's turn-of-the-century dictum that the job of baseball is to 'follow the flag around the world'.

NOTES

The author would like to thank Milton Jamail at the University of Texas-Austin for sharing his expertise in Latin American baseball and labour in the preparation of this chapter. Thanks also go to my colleagues at Northeastern University who read earlier drafts and offered advice: Daniel Faber and Luis Falcon.

1 After Jamaica and Laos, Dominican migration to the USA is the third highest in proportion to the size of the sending country (Grasmuck and Pessar, 1991: 25). In the aftermath of the coup to oust the elected Dominican President Juan Bosch, Dominicans began a trend of migration to the USA that would build to the present. Balaguer, who corralled the presidency afterwards also used emigration as a mechanism for ridding himself of potentially disruptive political forces. (The data in the remainder of this section are taken from Grasmuck and Pessar, 1991, with page numbers only given in parentheses).

2 Baseball-playing Latin American countries include, not only the Dominican Republic, but Puerto Rico, Mexico, Venezuela, Panama and Nicaragua. Cuba, the country most responsible for the spread of baseball after the USA and most successful in producing star baseball players, is not part of the organized professional competition that goes on among the first four of the above-mentioned countries. Partly because the Cuban revolution repudiates commercialism and professionalism as bourgeois, and partly because the USA has had a trade embargo against Cuba for over 30 years, Cubans have been denied access to this level of competition. Nevertheless, they have dominated baseball in the Pan American Games.

3 Professional baseball briefly allowed African-American players into its ranks during the 1870s and early 1880s before closing its doors for some 50 years (Tygiel, 1985).

4 Major league baseball signed a four-year contract with the CBS television broadcasting company, 1989–93, for $1.4 billion.

5 Each of the four teams will have a 26-man roster and at least four minor league teams (at various levels). Since each club will have about 35 men there will be an additional 140 minor league players per club in addition to the 26 in the parent team for a total of 166 new players. Altogether there will be 664 new professional players.

6 Certain of the lower minor leagues have clubs within their ranks that are not affiliated to any of the major league teams.

REFERENCES

Black, J.K. (1986) *The Dominican Republic: Politics and Underdevelopment in an Unsovereign State* (Boston: Allen & Unwin).

Blim, M. and Rothstein, F. (eds), (1992) *Anthropology and the Global Factory: Studies of the New Industrialization in the late 20th Century* (New York: Bergin and Garvey).

Brubaker, B. (1986) 'Inside the Dominican Pipeline', *Washington Post*, 20 March 1986.

Dixon, M. and Jonas, S. (1982) 'Reindustrialization and the Transnational Labor Force in the United States Today', in Dixon, M. and Jonas, S. (eds), *The New Nomads: From Immigrant Labor to Transnational Working Class* (San Francisco: Synthesis) pp. 42–54.

Fanon, F. (1967) *Black Skins, White Masks* (New York: Grove Press).

Frank, A.G. (1971) *Capitalism and Underdevelopment in Latin America*. (Harmondsworth: Penguin).

Gramsci, A. (1971) *Selections From Prison Notebooks* (London: Lawrence & Wishart).

Grasmuck, S. and Pessar, P. (1991) *Between Two Islands: Dominican International Migration* (Berkeley: University of California Press).

James, C.L.R. (1983) *Beyond a Boundary* (New York: Pantheon).

Joseph, G. (1987) 'Forging the Regional Pastime: Class and Baseball in the Yucatan', in Arbena, J. (ed.), *Sport and Society in Latin America* (Westview, CT: Greenwood) pp. 29–62.

Klein, A.M. (1988) 'American Hegemony, Dominican Resistance, and Baseball: A Preliminary Index', *Dialectical Anthropology*, 13,4, 11–27.

(1989) 'Baseball as Underdevelopment: The Political-Economy of Dominican Baseball', *Sociology of Sport Journal*, 6,3, 95–117.

(1990) 'Headcase, Headstrong, and Head-of-the-Class: Labeling and Socialization in Dominican Baseball', *Arena Review*, 14,1, 36–48.

(1991) *Sugarball: The American Game, The Dominican Dream* (New Haven, CT: Yale University Press).

LaFrance, D. (1985) 'A Mexican Popular Image of the United States Through the Baseball Hero, Fernando Valenzuela', *Studies in Latin American Popular Culture*, 4,1, 14–22.

Marx, K. (1964) *Capital* (3 Vols.) (Moscow: Progress).

Rhoden, D. (1980) 'Baseball and the Quest for National Identity in Meiji Japan', *American Historical Review*, 85,3, 511–34.

Ricardo, D. (1951) *The Works and Correspondence of David Ricardo*, P. Sraffa (ed.) (Cambridge: Cambridge University Press).

Rogosin, D. (1985) *Invisible Men: Life in Baseball's Negro Leagues* (New York: Atheneum).

Sassen, S. (1988) *The Mobility of Labor and Capital: A Study of Investment and Labor Flow* (Cambridge: Cambridge University Press).

Scott, J. (1983) *Weapons of the Weak: Everyday Forms of Peasant Resistance* (New Haven, CT: Yale University Press).

Spalding, A.G. (1991) *Baseball: America's National Game* (San Francisco: Halo).

Tygiel, J. (1985) Baseball's Great Experiment: Jackie Robinson and his Legacy (Oxford: Oxford University Press).

Wallerstein, I. (1979) *The Capitalist World Economy* (Cambridge: Cambridge University Press).

Whiting, R. (1979) *The Chrysanthemum and the Bat* (New York: Mentor).

14

Out of Africa: The 'Development' of Kenyan Athletics, Talent Migration and the Global Sports System

John Bale and Joe Sang

When Western Samoa, with a team made up of many talented players based in New Zealand, beat Wales in a game during the 1991 Rugby World Cup, it was widely inferred that such talent migration had contributed in no small part to Western Samoa's success. Similar comments have been made about many other sportsmen and women from a variety of sports, who live and train in countries other than their own. But there is always a danger that such conclusions result from the erroneous assumption that association implies causation. This chapter explores aspects of one such apparent association and one set of sporting migrants – Kenyan track and field athletes who have migrated to universities and colleges in the USA – and considers the impact of this migration on the so-called 'development' of track and field athletics in Kenya. The basic theme is that such talent migration, while having been substantial, must be seen within the broader global situation in which sports exist if its contribution to national sporting 'development' is to be accurately assessed. In other words, the chapter seeks to 'put talent migration in its place' and to view it as but part of a complex web of international flows. We accept that the development of sport in any country cannot be explained by studying events in that country alone and for this reason requires a more globally-oriented framework.

Our study begins by examining the claim that Kenya is today the 'giant' of African track and field, describing the absolute and relative 'production' patterns of Kenyan track and field athletics, in both an African and a global context in order to reveal the extent and nature of Kenyan sports development. The contribution of Kenyan talent migration to the USA is then assessed and we conclude with the view that this kind of migration cannot be causally associated with the development of the sport in Kenya, and indeed may have contributed in some respects to its underdevelopment and dependency.

WHAT IS 'ATHLETIC DEVELOPMENT'?

Widely regarded as the most 'athletically developed' nation in Africa, Kenya finished fourth in the unofficial, but widely publicized, medal table in the 1991 World Athletic Championships, behind such global mega-powers as the USA, USSR and Germany. The assumption that such sports success and the associated production of elite athletes is a 'good thing' can, of course, be interpreted ideologically and has been questioned by those who view the growth of western-oriented sports in third world nations as a form of cultural imperialism (for example, Galtung, 1984; Eichberg, 1984, 1990 and his chapter in this volume). If, however, it *is* considered desirable for a country to 'develop' athletically along a route which favours the production of an elite athletic force there is clearly a need to explore what 'development' actually means and how it can be operationalized in an athletic context. In this chapter we apply two simple measures; first, an index of per capita 'production' and second an index of the diversification (or specialization) of that production. Similar notions of 'development', related to mass participation, have been outlined by Mandle and Mandle, 1990 (see also Bale, 1985).

An initial indicator of athletic development might be that the nation should have a high level of athletic output in relation to the continental or global per capita level (depending at what geographical scale the analysis is being undertaken). In order to obtain a clearer picture of Kenya's present status in track and field athletics in both Africa and the world as a whole, we therefore present two analyses, one of the *relative* level of athletic 'production' at the scale of *continental* Africa and the other of Kenya's place on a *global* scale. Simple measures of athletic production can be undertaken by applying ideas used by Rooney (1972) and Bale (1982) in their work on the geography of American and British sports respectively (see also Bale, 1989). In order to compare the althetic productivity of different nations (or regions) of Africa, for example, a per capita index can be calculated for each country by applying the following simple formula:

$$I = (N/P) \times (A/1)$$

where I is the per capita index, N is the number of African-class athletes (defined as those capable of achieving a performance ranking in the top 50 in Africa in a given year; Abmayr, 1982) from a particular country, P is the population of the country, and A is the total number of African-class athletes per head of the total continental population. Kenya is easily the major producer of African talent in *absolute* terms, accounting for 31.7 and 32.7 per cent of superior African female and male athletes respectively. In 1984 there was one African-class athlete per 278,000 of the continental population. This figure is represented as an index of 1.00 (the African continental norm) against which national differences can be easily compared. If, for example, a country had an index of 5, it would be producing athletes at five times the continental norm; if, of the other hand, it had an index of 0.5 it would only be producing at half the continental average. In 1984 Kenya had an overall (men and women) index of 8.04, substantially higher than other comparable countries[1] (Figure 14.1) while the respective index for men was 8.01.

At the global scale Kenyan production of world-class athletes[2] has grown substantially since the 1950s and now lies well above the global per capita average. Whereas in 1956 Kenya was producing world-class male athletes at less than 0.2 times the global average level of production, by 1968 its level of output was over 4 times that of the global average and by 1972 over 6 times (Bale, 1979). Since then it has fallen to around about 4.5 times the world average level of per capita production but this remains higher than that of the UK.

The per capita index is a useful measure of national and international athletic productivity and in many respects more valid as an indicator of national 'output' than, for example, the Olympic medal count (Bale, 1985). But it needs to be complemented by a second simple numerical approach which explores the extent to which the production of athletes is diversified across the range of track and field events. This can be done by calculating a diversification index by the following simple formula:

$$DI = \sqrt{(P_1^2 + P_2^2 + P_3^2 + \ldots P_n^2)}$$

where DI is the diversification index and P is the percentage share of total athletic output in event 1, 2, 3 . . . n. The upper limit of DI is always 100, indicating that all athletes are in a single event; the lowest possible score which denotes the maximum possible degree of diversification, with the same proportion of total output in each event, depends on the number of events (n). Where $n = 18$, as in the present case, it is 23.59.

At the continental scale Kenyan men's track and field output was, in

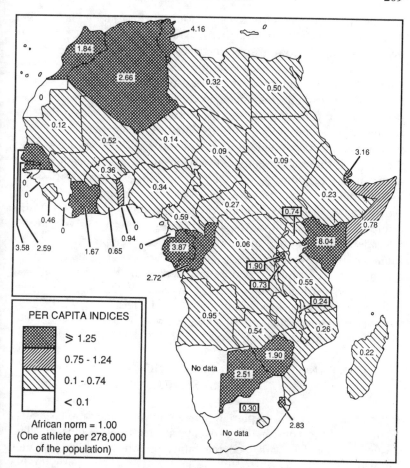

Figure 14.1 Per capita output of 'African class' track and field athletes in 1984.

1984, the most diversified in Africa (DI = 24.42), but very closely followed by Algeria (25.46) and Tunisia (25.84). Only Uganda (27.71) among other African nations had a diversification index of less than 30. At the global level, however, Kenya's world class output appears rather specialized, the contrast with the continental situation emphasizing the importance of the geographical concept of *scale*. Whereas in 1989 Kenya produced 43 world-class runners, it did not produce any such athletes across the entire range of field events. At this level it is clear that, in a *relative* sense, Kenya has not developed at all; indeed, it could be argued that in relative terms it has declined in terms of world-class athletic output in field events. Whereas in 1958, for example, a

Kenyan athlete could finish as high as fourth in an Empire Games field event (see below), the growing totalization process in modern sports since then has led to a greater specialization of performance among events. Contrast those events requiring the 'processing' of athletes (technical events) and those where 'raw materials' are utilized without the need for 'capital equipment' in the shape of expensive facilities (long-distance running). Hence, the developed world has displayed a comparative advantage in events needing technical expertise while the third world has depended on its raw materials. What we are saying, therefore, is that the development of Kenyan track and field has been partial in the extreme.

According to our criteria, Kenya is the principal athletic power in Africa and according to the crude medal tally following the 1991 World Athletics Championships, the fourth most powerful in the world. Considerable variations in national athletic development are to be found, however, among the various event groups. In women's track and field, for example, it is only in recent years that the traditional invisibility of African women in sport has changed though a number of distance runners are now competing at the highest level. In the 1991 world cross-country championships Kenya won both men's (senior and junior) and both women's races.

KENYAN TRACK AND FIELD MIGRATION TO US UNIVERSITIES

It is now appropriate to explore the extent to which migration of sports talent may have contributed to Kenya's athletic pre-eminence. The postwar period has witnessed the influx of foreign student-athletes from all over the world to college and university campuses of the United States as recipients of 'athletics scholarships' (Figure 14.2). Such recruits are found in many campus sports, with relatively high foreign proportions of the total student-athletic population being found in ice hockey, tennis and soccer (Bale, 1991). It has been estimated that among college track and field athletics in NCAA Division I colleges and universities in 1987, 5.3 per cent of the men and 4.5 per cent of the women were recruited from outside the United States (Bale, 1991). Such percentages represent over 700 foreign student-athletes (in track and field) in Division I schools alone and it is well known that significant numbers of foreigners are found in lower divisions, in NAIA institutions and in junior colleges. Many others remain in the United States when their time at college is over.

Among the foreign recruits in track and field have been a significant

Figure 14.2 A late twentieth-century scramble for Africa?

Table 14.1 Appearances by countries providing more than 3 per cent of foreign track and field athletes in NCAA championships (men), 1971–78.

Country	Number	Per cent
Kenya	**165**	**17.2**
Canada	120	12.5
Eire	102	10.6
United Kingdom	88	9.2
Sweden	58	6.0
Jamaica	53	5.5
Nigeria	52	5.4
Australia	47	4.9

Source: Hollander 1980

number of Kenyan athletes, the first Kenyan college-based athletes arriving in the late 1960s (Bale, 1991). The 1970s and early 1980s witnessed the most significant impact of Kenyan male athletes on US college sports. Between 1971 and 1978, 17.2 per cent of all NCAA track and field championship appearances by foreign athletes were by Kenyans (compared with 12.5 per cent by Canadians), while between 1973 and 1985 there were slightly more elite Kenyan runners in US colleges than there were Canadians (12.6 per cent compared with 12.2 per cent of all elite foreign recruits respectively).[3] During this period Kenya was the major source of elite foreign male track talent (Tables 14.1 and 14.2) though the import of Kenyan women athletes was non-existent. Since the early 1980s, however, the Kenyan presence has declined. By 1987, for example, only about 3.5 per cent of all foreign track and field athletes in NCAA Division I universities were from Kenya (Bale, 1991: 77). Whereas in 1982, 31.6 per cent of Kenya's national-class middle distance runners (defined as those achieving a standard of performance capable of ranking them in the top 50 Kenyans that year) were domiciled in the United States, the figure for 1986 was 15.4 per cent. If international-class runners (those ranked in the top 10 Kenyans) are considered, the respective figures were 68 and 25 per cent.

Although the total number of top-class Kenyans who were recruited to the USA between 1973 and 1985 were widely scattered across the nation, the pattern of their college destinations was neither regular nor random. Well-defined 'talent pipelines' can be identified where concentrations of national talent are found in particular institutions (Stidwill and Flath, 1985; Bale, 1991: 84–9). Such concentrations of Kenyans were found at Richmond, Iowa State and Washington State

Table 14.2 Major national donors supplying more than 3 per cent of superior foreign track and field student-athletes (men), 1973–85.

Country	Number	Per cent
Kenya	**77**	**12.6**
Canada	74	12.2
United Kingdom	54	8.9
Sweden	51	8.4
Jamaica	43	7.1
Nigeria	34	5.6
Eire	32	5.3
Norway	25	4.1
Ghana	18	3.0

Source: Bale 1991, 77.

Universities and, most notably, at the University of Texas at El Paso, reflecting well-established networks of contacts and rationalized recruiting strategies. UTEP won a large number of NCAA championship meetings with squads recruited largely from overseas. These recruits raised the visibility of an institution, off the beaten track and often with limited attraction for athletes from US high schools.

The relative emergence of Kenyan track and field during the period since 1950 is often illustrated by citing the number of medals won by athletes from that country at the Olympic and other games and championships. Certainly during the 1970s and 1980s Kenyan athletes were constantly in the headlines, names such as Henry Rono, John Ngugi, Mike Boit, Paul Ereng, Peter Koech and Julius Kariuki being prominent, and it is sometimes felt that the substantial migration of Kenyan atheltes to American universities has, in no small part, contributed to Kenya's rise in visibility and success in world running. A causal link between US domicile and development has been inferred by several observers of the international track and field scene. For example, in describing the African recruiting boom by US colleges it has been noted that 'young Kenyans on track scholarships in the United States *gain immeasurably* through competition with the best American runners. If they were at home they would stagnate through lack of competition' (quoted in Manners, 1975: 69, italics added). Similarly, a reaction to the decision of the NCAA to attempt to limit the number of foreign recruits taking part in inter-collegiate athletics claimed that it ignored 'the fact that athletes from the developing countries generally have little chance of an organized training programme and support system unless they are in the police or the

military, both of which are unavailable to high school age students'
(Boit, 1988). As an alumnus of an American university himself, Mike
Boit, the current Kenyan commissioner of sport, supports the view
that the American college system is an avenue for developing athletic
talent (though he does accept that it possesses some disadvantages). It
is, therefore, now appropriate to evaluate the argument that talent
migration has contributed to both the development and the underdevelopment of Kenyan athletics. There is no contradiction here; as
Klein (1991: 57–8) points out, it is important to define 'underdevelopment' at different levels – from individual to cultural. Hence, while for
individuals foreign migration *may* lead to both sporting and economic
enhancement, for the national sporting or movement culture, the very
same migration can lead to its underdevelopment. In cases of indigenous movement cultures it can be part and parcel of the process leading
to their total extinction.

US COLLEGE RECRUITMENT AS 'UNDERDEVELOPMENT'

We now explore in a little more detail the characteristics of Kenyan
athletic migration to the United States. There are three particular
areas to which we want to allude; first, the relationship over time
between the number of Kenyan recruits to US colleges and the global
status of Kenyan athletics; second, the event-by-event composition of
Kenyan recruits; and third, some cultural implications of foreign
recruiting of third world athletes in a Kenyan context.

The growth of Kenyan athletics
As at 1 January 1953 the top ten athletes of all time in each of the
Olympic track and field events did not include any from the nations of
Africa. Of the 176 athletes included in the all-time lists 93 were from
North America and 72 from Europe. One North African (Alain
Mimoun) was included but competed under the colours of France. By
1 January 1977 Africa had still to make much of an impact at the very
highest levels; only 5.5 per cent came from Africa though it might be
noted that 3.3 per cent came from Kenya alone. At the start of 1988
the percentage share of African athletes among the world's all-time
elite had reached 10 per cent with Kenya increasing its share to 4.6 per
cent. Such statistics need to be read in the context of the African and
Kenyan share of the world population – 10 per cent and 0.5 per cent
respectively. Africa, therefore, appears to contribute what would be
expected in per capita terms. Kenya contributes about nine times what
would be expected given its share of the world's population and seems

to be increasing its share of the world's greatest athletes at a rate of about 1 per cent every decade.

The first really world class Kenyan athlete was the middle-distance runner Nyandika Maiyoro who ran with distinction in the 1954 and 1958 Empire Games and the 1956 and 1960 Olympics. His initial appearance outside Kenya was at the (British) AAA championships in 1954. He astonished local observers with not only his barefoot running on London's White City cinder track but also by his uninhibited style whereby in the three-mile event he opened up a huge initial lead only to be eventually overtaken to finish fourth. Another Kenyan runner, Lazaro Chepkwony, also competed in this event but was injured and failed to finish. Maiyoro also ran well in the 1954 Empire Games in Vancouver, finishing in sixth place. Also in Vancouver, Maborra finished sixth in the javelin and Chepkwony seventh in the six miles. Even the more informed members of the athletics press covered these early international appearances with thinly veiled racism. The bizarre and exotic nature (as perceived) of the Kenyans often attracted attention, their uninhibited running often being described in derogatory or patronizing terms; one half-miler who built up a big lead on the first lap, only to fall away on the second, was termed the 'one-lap wonder'. Maiyoro was described by one of the foremost athletics journalists of the day as 'the popular Black Jack from Kenya' (McWhirter 1954).

In the 1958 Empire Games at Cardiff two Kenyan runners Anentia and Sum finished third and sixth in the six miles; Rotich won a bronze medal in the 440 yards hurdles and Leresae was fourth in the high jump. The Kenyan sprinter Antao was also prominent in the late 1950s and early 1960s. Although sprinters were as prominent as distance runners in Kenya's early successes, Maiyoro in particular seems to have provided an important role model for younger Kenyan runners, and in the 1960s his place was taken by Kipchoge Keino. By 1968 the Kenyans were able to demonstrate a remarkable presence at the Mexico City Olympics, featuring such athletes as Keino, Jipcho, Biwott and Temu. The country won no fewer than eight medals – all in running events. Although the 40 x 400 metres relay team won a silver medal behind the world-record breaking US squad, a specialization in distance running had emerged, in contrast to the more diversified collection of athletes who had competed in international competition in the 1950s.

The crucial point here is that the development of Kenyan athletics owed nothing at all to the out-migration of Kenya's athletes: none of the athletes named above attended US universities. The first migration

to the colleges of the United States did not occur until the late 1960s
by which time Kenya was already establishing itself as an emerging
athletic power. The first Kenyan of any note to arrive in the United
States was Steve Machooka, a strong cross-country runner who won
several east coast titles and attended Cornell. More aggressive recruit
ing in the early 1970s resulted in other recruits, notably Julius Sang and
Robert Ouko to the black southern university, North Carolina
Central, but it was not until the mid-1970s and 1980s that the
overwhelming majority of Kenyans were recruited to the United
States. Some of these athletes were proven high school runners but
many were of more mature years. Either way, the seeds of their
athletic development had been sown in Kenya; the US colleges
basically *exploited* existing talent – they did not develop it. Indeed, the
growth in the number of Kenyan athletes migrating to the USA
coincided with a fall in Kenya's global per capita index, the index
starting to fall just before the number of elite Kenyans on US
campuses peaked (Bale, 1991: 80). More recently, the number of
Kenya's athletes domiciled in the USA has fallen significantly. Wher
eas in 1982 there were 67 Kenyan athletes based in the USA, the figure
for 1986 was 34.

The division of labour among Kenyan recruits
The sport is known as track *and field* yet at the global level Kenya's
talent is almost entirely restricted to track events. Of the 67 Kenyans
domiciled in the USA in 1984 the number from the entire range of field
events was three. A more detailed presentation of the event-group
specificity of American recruiting is shown by the fact that of Kenya's
165 NCAA track and field championship appearances between 1971
and 1978 151 were in the running events (132 in the longer distances)
with only 14 in the field events (Hollander, 1980). What we see here is
the exploitation of specific skills which needs to be seen in the context
of an international division of sporting labour. For the US colleges,
Kenya supplies the distance runners, the Caribbean and West Africa
the sprinters and Scandinavia the throwers (Bale, 1991: 77). Even if a
tenuous connection could be made between the growth in the number
of athletes with sojourn in the USA and the development of a plethora
of Kenyan runners, it would have done so at the expense of Kenya's
sprinters and field event athletes. Let us examine this assertion a little
further.

At the African level of scale Kenya is the major *absolute* producer of
athletic talent in three of the major event groups, Senegal producing
more sprinters than Kenya but Kenya producing twice as many
distance runners, jumpers and throwers as any other African nation.

But Kenya is the major continental per capita leader in only one of the event groups, ironically in the group where American talent migration has been least evident (indeed, virtually non-existent) – the throwing events (Table 14.3). In other event groups, however, the level of Kenyan per capita production is higher than in the throws, reflecting the greater divergence of national outputs in the sprints, distances and jumps and the greater convergence of national outputs in the more poorly developed throwing events. As noted earlier, at the global level the production of Kenyan field event athletes is very weak. Even if the US colleges could be viewed as aiding Kenyan athletics by producing world-class athletes, it is obvious that such talent production is highly selective and that at the global level Kenyan field events languish at very modest levels compared with those on the track and with its position in Africa.

Cultural imperialism and underdevelopment

We now explore the contribution of US colleges to Kenyan athletic development from a different perspective. Kenyan talent migration to the United States can be interpreted as a form of cultural imperialism and the underdevelopment of local sporting resources. Part of the globalization of sports involves the erosion of regional cultures (Peet, 1986) and the devaluation of indigenous values and movement cultures. This had started long before the 1960s, of course, and in this respect the migration to the USA can be viewed as the apogee of foreign tampering with African body cultures.

It is possible to interpret the widespread foreign migration of athletic talent as having had a negative effect on Kenyan athletics. For example, with overseas migration, athletes come to devalue their own country, its traditions and its culture. Competing for a university or college in small-town America becomes more important than representing one's own country. This did cause some concern within Kenya and in the 1980s some hesitant attempts were made at 'unlinking' Kenya from this aspect of the global sports system by refusing to select US-based athletes for certain events. Such interference was doomed to failure, however.

Associated with foreign sojourn can come the widely voiced opinion that African athletes are often exploited in US universities, being seen as point-scoring machines rather than human beings, and widely subjected to racial discrimination. It is claimed by Ballinger (1981: 60), for example, that African athletes in US colleges 'have been threatened on many occasions with deportation if they don't do as they are told, if they don't race in every meet that comes along'. While Swedish hammer throwers might be welcomed, Kenyan distance runners are

Table 14.3 Major producers of athletic talent in the conterminous nations o
Africa, 1984. Shown by (a) nation, (b) absolute production, and (c) per capit
index

SPRINTS			DISTANCES		
(a)	(b)	(c)	(a)	(b)	(c)
Gabon	8	8.57	Djibouti	5	12.13
Senegal	44	8.42	Swaziland	8	10.86
Congo	11	7.79	KENYA	249	10.68
Gambia	4	7.67	Tunisia	48	5.98
Ivory C	30	3.77	Botswana	4	3.19
KENYA	41	2.45	Algeria	74	3.01
Zimbabwe	17	2.39	Zimbabwe	28	2.82
Algeria	39	2.21	Morocco	26	2.05
Tanzania	35	1.92	Somalia	9	1.71
Malawi	1	1.77	Congo	3	1.52
AFRICA	424	1.00	AFRICA	592	1.00
JUMPS			THROWS		
(a)	(b)	(c)	(a)	(b)	(c)
Gabon	9	10.28	KENYA	94	5.94
KENYA	119	7.58	Tunisia	24	4.44
Senegal	26	5.30	Gabon	3	3.41
Tunisia	23	4.26	Algeria	46	2.77
Algeria	49	2.96	Ivory C	20	2.67
Togo	6	2.66	Morocco	38	2.27
Morocco	26	2.27	Senegal	9	1.83
Congo	3	2.26	Zimbabwe	12	1.80
Ivory C	9	1.20	Cameroun	11	1.46
Angola	8	1.20	Egypt	50	1.40
AFRICA	398	1.00	AFRICA	399	1.00

not, beyond scoring points for the university. Having questioned th
role of the US colleges in the development of Kenyan athletic talen
we next speculate about a more global approach to the explanation o
Kenya's African athletic development. This is done by briefly notin
two other 'naive' explanations of such development before explorin
the large number of other 'actors' on the Kenyan sporting stage.

'NAIVE' OR RACIST EXPLANATIONS OF THE GROWTH OF KENYAN TRACK AND FIELD

A number of what we shall call 'naive' explanations have traditionall
been used to explain the pre-eminence of Kenya as a major Africa

athletic nation. Among these is the notion that Kenyan development has been undertaken by athletic departments in American universities, something we hope we have been able to critique in the previous sections of this chapter. The growing success of Kenyan athletics which, as noted above, was most demonstrably evident among middle and long-distance runners has also been popularly attributed to crudely environmental factors or to almost folkloric or racist stories of the cultural background of Kenya's runners. In particular, the high elevation of much of the Kenyan countryside and the propensity of many Kenyans to engage in large amounts of physical exercise as children were popularly cited as explanations of Kenyan running success. The East African plateau undoubtedly has the effect of encouraging aerobic powers as a result of the thinner atmosphere but other countries of high relief, not only in East Africa but elsewhere in the world, are nowhere near as prolific in terms of athletic production. In East Africa, for example, Ethiopia and Tanzania, while producing some very eminent long-distance runners, were, in 1984, producing respectively only 0.14 and 0.69 of the continental norm.

Such a view also ignores the fact that the early success of Kenyan athletes was distributed across a variety of events. In addition, it ignores the concept of the 'ecological fallacy'; that is, in this context, that while on average Kenya is a nation of high athletic productivity and a high-altitude country, it is not necessarily the case that all the best athletes come from high-altitude areas. Indeed, in some cases, such as that of marathon runner, Douglas Wakihuri, leading runners were born in coastal Mombasa.

TOWARDS A GLOBAL SYSTEMS VIEW

In a seminal paper written over a quarter of a century ago Heinilä (1967) drew attention to the fact that the success of a nation's athletes in international competitions was no longer 'a matter of individual effort and the resources of the participant but instead a matter of the effectiveness and total resources of the whole *national sports system*' (emphasis added). This system, he went on, was made up of human resources in sports, the level of knowledge of sports science, the efficiency of organizations and of training systems, etc. 'In other words, the success and effectiveness of the individual athlete or the single team depend more and more on the resources and effectiveness of the total systems of national sport and less on effort independent of the system as a whole' (Heinilä, 1967: 348). Some years later Heinilä (1984:23) continued to emphasize that 'although athletes still seemingly fight for superiority among themselves, success in top-level spor depends increasingly on the background forces in sport, the perfor mance capacity of the system in which the athlete/team is a representa tive. As a result of this, international sport has become increasingly more total, a contest between systems of sport.'

Our basic contention is that it is no longer tenable to attribute national success or failure in international sport and in athletie productivity (the ability of a nation to produce athletes of high quality to national sports systems alone; instead we now need to take into account an international or *global* sports system. The totalization process in sports has transcended national boundaries and today national sports output often results from the workings of globa mechanisms and systems. The global sports system shares severa characteristics with the world political and economic system. There exists a three-tiered structure of inequality with a sports-core, a semi periphery and a periphery. Countries at the core have incorporated those at the periphery into a global system of Eurocentric sports competition, sports aid, and the importation of (sporting analogues of) natural resources. An essential component – but only one component – of this system is hence the trans-national migration of sports talent. In the context of Kenyan athletics we can identify several dimensions of the global system which need to be taken into account, in addition to the 'naive' explanations which we have already noted. These include a number of historical, more recent and contemporary interactions with various parts of the world.

The Imperial legacy
The tradition of 'muscular Christianity' (Mangan, 1986), so well known as an agent of socializing people in colonial countries to the ways of white imperialists, was an important factor in the introduction of western forms of body culture to Kenya – a nation rich in indigenous forms of movement culture. Particularly important as an imperial influence was the longstanding headmaster of Alliance High School, founded in 1926. Carey Francis was a product of Trinity College, Cambridge, and a great believer in Christianity and games, and in his period as head, from 1940 to 1962, he encouraged every student to participate in athletics (Stabler, 1969: 106). Alliance, and other such schools, were moulded on the British public school model and, in some cases, appeared more British than the British! Such an approach was typified also by the Kenyan independent school system (the Kikuyu Independent Schools Association for example) which, while resulting from a desire to curb British moves to destroy certain Kenyan cultural

practices, notably female circumcision, accepted much of what the English system had to offer, and recognized that an English curriculum would lead to social and economic mobility. The schools certainly fully accepted western sports and engaged in inter-school events from the 1930s onwards. Mission schools such as St Patrick's at Iten and Cardinal Otunga High School at Kisii were established in the early 1960s. The former, in particular, has been of considerable significance in socializing young athletes into the achievement sport ethos under the coaching of Brother Simon and more recently by Brother Colm O'Connell. Many of Kenya's most famous athletes attended St Patrick's, a school whose main rival is the aforementioned Cardinal Otunga School, which has also produced many famous Kenyan runners.

In addition to such schools, the army and police – extensions of European imperial rule – have long had an athletic role. As early as 1902, a graduate of Harrow school, Colonel Meinertzhagen, introduced a form of athletics to his King's African Rifles and while based at Muranga organized a two-and-a-quarter mile foot race, recording that the winner covered the course in 14 minutes (Meinertzhagen, 1957: 22). During the Second World War it was noted that Kenyan runners outclassed British, American, Indian and Chinese runners in military athletic events in Burma. Significant individuals in the police force were also important. A police administrator who did more than anyone else in this sphere to encourage athletics was R.G.B. Spicer, commissioner of police from 1925 to 1931. Police athletics programmes were established and the police system subsequently contributed to the emergence of Keino and others.

Interestingly, little if any indigenous resistance appears to have been employed against the introduction of western sports in Kenya. Nationalistic movements, including the Mau Mau, do not seem to have included any anti-western sentiment with regard to sports. Indeed, Jomo Kenyatta, the first national president following independence, whose daughter Jane was a talented high school runner, tended to embrace sports as a form of national promotion.

Kenyan migration to other foreign countries
A phenomenon of recent years has been the increase in the number of Kenyan athletes who choose to live outside Kenya but not in the United States, further illustrating the dependency of the periphery on the core. In some ways this migration is similar to economic-based

immigration but differs in the fact that residence in the core is temporary. These athletes fall into two groups, the first made up of those who are domiciled abroad on a long-term but not permanent basis, the second being those who are essentially *seasonal* migrants. Several Kenyan athletes have taken up residence in Japan, the most notable being marathon runner Douglas Wakihuri. Others live in Germany, Spain, Scandinavia and Italy and hence gain access to the lucrative European running 'industry'. The second group of seasonal migrants tends to live and train in various parts of Europe during the summer grand prix season. A newer trend has been for groups to reside in Britain during the winter months in order to benefit from access to the newly inaugurated grand prix cross-country events, held in several countries in western Europe. In Britain at least two groups who have taken up seasonal domicile during the summer months can be identified. The first is focused in the north-west of England while the second is based in the London area, benefiting from facilities available at a west London college during the summer vacation. Crucial actors in the organization of such groups are European agents who organize races and accommodation for such migrant athletes. But such a migration further illustrates the Eurocentricity of international sports. In order to compete in grand prix events African athletes are forced to labour in the core nations where the events are held. In order not to compete at a disadvantage they require temporary residence away from home.

Sport investment in Kenya by overseas nations
In addition to the outflow of human sporting capital there has been a inflow of sport investment by overseas donors, basically an extension of existing economic relations. The two major nations involved in the Kenyan case have been China and Germany. Curiously, in spite of a different sporting ideology from Kenya, China has helped develop a modern sports complex with a 60,000 seater stadium and high quality international facilities. This has resulted in some subsequent economic linkages with China from where maintenance and spare parts for stadium equipment are obtained. German aid, on the other hand, is channelled through the German Agency for Technical Assistance and between 1981 and 1985 this project helped train about 250 coaches. The programme also provided Kenya with a German national coach from 1980 to 1985 (Abmayer, 1984). There has been a reciprocal arrangement whereby Kenyan coaches have spent time in Germany.

In addition, British coaches have visited Kenya to undertake coaching clinics.

Other foreign agencies

As part of the attempt to globalize track and field athletics the International Amateur Athletics Federation, in co-operation with the Kenyan AAA, established an IAAF training centre at Nairobi in 1986. This provides a focus for carrying out training clinics and seminars, for Kenyans as well as athletes from other African countries. The role of the IAAF also extends to help in financing Kenyan athletes with international travel and competition. The IAAF's role in Kenya shows how trans-national bodies are actively involved in the promotion of their interests and hence the internationalization of sports. Since such a body is mainly western in its biases, it helps in spreading the cultural values of the western world in a more subtle way since it cannot be readily identified with any particular national government. In this way it is probably a more efficient means of diffusing western notions of body culture than agencies more obviously linked to a particular country.

Private sports investment, on the other hand, is reminiscent of the situation which existed in the third world in the 1970s when private banks assumed the role of governments in the provision of loans and investments. As part of the development of Kenyan athletics an American firm, John Hancock Financial Services of Boston, has recently signed a contract with the Kenyan AAA which sponsors the development of track and field to the amount of 1.2 million Kenyan shillings. This reduces dependency on the government but private firms tend to be driven by profit motives and self-interest.

Kenyan Influences

The previous paragraphs show that in addition to US college migration, the international sports system has impacted in a number of ways on the development of Kenyan track and field. Kenya itself, of course, is part of that system and the development of various heroic role models (Maiyoro, Keino, Jipcho) cannot be underestimated in the range of factors influencing the growth of Kenyan sports. President Moi, a great lover of sport, has also played a leading role in sports development, culminating in the establishment of a separate department of sport. The government is also likely to provide support for sport, given that track and field – while not as popular as soccer in Kenya itself – is probably *the* major focus for image projection overseas.

CONCLUSION

We have yet to identify the precise roles of several of the elements of the system which has been identified in this chapter. There is also much to be done in the exploration and explication of analogies and homologies between the global sports system and the global economic system and corresponding relationships between sports and societal development. What we have done, however, is to question the causal link between the recruitment of Kenyan athletes to US colleges and the growth in prominence of Kenyan track and field. In this way the notion of 'Americanization', while far from absent, seems to be a less appropriate notion than globalization – or 'mundialization' in Wagner's (1990) terms. We have suggested that much of Kenyan athletics remains underdeveloped, notably in the various field events at the global, though not continental scale. Finally, we have tried to counter Heinilä's suggestion that elite sports should be viewed as the outcome of national systems and have, instead, suggested that a global system approach must be invoked in order to appreciate fully the changes in national body and movement cultures.

NOTES

1 1984 is regarded as a typical year. We are not yet in a position to explore long-term changes in the athletic map of Africa.
2 By world-class is meant those athletes achieving a performance capable of being ranked in the top 100 in the world in any one year. Such world ranking lists have been produced annually since the early 1950s (for example, Matthews, 1989).
3 By elite is meant those college athletes included in the US top 50 for any year. Such ranking lists have been published annually in *Track and Field News* since the late 1940s. Foreign athletes are usually identified by national origin and college attended.
4 These data are taken from various issues of the *International Athletics Annual*, published by the Association of Track and Field Statisticians since the early 1950s (for example, Matthews, 1989).

REFERENCES

Abmayr, W. (1982 *et seq*) *Track and Field Best Performances, Kenya* (Nairobi: Abmayr).
Bale, J. (1979) 'A Geography of World Class Track and Field Athletics', *Sports Exchange World*, 4, 26–31.
(1982) *Sport and Place* (London: Hurst).
(1985) 'Towards a Geography of International Sport', Occasional paper No. 8, Department of Geography, Loughborough University.

(1989) *Sports Geography* (London: Spon.).

(1991) *The Brawn Drain; Foreign Student-Athletes in American Universities* (Urbana, Il: University of Illinois Press).

Ballinger, L. (1981) *In Your Face! Sports for Love or Money* (Chicago: Vanguard)

Boit, M. (1988) 'Track Scholarships: The Pros and Cons', unpublished paper, Department of PE, Kenyatta University.

Eichberg, H. (1984) 'Olympic Sport: Neo-colonialism and Alternatives', *International Review for the Sociology of Sport*, 19,1, 97–105.

(1990) 'Forward Race and the Laughter of Pygmies; On Olympic Sport', in Teich, M. and Porter, R. (eds), *Fin de Siècle and its Legacy* (Cambridge: Cambridge University Press) pp. 115–31.

Galtung, J. (1984) 'Sport and International Understanding: Sport as a Carrier of Deep Structure and Culture', in Ilmarinen, M. (ed.), *Sport and International Understanding* (New York: Springer-Verlag) pp. 12–19.

Heinilä, K. (1967) 'Notes on Inter-group Conflict in International Sport' in Dunning, E. (ed.), *The Sociology of Sport* (London: Cass).

(1984) 'The Totalization Process in International Sport' in Ilmarinen, M. (ed.), *Sport and International Understanding* (New York: Springer-Verlag).

Hollander, T. (1980) 'A Geographical Analysis of Foreign Intercollegiate Track and Field Athletes in the United States', unpublished master's dissertation, Eastern Michigan Univesity.

Klein, A. (1991) *Sugarball: the American Game, the Dominican Dream* (New Haven, CT: Yale University Press).

Mandle, J.R. and Mandle, J.D. (1990) 'Basketball, Civil Society and the Post Colonial State in the Commonwealth Caribbean', *Journal of Sport and Social Issues*, 14,2, 59–75.

Mangan, J. (1986) *The Games Ethic and Imperialism* (London: Viking).

Manners, J. (1975) 'African Recruiting Boom', in Prokop, D. (ed.), *The African Running Revolution* (Mountain View, CA: World Publications).

Matthews, P. (ed.) (1989) *Athletics '89/90: the International Track and Field Annual* (London: Sports World).

McWhirter, N. (1954) *Athletics World*, 8.

Meinertzhagen, R. (1957) *Kenya Diary 1902–1906* (London: Oliver & Boyd).

Monnington, T. (1985) 'The Politics of Black African Sport', in Allison, L. (ed.), *The Politics of Sport* (Manchester: Manchester University Press).

Peet, R. (1986) 'The Destruction of Regional Cultures', in Johnston, R. and Taylor, P. (eds), *A World in Crisis? Geographical Perspectives* (Oxford: Blackwell).

Rooney, J. (1972) *A Geography of American Sport: From Cabin Creek to Anaheim* (Reading, MA: Addison-Wesley).

Stabler, E. (1969) *Education Since Uhuru* (Middletown, CT: Wesleyan University Press).

Stidwill, H. and Flath, A. (1985) 'The Internationalization of Track and Field at American Universities', *Journal of Comparative Physical Education and Sport*, 7,2, 26–42.

Wagner, E. (1990) 'Sport in Asia and Africa: Americanization or Mundialization?', *Sociology of Sport Journal*, 7,4, 378–88.

15

American Labour Migrants, Globalization and the Making of English Basketball

Joseph Maguire

For those directly involved in English basketball, the players, officials and spectators, a grasp of the interconnections between the movement of players from one country to another, the cultural meaning and significance of the game and its place within the development of global sport is probably lost in an understandable concern with what appears to be the 'here and now'. Though this 'involved' perspective is vital in probing how those caught up in sports labour migration experience this process, a more 'detached' perspective is also needed in order to place the experience of any one individual on a broader canvas.

The trans-national migration of sports talent, whether in basketball or in other sports, captures but one, albeit important, part of global sports development which is, in turn, interconnected with broader global change. There are arguably other elements involved which need to be probed in conjunction with the global movement of sports labour. These elements include cultural, technological, ideological and economic processes which are trans-national in character (Maguire, 1991). It is the intention of this study critically to explore the transformation of English basketball in the light of these issues.

SPORTS MIGRATION AND GLOBALIZATION

When reference is made to the idea of a global culture there is a danger, as Featherstone has noted, in overstating the case for homogeneity and integration (Featherstone, 1990). This tendency is in no small measure due to the potentially unwise association of the idea of a global culture with the culture of any one nation-state. A process-sociological perspective tackles the problem in terms of the globalization of human interdependencies (Mennell, 1990). Indeed, such an approach also suggests that the tendency towards dichotomous thinking regarding global culture is also inappropriate. Instead of endlessly arguing about whether homogeneity or heterogeneity, integration or disintegration, unity or diversity are evident, it is more adequate to see these processes as interwoven. nor is it a question of either/ors but rather of balances and blends.

If the analysis moves towards a concern with what Sklair (1991) describes as trans-national practices, then the observer is better placed to note that there is something more at work than merely flows between nation-states. It may well be that trans-national practices, which take a variety of cultural forms, gain a degree of relative autonomy on a global level. Referring to what he terms trans-societal processes, Robertson (1990) maintains that it is these which sustain the exchange and flow of goods, people, information, knowledge and images. It is not difficult to see how sports labour migrants in general or American basketball players in particular fit in as part of this overall process.

It is important to probe the existence of these relatively autonomous trans-national practices, seemingly possessing a dynamic of their own. But in so doing, it is also important not to overlook the fact that national agencies and trans-national agencies such as the International Olympic Committee, or groups such as those which Sklair (1991) terms the 'transnational capitalist class', will attempt to manipulate and control such practices. Such interventions give rise to cultural struggles of various kinds and at different levels. These issues also surface in the transformation of English basketball and will be returned to in due course. For now, it is important to note that these trans-cultural or globalization processes emerged between the fifteenth and eighteenth centuries and have been gathering momentum since the turn of the present century (Robertson, 1990).

A number of the more recent features of these processes can be identified. These include an increase in the number of international agencies; the growth of increasingly global forms of communication; the development of global competitions and prizes; and the development of standard notions of 'rights' and citizenship that are increasingly standardized internationally. The emergence and spread of sport is clearly interwoven with this overall process. The development of international sports organizations, the growth of competition among national team, the worldwide acceptance of rules governing specific sport forms, and the establishment of global competitions such as the Olympic games and soccer's World Cup tournament are all indicative of the occurrence of globalization in the sports world.

If Robertson is correct, then neither the broader globalization processes nor those identified here which relate to sport are the direct outcome of inter-state processes. Rather, these processes need to be accounted for in relation to how they operate relatively independently of conventionally designated societal and socio-cultural processes. It is perhaps a point which those researchers who have examined the development of sport have yet to appreciate fully. While the globalization of sport is connected to the intended ideological practices of specific groups of people from particular countries, its pattern and development cannot be reduced to these ideological practices. Out of the plans and intentions of these groups something that was neither planned nor intended emerged: the globalization of human inter-dependencies.

In this connection Appadurai (1990) is, in part, correct to emphasize the disjunction between the cultural flows which he sees as characterizing globalization processes. Global flows are seen to occur in and through the growing disjunctures between what he calls 'ethnoscapes', 'technoscapes', 'financescapes', 'mediascapes' and 'ideoscapes'. The sheer speed, scale and volume of each of these flows is such that the disjunctures have become central to the politics of global culture. Given the concerns of the present study, it is necessary to consider these cultural flows in a little more detail: 'ethnoscapes' involve the international movement of such people as tourists, migrants, exiles and guestworkers; 'technoscapes' are created by the flow between countries of the machinery and plant produced by corporations (transnational as well as national) and government agencies; 'financescapes' centre on the rapid flow of money and its equivalents around the currency markets and stock exchanges of the world; 'mediascapes' entail the flow of images and information between countries and are produced and distributed by newspapers, magazines, radio, television and films; and, finally, 'ideoscapes' are linked to the flow of ideas centrally associated with state or counter-state ideologies and movements.

The speed, scale and volume of sports development is interwoven with these global cultural flows: a probing of sporting 'ethnoscapes', for example, reveals that the global migration of both professional and college sports personnel was a pronounced feature of sports development in the 1980s. The flow from country to country of sports goods, equipment and 'landscapes' (for example, golf courses or artificial playing surfaces) has grown to such an extent that it is currently a multi-billion dollar business and represents a development in sports at he level of 'technoscapes'. At the level of 'financescapes' stands the act that the flow of finance in the global sports arena has come to entre not only on the international trade in sports personnel, prize noney and endorsements, but on the marketing of sport along pecific, often American, lines. The transformation of English and ndeed European basketball is no exception to this.

Crucial in all these regards, of course, has been a development at the evel of 'mediascapes', more particularly the development of a 'media–port production complex' which projects images to large global udiences. Attention will be paid to this in the concluding section to his chapter. It can also be observed that, at the level of 'ideoscapes', lobal sports festivals such as the Olympics, the Asian games and the 'an-American games have come to serve as vehicles for the expression f ideologies that are not only national in character (the Berlin, Moscow and Los Angeles Olympics) but are also trans-national in heir consequences. Though these cultural flows do interweave in a vay which has a relative autonomy from the plans and intentions of articular groups of people within any one nation-state, trans-national orporation or sports organization, it is also necessary to probe how uch groups attempt to define and regulate the cultural access for hemselves and others to these cultural flows. These attempts are also ound up in a series of power struggles (Maguire, 1990).

As sports migration is the central concern in this context, it is ppropriate to concentrate on one aspect of the cultural flows dentified, namely changes at the level of 'financescapes'. Here hanges have centred on the demonopolization of economic structures n the world economy, with the concomitant deregulation and globali-ation of markets, trade and labour. The globalization of capital has lso entailed the globalization of the market in services to finance, ommerce and industry (Dezalay, 1990). Crucially, this has led to a lew category of professionals. These include international lawyers, orporate tax accountants, financial advisers and management consul-ants. It is this group which emerged in the context of the attempts by rans-national corporations to chart and formalize the newly globalized conomic arena. In certain key respects, some elite sports labour nigrants embody the characteristics of this new breed of entre-reneurs. Reference to how Dezalay reviews the activities of the new rofessionals identified can help illuminate this issue:

> In putting themselves at the service of the market, and becoming entrepreneurial service providers who are more interested in economic return than justice, aren't these new mercenaries

('hired guns') in the employ of capital squandering the stock of legitimacy and credibility built up by their 'gentleman lawyer' predecessors? (Dezalay, 1990: 279).

For Dezalay the deregulation and globalization of the market for legal and financial services has led to an emphasis in the professional craft of those involved which centres on technical competence aggressive tactics and a meritocratic ethos. Gone are the quasi aristocratic 'fair play' values of an older generation of lawyers and advisers. These new professionals present themselves as sweeping away archaic practices, replacing them with modern and highly rational decision-making. Yet, as Dezalay remarks, 'their real ambi tion is to occupy a strategic and intermediary position as much a relating to internal transactions in the field of economic power as to those that mesh with the field of political power' (Dezalay, 1990: 284) The prototype of this new regime is the corporate law firm of the United States. For Dezalay, a complete remodelling of legal culture has occurred and can be said to involve a process of Americanization Dezalay concludes:

> The opening and expansion of the market in legal services has unleashed a process of homogenization and of interconnection between national legal systems which until now have strongly preserved their own identities. The breaking down of barriers favours the strongest performers – in this case, the great North American firms – and forces the others to align themselves on their model if they wish to survive (Dezalay, 1990: 285).

Before consideration is given to both the adequacy and applicability of this analysis to the issue of sports migrants, one further point regarding the deregulation and globalization of activities within other professions is required. Reviewing King's (1990) work on design professionals in areas such as architecture and advertising, Feather-stone observes that this new band of specialists not only work outside the traditional professional and organizational cultures of the nation-state, they also experience the problems of inter-cultural communica-tion at first hand. Further, the constant moving back and forth between different cultures means that such groups must develop new types of flexible personal controls, dispositions and means of orien-tation. In developing this new type of habitus, such people frequently work in and inhabit a specific type of urban space: the redeveloped inner-city areas.

Though there is as yet no systematic research on the details of these
ssues, from the evidence so far to hand it does appear that there are
ome parallels between these 'new professionals' and sectors of elite
ports labour migration. The introduction of competition and market
mperatives in the world of law has also been a more pronounced
eature of the sports world over the past decade. The quasi-aristocratic
otions of the legal profession and the amateur ideology of elite sports
dministrators have been superseded by the need to compete in the
narket place. The globalization of the market for legal services is also
aralleled by the globalization of the market for sports services.

With the removal of the 'old-boy' networks, a new generation of
gents and organizations, such as Mark McCormack and his Inter-
ational Marketing Group, entrepreneurs establishing grand prix
ircuits in sports such as tennis and athletics and media-sport produc-
ion executives creating sport spectacles by employing elite sport
nigrants to perform exhibition bouts or contests – the equivalent of
Dezalay's 'hired guns' in North American law firms – have traversed
he globe in search of new markets. As with the globalization of legal
ervices, so too in relation to sport are elements of an Americanization
process evident (Maguire, 1990). The pervasiveness of this American
practice in sports such as American football, basketball and baseball
as forced a range of sports to align themselves to this model if they
vish to survive in the global media market place.

Whereas the new generation of lawyers are less tied to notions of
community and disavow a sense of *noblesse oblige*, they actively
embrace the marketing techniques disdained by their predecessors.
Likewise, the new generation of sports migrants – such as tennis star
van Lendl, the Romanian middle-distance runner Doina Melinte, or
he Americans plying their trade in the World League of American
Football – appear to have little sense of attachment to a specific space
or community. Observe the phenomena of a former English international soccer player (Jack Charlton) managing the Eire national
soccer squad or of South Africans such as Zola Budd and Alan Lamb
epresenting Great Britain in athletics and England in cricket respect-
vely. Though varying in form and intensity, and from one sport form
o another, elite sports migrants increasingly demand and, to a degree,
chieve, 'freedom of contract' and free movement of labour rights.
Their talent is determined by highly rational and technical criteria and
heir worth assessed according to market value. Just as the new
generation of lawyers stress technical competency, aggressive tactics
and a meritocratic ethos, sports migrants embrace the ethos of hard

work, differential rewards and a win-at-all-costs approach. The occu pational subculture of some elite sports migrants, in ice hockey for example, is dominated by aggressive and violent tactics (Smith, 1983). Those who cannot take the pressure, 'burn out' and become expend able: young women tennis players, for example.

As Dezalay noted, those lawyers who adopt such practices are thus 'perfect auxiliaries to the new breed of corporate raiders'. One has only to think of the 'rebel' cricket and rugby union tours to South Africa to understand how sports migrants can act as mercenaries for 'big business'. In some instances, the link between corporate raider and sports migrants is only too clear. Take, for example, the World Series Cricket organized by Kerry Packer or the activities of Alan Bond with the America's Cup sailing competition.

Sports migrants also have elements in common with the new generation of design professionals. They, too, work outside the traditional professional and organization cultures of the nation-state. By definition, sport migrants are on the move. In some sports, such as in golf, tennis, formula one motor-racing and Alpine skiing, the sport migrant has an almost nomadic lifestyle. In other sports, for example cricket and rugby, there is a seasonal dimension, sports migrants moving between the northern and southern hemispheres.

Along with this movement come problems of 'dislocation' and, as King noted, problems of inter-cultural communication. Witness the 'babel-like' quality of global sports festivals or tournaments. For sport migrants such a social milieu involves a multi-layered form of inter cultural communication centring on interaction with fellow players, coaches, officials, the crowd and media personnel. As with design professionals, so too with sports migrants: such interaction necessitates the adoption of new types of flexible personal controls. In the world of European soccer, Swedes, Danes, Dutchmen and Germans appear adept at handling this process, often communicating with ease in several different languages. For people from some cultural back grounds, however, it may be that specific problems are more evident. The experience in Italy of British soccer players such as Denis Law and Ian Rush highlights how being a sports migrant can engender a sense of 'dislocation'. A number of elite sports migrants, in a manner similar to design professionals and lawyers, also work in and inhabit a specific type of urban space. Think of the redeveloped city areas now occupied by sport-workplaces such as the Skydome in Toronto, the Globe in Stockholm and the Palais Omnisports in Paris.

At this point it is appropriate to consider how research findings illuminate the way in which the transformation of English basketball, and the role played by American sports migrants in this process, is part of the globalization processes so far identified.

AMERICAN SPORTS MIGRANTS, NEW CAPITAL AND THE TRANSFORMATION OF ENGLISH BASKETBALL

Since the foundation of the National Basketball League (NBL) in 1972, English basketball has undergone a transformation in a number of key respects. Elite participants have shifted from being amateur 'home-based' players to achievement-oriented migrants and 'indigenous' workers. The game itself has become a commodity competing in the media and sponsorship market place. As part of this process of competing with other sport forms, the cultural meaning of the game has shifted in the direction of 'spectacle'. This overall commodification process has engendered a number of strains and tensions which are also bound up with the 'Americanization' of the game. This is evident in the expansion of the league, the concomitant growth in attendances and increased media coverage and sponsorship.

Dovetailing with this commodification process, Americanization involved the recruitment of American sports migrants as players and coaches, the adoption of American-style marketing strategies and media coverage, and a change in the ideological messages underpinning the game centring on American spectacle and entertainment. Centrally, these processes were marked by conflicts between the desire of a new breed of club owners and their auxiliaries, the American sports migrants, to provide an instant commercial product to 'display' to spectators, and the aspiration of more established officials of the English Basketball Association (EBBA) to build the foundations for the long-term playing success of 'English' basketball.

Some of these trends did not escape the notice of commentators within the game. Take the following remarks made in 1985 by Richard Taylor, then editor of the sport's premier magazine *Basketball Monthly*:

> Coaches, usually Americans, respond to the pressures on them in totally understandable ways. When they have the money they recruit new players, with dual nationals, former dual nationals and naturalised Americans almost always to the fore, to add to their two foreign (American) players (*Basketball Monthly*, March 1985).

Such comments provide anecdotal evidence to support the notion

Table 15.1 Sports migrants and 'indigenous' labour in Division One of the English National Basketball League.

Year	Sports Migrants American	Dual/English acquired	Indigenous English	Total	% Foreign
1982–83	26	12	93	131	29%
1983–84	28	11	98	137	28.4%
1984–85	31	16	114	161	29.1%
1985–86	35	16	103	154	33.1%

that a process of sports migration, closely linked to the movement of people from one specific society to England, took place during the 1980s. The available substantive evidence appears to bear out this conclusion. Table 15.1, based on an analysis of players rosters of first-division clubs between 1982 and 1986 highlights the significant involvement of American migrants.

In the first year of the NBL only two sports migrants were registered. However, between 1982 and 1986 American sports migrants accounted for some 20.5 per cent of the total number of players. When players designated as 'dual nationals' or 'English acquired' are combined with 'Americans', the trend towards Americanization is further established. In all cases those players classified as 'dual nationals' or 'English acquired' grew up and learned their basketball in North America. 'Foreign' thus denotes a combination of these two categories. Between 1982 and 1986, therefore, the involvement of 'American' sports migrants averaged 30 per cent. The central importance of these sports migrants to team success is revealed by Table 15.2. In each of four performance measures, these Americans were much more successful than English players.

Offensively, Americans dominated the top ten ranking positions throughout the period under consideration. They were key performers in terms of assists, scoring and rebounding. This evidence indicates both the extent of sports migrant involvement and their domination of teams in terms of 'starting fives' and court time. The English players tended to occupy supporting positions. In addition, while this evidence does not reveal it, the gradual erosion of the dominance of those white Britons who had traditionally played the game also involved a shift in the ethnic composition of teams.

This phenomenon is of interest to a wider study of sports labour migration, raising issues of both racism and ethnicity within American college sport and the post-college experiences of large numbers of

Table 15.2   Analysis of Top 10 Performers in Division One of the English National Basketball League

Year	Points			Rebounding			Floor shots			Assists		
	A	D	E	A	D	E	A	D	E	A	D	E
1982–83	9	1	0	7	2	1	7	1	2	5	3	2
1983–84	9	1	0	9	1	0	6	2	2	7	1	2
1984–85	8	2	0	8	1	0	7	3	0	8	0	2
1985–86	9	1	0	9	1	0	6	2	2	8	0	2

Key: A = American, D = Dual national = Sport migrants. E= English = Indigenous labour. N = 10.

black Americans. For present purposes, it is necessary to focus on how the general American sports migration process identified has been bound up with the commodification process referred to earlier. What were the essential developmental characteristics of this process? Formed in 1936 as the Amateur Basketball Association, the governing body of the English game assumed its present title, the English Basketball Association, in 1974. During the hegemony of the ABA, there were several attempts made to form a national league. None was successful. Up to the late 1960s, the game remained amateur, tied to voluntary organizations and university teams, and was supported by only a small band of devotees. By and large, it was played, controlled and administered by the same group of British nationals.

It was not until 1972 that the present National Basketball League (NBL) was formed. In order to accomplish this, the EBBA, and not the clubs, made available a significant sum of money from its reserves. Of the six teams involved in the NBL in 1972–73, one was connected with a voluntary organization and another represented a branch of the armed services. The remaining teams were, by and large, unsponsored and 'amateur' in outlook, but occasionally playing an overseas player who 'happened' to be living, working or studying in the local community. A sense of continuity with the past was evident.

A number of processes were at work, however, which contributed to a desire to attract income from both paying spectators and sponsorship. By the following season, at least four of the eight teams involved were formally sponsored by such companies as the tobacco firm WD & HO Wills. This was to prove catalytic in both the commodification of basketball and the American sports migration process that went along with it. Between 1972 and 1988, the league expanded from 6 to 52 teams, 45 of them defined as 'senior'. This process of expansion is shown in Table 15.3.

Table 15.3   The expansion of the National Basketball League, 1972–88

	NBL TEAMS				
	Division 1 Men	Division 2 Men	Division 1 Women	Division 2 Women	Junior Men	TOTAL
1972–73	6	0	0	0	0	6
1973–74	8	0	0	0	0	8
1974–75	10	0	0	0	0	10
1975–76	10	7	6	0	0	23
1976–77	10	11	8	7	0	36
1977–78	10	11	8	6	7	42
1978–79	11	10	8	10	11	50
1979–80	10	8	8	12	15	53
1980–81	10	9	8	13	13	53
1981–82	12	9	9	14	16	60
1982–83	13	12	10	15	18	68
1983–84	13	13	10	14	21	71
1984–85	14	12	12	9	19	66
1985–86	15	12	12	10	18	67
1986–87	13	11	11	10	17	62
1987–88	15*	10	10	10	7	52

* During the 1987–88 season, the owners of the Division One Men's clubs formed their own league.

The data indicate a significant expansion of the NBL over the period but do not however, reveal the degree of volatility in the NBL: although the *overall* number of teams in the league may have remained the same, or indeed increased from one season to the next, there was in fact a significant turnover in the participating clubs. This took two main forms: teams either went out of existence or changed the name of their club on several occasions. None of the original founding men's clubs is presently in the league and some 27 others have also folded or withdrawn (EBBA, 1987). A number of teams playing in the league in the late 1980s, such as Leicester Riders/City Bus and Polycell Kingston have had several different previous names. In the case of the club currently located in Kingston, a suburb of London, the club has not only had at least seven name changes but was also relocated to Scotland only to return subsequently to its original home. More often than not, such changes have been connected to changes in ownership or sponsorship. This growth in sponsorship is shown in Table 15.4.

Table 15.4 charts the position of all the men's teams in the NBL between 1972 and 1987. If one looks only at division one clubs, the growth of sponsorships is even more dramatic. Division one clubs

Table 15.4   NBL Men's Division One and Two Teams including the name of a sponsor in their Official Title, 1972–87

	Sponsored	Unsponsored		Sponsored	Unsponsored
1972–73	0	6	1980–81	10	9
1973–74	4	4	1981–82	10	11
1974–75	4	6	1982–83	11	14
1975–76	6	11	1983–84	16	10
1976–77	8	9	1984–85	16	10
1977–78	11	10	1985–86	16	10
1978–79	13	8	1986–87	14	10
1979–80	10	8			

Table 15.5   Sponsorship of the National Basketball League 1972–88

	Sponsor		Sponsor
1972–73	None	1981–82	Just Juice
1973–74	Clark's Men's Shoes	1982–83	Just Juice
1974–75	Clark's Men's Shoes	1983–84	Wimpey Homes
1975–76	None	1984–85	Wimpey Homes
1976–77	None	1985–86	Carlsberg
1977–78	None	1986–87	Carlsberg
1978–79	Rotary Watches	1987–88	Carlsberg
1979–80	Rotary Watches		
1980–81	Rotary Watches		

nearly always include the name of a sponsor in their official title. As early as 1973–74, the NBL itself was sponsored and renamed the Clark's Men's Shoes League. Since then, the league has continued to be associated with a sponsor and, as Table 15.5 shows, has been named after a number of different companies.

Sponsorship of the league was also combined with sponsorship of clubs. Initially the sponsors of teams tended to be small companies from the local area. Teams such as Wilson Panthers, Magnet Wicksteed Metros and Swithland Motors All Stars were soon displaced, however, by teams with larger budgets sponsored by national and trans-national corporations. These corporations, competing as they were in the global market place, were well aware of the marketing potential of sport to cross national boundaries. In fact since the foundation of the league there has been an increasing trend for trans-national corporations such as Fiat, Talbot Cars, Cinzano, Nissan and

Sharp to sponsor specific teams. The influx of money allowed clubs to establish themselves as limited companies. Thus, by 1984–85, of the 26 men's teams playing in the first two division of the NBL all but two were listed in the league handbook as being limited companies.

Increasingly the game became subject to market pressures: its success being tied to its market value. That is, the viability of clubs became more and more dependent on income derived from spectators and sponsors. This commodification process allowed the recruitment of American sports migrants to become a formal strategy of the clubs. Those clubs who were in favour of recruiting Americans tended to couch their arguments in terms of the advantages gained in relation to playing standards, entertainment value and increased gates. Take the comments made by Mike Ainger, a member of the Sutton and Crystal Palace club, in 1975: 'The introduction of American players . . . has [led to] increased publicity, which can only be good for English basketball . . . Please administrators, encourage top Americans to come to England' (*Basketball Monthly*, Spring 1975).

The utilization of American imports was, in fact, initially promoted by all groups connected with the game. The hope was that the 'entertainment' they would provide would produce several benefits, but above all more sponsorship and media coverage, increased attendance figures, greater participation rates and improved playing standards. That some of the aims of the advocates of these benefits have been achieved can be shown in several ways.

In 1972–73, total NBL attendance figures stood at 7.500. By 1984–85, the number of spectators watching NBL games had risen to over 330,000. Attendance figures at the National Championship Play-offs had grown from 650 in 1970, to 8,000 in 1978, and to 18,300 in 1984 (EBBA 1987). Regular participation in basketball both in schools and in local clubs had also increased from 240,000 in 1972 to 1,150,000 in 1981 (EBBA 1987). Accompanying this expansion was an increase in media attention. Table 15.6 highlights the growth in national and regional television coverage.

Over the period in question, the commodification and Americanization of the game brought major changes. The structure of the league had expanded. The game had grown at the grass roots level but was also increasingly 'sold' as a commodity to the media–sport production complex. The status and competition of the playing personnel had also undergone changes. Now players were workers who, by and large, were drawn from foreign lands. These processes had also entailed a shift in the ownership and control of the game. New entrepreneurs have moved into the game and struggled with 'traditionalists' who

Table 15.6   National and Regional Television Coverage of the NBL, 1976–84.
(EBBA 1987)

	Number of Minutes		Number of Minutes
1976–77	40	1980–81	600
1977–78	Unavailable	1981–82	640
1978–79	250	1982–83	1500
1979–80	580	1983–84	1640

sought to develop the game along a different trajectory. In order to trace how the issue of American sport 'imports' was bound up, and arguably seen as a symbol of, this contested commodification process, reference to the competing plans and intentions of the different groups surrounding the transformation of English basketball is required.

AMERICAN BASKETBALL MIGRATION AS CONTESTED TERRAIN: A PLAYER CIRCUS OR ROLE MODELS FOR 'NATIVE' BRITONS?

Up to 1975, the number of American players involved in English basketball was limited but growing. Indeed, their continued recruitment was seen as essential to attracting publicity which would lead to greater sponsorship. Vic Ambler, then England coach, appears to have recognized this when he wrote in the summer 1975 edition of *Basketball Monthly* that 'the building of a cultural image of basketball via publicity is crucial to our problems'. Discontent, however, was beginning to emerge. The comments of Roy Packham, another English coach, were indicative of this discontent:

> The amount of effort and publicity that is devoted to the promotion of senior basketball through the press, television etc. is very apparent, but how much of our administration is given over to the promotion and encouragement of junior basketball? By concentrating so much on senior basketball, are we not attempting to build a pyramid from the top to the bottom? (*Basketball Monthly*, Easter 1975).

Packham's comments illustrate a central focus of the tensions which then existed in the sport and were also a precursor for a more vehement debate. The impact of the trends which Packham was critical of had, however, a more immediate effect. Financial problems dogged two of the original founding clubs, Avenue and Loughborough All Stars. An anonymous writer commented on this situation: 'Avenue and Loughborough All Stars have always concentrated on producing their own players. But without money or Americans, they may find the problem of keeping up with the top squads is too much for them' (*Basketball Monthly*, Autumn 1976).

By 1977–78, both sides had withdrawn from the league. The university and college teams which had contested nine finals between 1961 and 1972 also withdrew at the end of the following season. This turnover of clubs continued to characterize the development of the league. The strongest sides were those who combined the recruitment of top Americans with significant sponsorship from large transnational corporations. Despite some internal dissension, the EBBA publicly welcomed this commercialization and in its annual reports of 1977–78 and 1978–79 praised the increased media attention and growth in sponsorship.

During 1977–78, the influx of American sports migrants began to cause concern to the National Executive Committee of the EBBA. At a meeting in April 1977, while it agreed that two foreign migrants per club would continue to be permitted, it also expressed reservations regarding this influx. In the same month, Ian Day, a leading English player, critically reviewed the trends towards the commodification of the game and the recruitment of overseas migrants:

> Basketball has become a commercial enterprise where the Americans are viewed in terms of financial investment. Money buys better players which buys success which in its turn buys more money from the sponsor. It has been proven that you can buy success (*Basketball Monthly*, April 1977).

The recruitment of this American migrant labour stemmed from the perceived need to compete with other sport forms in marketing the game to the media–sport production complex. Writing later in the same year, an anonymous author made a number of observations which bear this out:

> The media have shown more interest on account of increasing crowds and the sponsors have ploughed in large sums of money. Dare our sport, on the point of a major breakthrough into TV risk losing the crowds, the media and with them the sponsors? [The] Americans are needed to retain spectator interest and with it the sponsors (*Basketball Monthly*, Summer 1977).

Such observations not only highlight what one might call the commodification and 'spectacularization' of the game, but also illustrate the struggle for ascendancy in basketball. Fear of the commercial consequences of the removal of the American sports migrants from the league and a relative loss of power to the increasingly commercially oriented clubs, resulted in English players, coaches and the EBBA becoming marginalized. The number of Americans allowed per club remained at two. Some officials within the EBBA, however, did seek to limit even further the number of sports migrants being recruited by the clubs. The coaching subcommittee of the EBBA recommended, for example, the restriction of American players to one per club. A writer in *Basketball Monthly* (Summer 1977) noted that the proposal faces a predictably rough passage' at the hands of those 'concerned to attract spectators to the game'.

Officials and coaches concerned with the development of native English players were losing ground to those who advocated the need to recruit American players in order to provide an entertainment package which would attract spectators, media coverage and sponsorship. Highlighting the last two, Peter Sprogis, then Development Officer of the EBBA, whose duties included media relations and sponsorship, argued with respect to attendances and media coverage that:

> The two go together, because until we get big crowds for all the clubs the media will not be really interested from the point of view of their readership. I would like to bring a top NBA promoter over from the States for seminars (*Basketball Monthly*, February 1978).

These comments not only reveal the extent to which officials of the EBBA were, by that time, concerned to market the game, but also indicate that Americanization was not confined to player imports. Looking across the Atlantic for models to follow, the EBBA focused its attention on the marketing strategies adopted by the National Football League and the National Basketball Association.

As with the law firms described by Dezalay, the North American marketing models were setting the agenda for sports organizations. In particular, the EBBA proposed the adoption of a 'group marketing philosophy' in which all clubs in the league would be marketed as a single package to sponsors. The following comments by Mel Welch, a leading figure in the EBBA, illustrate the extent to which American marketing models were dependent upon access to the media–sport production complex:

Ten years ago, basketball in Britain was a sport for enthusiastic players. There was little spectator following and virtually no media coverage. Then came sponsorship, and basketball is now on the verge of being regarded as a major sport in this country. Basketball has exploded. But as with any explosion, there have been casualties. Sponsorship is like a drug in that, just like with an addict, there are withdrawal symptoms. . . . [But] sponsorship, basketball and television are now inextricably linked, and sponsorship of basketball will continue to increase as TV coverage increases (*Basketball Monthly*, February 1980).

The 'casualties' to which Welch referred have involved changes which may be seen as those which accompany any sport which undergoes rapid commercialization. As has already been noted, at least 27 clubs had left the league by the late 1980s and spectators at most clubs had been faced with several changes to the names of the teams they followed. Not only have teams changed their names but a number have been taken over and their league franchises transferred to different parts of the country. The entry into the league of two teams owned by soccer clubs, Manchester United FC and Portsmouth FC, are examples of this process. Previously they had been owned by local entrepreneurs, from Manchester and the West Midlands respectively. Yet this involvement was short term. Both soccer clubs had ended their involvement by the late 1980s.

The recruitment of American sports migrants paralleled these developments. Whereas in the early stages of the NBL, concern had been expressed over the number of American imports, towards the end of the 1970s and in the early 1980s criticism of the number of 'dual nationals' began to rise. The system of 'dual nationality' involved the fact that, while a particular team could have two foreign players on its roster, they could also add Americans to their squad if they could claim British nationality. Given the rationale underpinning the commodification of basketball, it is not surprising that clubs sought to exploit this loophole.

By the early 1980s, the question of dual nationals had become, according to Richard Taylor 'the most contentious issue in English basketball' (*Basketball Monthly*, January 1981). In the preceding month, the National League Committee recommended that teams should be allowed only three spots for non-English players. Taylor subsequently suggested that 'legal action and withdrawal from the league were mentioned as possible outcomes if this proposal was accepted by the National Executive'. The fact that the National

Executive did not endorse the recommendation is arguably indicative of the erosion of EBBA power in the wake of commodification. Within ten months, the EBBA was issuing temporary British licences to Americans who had not yet received British passports! The growth in the number of migrants designated as 'dual nationals' and 'English acquired' – players who had served a minimum residence period – continued. The recommendations by the National League Committee had, however, sown the seed of dissent among the clubs. Not content just to frustrate these recommendations, the clubs sought to increase their power. It was noted that:

> Division One Men's clubs are moving towards the formation of a new body to represent their views within the spectrum of English basketball. The former National Basketball League Committee was not reconstituted after the Annual Meeting . . . and talks have been held to replace it. The old NBL Committee was itself formed at the wishes of the clubs, but pressure began building against it after a number of recommendations were poorly received, particularly one concerning the eligibility of foreign and dual national players (*Basketball Monthly*, December 1981).

The recommendations centred on limiting the number of American migrants but the clubs' dissatisfaction with the governing body also involved the distribution of the income derived from sponsorship. Responding to this criticism, the EBBA adopted a group marketing strategy. This move, however, can also be seen as symptomatic of the commodification of the game and as the initial step in a move by the clubs to break away from the EBBA and to form their own league. The formation of what came to be called the 'Carlsberg League' took place in time for the start of the 1987–88 season.

In the early 1980s, the move of the EBBA towards group marketing appeared to be successful. According to its own figures, media coverage had increased by 77.9 per cent in 1980–81 compared with the previous season, and a large sponsorship of the league had been secured. The EBBA realized that it was now essential to secure substantial television exposure. This was not long delayed. Peter Sprogis commented on the significance of the television contract worked out in that context:

> These deals will totally change basketball in this country . . . It's the first time in Europe that clubs in a league have agreed to give up their own individual sponsorship deals and pool their market-

ing rights . . . It will put English basketball on a business footing comparable to the way pro-basketball, football and soccer are run in the United States (*Daily Mail*, 20 January 1982).

In placing basketball on what Sprogis termed a 'business footing' (in other words, the American model), the game came under increasing pressure not simply to perform in front of the cameras but also to entertain. Take the remarks made by Adrian Metcalfe, the Commissioning Editor for Channel Four TV:

The clever clubs will learn from how television markets the game and make it attractive as an entertainment package . . . Basketball has got to get it right, because as committed as we are to the sport, Channel Four will survive without it (*Basketball Monthly*, February 1982).

Illustrative of this shift in emphasis was the pressure that coaches came under not to employ what was described by a writer in the *Guardian* on 6 November 1982, as 'boring zone defences for long periods'. This pressure, coupled with the influx of Americans and the distribution of the wealth coming into the game, prompted a number of criticisms. In a wide-ranging critique of the changes then occurring, Dave West, coach of Stockport Thoroglaze Belgrade, writing in 1982, called on the EBBA to enforce regulations to safeguard the future of England's juniors:

We sacrifice the future of the game for the Americans. Since the majority of First Division teams have two foreign and one dual national player, this can absorb up to 75% of a club's annual budget . . . We must have the only national team in European basketball that speaks with an American accent. The introduction of the foreign player has helped to popularise the game . . . But their numbers must be controlled to create opportunities for our own players to develop. The destiny of the game lies with the Association. They represent the interests of its affiliated members and they must protect and be responsible for its future development (*Basketball Monthly*, December 1982).

Although West suggested that the English national team was the only one in Europe to 'speak with an American accent', the processes in question were occurring to varying degrees throughout Europe

Olin, 1984). Such comments, however, vividly highlight the contested ature of the recruitment of sports migrants and the commodification nd shift of the game towards spectacle. In addition, while West rgued that the 'future of the game lies with the Association', he verlooked the extent to which the power of the EBBA had declined. he growing power of Basketball Marketing Limited, the company set p by the EBBA and the clubs, and the growing ownership of clubs by ew entrepreneurs were indicative of this. While West questioned the isdom of the recruitment of American players, others criticized the ommodification of the game in general. Take, for example, the omments expressed by the England player Ian Day:

> Survival of our game rests purely and simply with the wealthy businessmen . . . We are at the mercies of the bon viveurs' whims and fantasies. Are we not falling into the same trap as our social system where we create opportunities for all, but restrict them to a few? (*Sunday Times*, 23 January 1982).

Day was not alone in this perception. In March 1983, Bill Beswick, he England coach, was reported in the *Guardian* as stating that 'as our oaching and preparation of players gets better, I can now envisage the lay coming when English players are competing in the market place gainst Americans'. Beswick's remarks are significant for two reasons. irst, he defined the worth of players in terms of their 'market value'; he players had become commodities! Second, he commented in the uture tense – he could 'now envisage the day' when English players vill compete in the market against Americans. In 1983, however, it vas the American migrants who were the paid employees: the English layers were their unpaid assistants.

During the early 1980s, money was certainly flowing in. In February 983, the group marketing company signed a two-year footwear and lothing contract with Adidas. In June that year, it was reported that ver £450,000 worth of sponsorship money had been secured. By November, *Basketball Monthly* noted that attendances were up by 8.3 per cent. By 1984–85, the total income of the clubs was estimated t £1,196,000. As well as their own team sponsorship, the clubs were eceiving money from the EBBA via its national agreements with Carlsberg, Prudential Insurance, Just Juice, Bell's Whisky, Adidas, Mikasa and U-Bix Copiers. Despite this, the clubs were still not content. In the same month as the above attendance figures were ssued, nine of the first-division clubs set up the Basketball Owners' Association (BOA). Highly critical of the EBBA, the BOA wanted

greater autonomy and to maximize financial returns. In an articl
critical of the BOA, Chris Lightbown commented:

> Should they lose them, clubs have no alternative income t(
> sponsors. Sponsors and TV itself are like the first America1
> players to come to England, a shield behind which the domesti(
> game can be gradually developed. It has not happened and th(
> BOA said nothing about this . . . Young English basketball, th(
> game's greatest asset, barely exists . . . From this meagre poo(
> must come the future of English basketball. If the pool gets n(
> larger, basketball will have to become a TV-imported playe1
> circus. The BOA said . . . yes (*Basketball Monthly*, Februar)
> 1984).

The struggle over the import of American migrants continuec
throughout the 1980s. In commenting on an alternative to the BOA'!
policy, Beswick, the national coach, argued that, if elected to th(
National Executive Committee, he would align himself

> with those concerned with the development and progress of ou1
> sport as a healthy, exciting and wholesome game . . . Basketbal
> is temporarily the responsibility of the generation who have a
> moral obligation to hand it over in better shape to the next
> Basketball is not owned by anyone (*Basketball Monthly*, Febru-
> ary 1984).

With the rise of the BOA, it would appear that the position of thosε
with whom Beswick sought to align himself had been further eroded
At the start of the 1984–85 season, however, the game went intc
recession: TV coverage was reduced, a number of sponsors withdrew
and recriminations followed. Given this economic downturn, it is no1
surprising that the BOA was vociferous in its criticism of the EBBA
Take, for example, the comments of David Last, a key official of thε
Crystal Palace club:

> It's all too late. The amateurs who run the game didn't decidε
> whether it was a TV entertainment, a spectator sport or partici-
> pant game. Result, we never developed something that coulc
> compete with other TV sports . . . We'll be back in the schoo
> gym era with no-one to blame but ourselves (*Sunday Times*, 3(
> September 1984).

The struggle between those seeking to develop the sport as TV entertainment and those who sought to promote it as a participant game has continued to mark English basketball up to the present day. As this conflict has taken place, the concomitant Americanization of the game has accelerated. By January 1984, Beswick appears to have felt that this process had gone too far:

> Basketball in this country without a well-thought-out, properly organised structure and not governed with imagination and firmness by those elected to lead will deny national teams their rightful place, will fragment and alienate the various areas of development, and will leave the N.B.L. an over-commercialized, over-Americanized entertainment package with little or no relationship to the real game . . . in this country (Philips World Basketball Series programme, January 1985).

Since that point, power within the game has shifted even further in the direction of the owners and away from the EBBA. Direct sponsorship had increased to £900,000 by the 1985–86 season. It was accordingly not surprising that the owners would be resistant to any changes which would be detrimental to their position. In fact, as noted earlier, in tandem with this increase in sponsorship, the leading first-division clubs decided in April 1986 to form a breakaway league under their own control. In the power struggle which ensued, the EBBA, urged by its National League Council not to recognize the breakaway league, opposed the move. They warned the clubs involved that the new league would be outside both its and the international governing body, FIBA's, jurisdiction. In consequence, none of the clubs would be able to enter European competitions and none of the players would be able to play for their country. In June 1986, the Sports Council, a quasi-state body, acting as arbiter, broke the impasse. Under the agreement the clubs would take over the responsibility for the administration and management of division one, renamed the Carlsberg League, from the 1987–88 season. By the end of the 1980s the entrepreneurs had got what they wanted! While the development of English basketball in the early 1990s is yet to be charted, the general trend towards basketball becoming a commodity to be sold and to be consumed as a spectacle is evident.

These processes were not confined to England. Given that over 400 Americans currently play at elite level in west European basketball leagues, the same situation may hold true in that wider context (FIBA, 1989). Those leagues which have undergone the most successful commercialization processes – many Italian and Spanish clubs are closely connected to trans-national corporations – tend to recruit higher quality American migrants. Further, just as English officials looked across the Atlantic for marketing models to follow, European basketball officials have been reported as considering:

> Their own version of the NBA . . . creating a league of top clubs from across the continent [and] plans also are under way for creation of a world club championship tournament that would be an expanded version of the four-nation McDonald's Open (*USA Today*, 14 November 1990).

Teams such as the Denver Nuggets, the Boston Celtics and the New York Knicks have competed in the McDonalds' Open tournament. In the most recent competition, held in Paris, a Spanish team. Badalona, nearly succeeded in beating the Los Angeles Lakers. Reflecting on the game, one of the Spanish team's American migrants, Harold Pressley, who had previously played for four years with the Sacramento Kings, spoke for the other American players when he remarked that 'the fact that we're not trying to get back to the NBA really relaxes us and makes us better as a team' (*Basketball News*, November 1991). As in the English case, a number of American migrants are beginning to 'settle' in other European countries.

During the last decade, Americanization has therefore involved not simply the quick raising of playing standards, but also the transformation of the structure and meaning of the game in Europe. During the 1980s, the adoption of American marketing strategies involved not only the forming of a cartel to deal with potential sponsors and the media but also the presentation of an event. Where once devotees watched a game, spectators now consumed a show with glitz! American music now accompanies the presentation of teams, time-out and intervals. Cheerleaders, dressed in a style reminiscent of North American sporting occasions, entertain the crowd and Disney-like figures parade around the courts. In several respects this development mirrors that launched by the National Football League (NFL) in its marketing of American football both in specific countries and with regard to the formation of the World League of American Football (Maguire, 1990; 1991).

These processes are not confined to England or to Europe, but are at work to greater or lesser degrees on a global basis. The 1990–91 NBA season's opening matches were held in Tokyo with the series being seen as 'a giant marketing test for the NBA'. Games were reported as having 'had an undeniable NBA stamp' (*Sports Illustrated* 16 November 1990). This marketing image included official NBA clocks, baskets and floor with the whole operation being supported by official NBA entertainment in the form of 'The Famous Chicken' and the Memphis State Pom-Pom Girls. The NBA Commissioner, David Stern, is reported as 'seeing the world as one big NBA supermarket' and Charles Grantham, the executive director of the NBA Players' Association, though conscious of the demands on American players, recently concluded 'just think of this global picture as a big pie. The bigger the pie gets, the bigger the piece for the players' (*Sports Illustrated*, 16 November 1990). The squeezing out of indigenous players is overlooked by Grantham (Maguire, 1988).

Commenting on the marketing agreement reached between the NBA and a Japanese company, *Sports Illustrated* noted that 'last week's series was, in the words of Masanori Otsubo, a C. Itoh executive, "a kick off event" to promote the NBA in Japan. In other words, citizens of Japan, look for a blitz of those two big American T's–TV and T-shirts' (*Sports Illustrated*, 16 November 1990).

ENGLISH ELITE BASKETBALL AS A COMMODITY AND MIGRANT SPORTS LABOUR MARKET: AN EVALUATION

The changes in English basketball which have occurred over the last 20 years have been contoured by a number of interwoven processes which are themselves bound up in the global development of sport. These changes centred on a number of key areas. New patterns of independence with respect to the ownership and control of the sport emerged. Commodification along American marketing lines attracted entrepreneurs who either directly, in terms of the ownership of clubs, or indirectly, in terms of agents, exercised varying degrees of control over the sport. The sovereignty of the governing body was also eroded by a number of sources. For example, the influence which the media–sport production complex and sponsoring companies brought to bear on decision-making processes all undermined the earlier power ratio and weakened the relative power superiority of the governing body.

The struggle over the form in which the game was to develop relates to another feature which was propelling these chances, namely that of the Americanization of the game and the associated tensions raised by both issues of nationalism and the position of different ethnic groups within the basketball subculture. Interwoven with commodification, Americanization involved the recruitment of American players and coaches and the erosion of the position of their English counterparts. But this transformation also entailed a shift away from a game played, by and large, by Anglo-Britons to one in which the involvement of black Americans and Afro-Caribbean Britons has increased significantly.

Questions regarding the over-dependency on foreign migrants for sports development arise in this connection. While a market for a specific cultural product had been created, English basketball was arguably being actively underdeveloped. The nature of this process is made more complex by the fact that it meshed with the issue of 'racism'; that is, Americanization centrally involved black Americans having to ply their playing talents around Europe. The issue of such labour movement and the reception received by such black Americans raises further as yet unanswered questions. In addition, Afro-Caribbean Britons have increasingly taken to the game, possibly as a result of role-modelling those black American players recruited as a consequence of the game's professionalization. It would appear ironical that this involvement is seen as a sign that English basketball can serve as an avenue of social mobility when the very players role-modelled have themselves a rather tenuous career expectancy. Yet for young Afro-Caribbean Britons, basketball may well serve as a source of meaning in their lives. The promise of basketball serving as an avenue of social mobility for women either as migrants or indigenous labour, however, is less realistic.

Despite the overall commodification of the sport, women's basketball has become increasingly marginalized in Britain. Underfunded and lacking adequate access to facilities or coaching personnel, the players regularly have to pay to play. Relatively few women sports migrants have been seen in English basketball: systematic research of their experiences is yet to be conducted.

The processes of Americanization and commodification also manifested themselves in terms of the cultural meaning and function of the game. Changes took place in the structure of the sport, above all in its constitutive rules designed to speed up the action, increase ease of scoring and introduce 'sudden-death' play. The main consequence of these changes has been an increasingly spectacle-centred sport. In addition, the timing of events was changed in order to meet the needs of the media and/or of the sponsors. The emphasis increasingly focused on changing the structural characteristics of the product in order to enhance its appeal as something to be consumed.

Closely linked to this shift were the changes which have taken place with respect to the form of the sport, including its regulative rules.

Here one observes the growing ascendancy of values governing the conduct of play which emphasize display, glitz and entertainment. In the pursuit of spectacle, the old aesthetic values have lost ground. Players and coaches have become more concerned with the outcome and the need to satisfy the audience than with the experience of playing as a pleasurable end in itself.

It is possible to conclude that basketball became something to be marketed, packaged and sold as part of a consumer-oriented and media-tempered package. In order to be initially recruited and retained on teams, sports migrants have increasingly had to display their labour in an entertaining way. Decisions about the structure, form and organization of the sport, and about the nature and extent of migration, have come, in part, to reflect the dominance of business criteria and interests. The playing of elite basketball has thus increasingly assumed work-like characteristics. Before this transformation, players or ex-players administered and organized the game themselves. Performances tended to be more related to intrinsic values than to the need to 'display' and earn a salary. While the relative erosion of the power of English players and coaches is perhaps the most visible feature of this process, American players and coaches were and are no less affected. Indeed, the Americanization of English basketball relates not only to questions regarding sport underdevelopment in Britain but also reflects, as noted, the marginal position of college and pro-basketball players in the USA and their need to migrate to Europe and other parts of the globe to pursue a sport career.

GLOBALIZATION, SPORTS MIGRATION AND THE MEDIA–SPORT PRODUCTION COMPLEX

Extensive reference has been made in the case study of English basketball to the process of Americanization. At first sight such an approach would seem to have fallen into the trap outlined at the outset of this chapter; namely, that this approach represents an example of the unwise association of the idea of global culture with the culture of a single nation-state. This is not what I have been arguing for. As the work of Dezalay highlights, Americanization can occur within the context of global cultural flows. Besides, the analysis of English basketball emphasized how Americanization was interwoven with commodification processes which characterize the global capitalist system, which itself is not the preserve of any one nation-state.

What is being argued is that one of the dominant, but by no means exclusive, themes of global sports development in the late twentieth century is Americanization. It is also legitimate, however, to talk of competing cultural flows including Japanization, Europeanization, Asiaticization, Africanization and Hispanicization. As a result, the very notion of 'sport', as well as that of 'development', becomes problematic. The analysis is not therefore overstating the case of homogeneity and integration. The broad cultural processes identified interweave and manifest themselves along the cultural flow lines identified by Appadurai: out of this interdependency something emerges which was neither planned nor intended and which both reflects and contributes to the broader globalization process. Two further points need to be made. Although sports migrants, officials and consumers are no less caught up in this unfolding globalization process, they do have the capacity to reinterpret cultural products and experiences into something distinct. Furthermore, the receptivity of national popular cultures to non-indigenous cultural wares can be both active and heterogeneous. These are areas in which much more work needs to be done.

But while it is important to probe the existence of these relatively autonomous trans-national practices, this should not, as was noted at the outset, lead the analyst to overlook the fact that national and trans-national agencies, including such sports organizations as the NBA and the NFL, will attempt to manipulate and control such processes (Maguire, 1990; 1991). It is also legitimate to note, though more particularly with reference to specific sports, that a process of commodification/Americanization has occurred. This can take several forms: the global migration of American sports personnel, the global spread of American sports forms and the global adoption of the marketing of sport along American lines. Though these forms have developed to varying degrees in different countries and continents, more usually they interweave in a mutually reinforcing manner.

That is why Appandurai (1990) is only in part correct to emphasize that global flows 'occur in and through the growing disjunctures between "ethnoscapes", "technoscapes", "financescapes", "media-scapes" and "ideoscapes" '. Both existing and future global sports development, and as part of that, sports labour migration, are and will be clearly affected by and interwoven with these cultural flows. These flows are themselves characterized by both unintended inter-dependency chains and conscious interventions by more or less powerful groups. Given the concerns of the present study, the mediascape cultural flow is of especial significance, and can serve to highlight the nature of the argument being proposed.

The media-sport production complex is arguably made up of three key groups: sports organizations, media and marketing organizations and media personnel, notably broadcasters and journalists. The nature and form of their interdependency has varied over time and within and between continents. There are, for example, important differences in this regard between North America and Europe. Indeed, in the United States there is greater cross-ownership of sport and media organizations than at present exists in Europe. Further, the nature of this interrelationship also varies from one sport to another. Some sports organizations, notably well-established male sports, are more successful than others. All sports organizations tend to negotiate separately with the media.

Sports have a largely dependent role in this media-sport production complex. That is, sports organizations have little or no control over the nature and form in which 'their' sport is televised, reported or covered. Given the relative power of the NFL in its negotiations with the media, this observation, however, may apply less to American football than to other sports. Nevertheless, this dependency appears to have grown over time and is arguably connected to sports organizations relying increasingly on revenues derived from sponsorship and marketing rather than from more traditional sources such as spectator receipts and patronage. Sports organizations thus have to ensure that they gain sufficient exposure and are visible in the sponsorship and endorsement market place. Media coverage ensures this. Because of the hegemonic position enjoyed by specific sports within the media-sport production complex, the manner and form in which they are currently developing can be a powerful benchmark by which other sports are judged. Since other sports are being forced increasingly to survive in such a market place, it is perhaps not surprising that they have begun to adopt marketing strategies and business ethics the same as or similar to those associated with American sports production (Maguire, 1991).

With reference specifically to English basketball, it appears that the EBBA, unlike the NBA and the NFL, has been more concerned to market the game *per se* rather than with launching into a large-scale marketing/endorsement operation. This is not to suggest that the EBBA did not seek to commercialize its product: it did so through direct sponsorship of the clubs and the league which was itself arguably secured by the guarantee of media coverage, the latter being dependent on providing a 'quality' product, hence the role of the American sports migrants. But the EBBA seemingly had less control or influence over the media, especially Channel Four, and, during the late 1980s, television coverage of the game decreased dramatically. The balance of power between the EBBA and the media decisively favoured the latter. Though still part of the overall English sports culture, the game is marked by instability at a number of levels. Hence the position of American sports migrants is marked by insecurity. Indeed, the speed, scale and volume of existing and future sports labour migration in general are arguably closely tied to these issues.

The balance of power involved in the emergence of American football on the British, European and the global scales has been more complex. It has been contoured by the meshing of interests among three key groups: media organizations, sponsoring corporations and the NFL. The consumption of the trans-national practices of American football and basketball has clearly been influenced by a conscious strategy adopted by the NFL and the NBA. With regard to England, key NFL officials have been able to secure more advantageous terms and coverage for American football than either the EBBA or, up until now, the NBA, has for basketball. From the anecdotal evidence to hand it appears that the owners of American baseball are attempting to follow the example of these sports organizations and to develop on a global basis (Maguire, 1991). In some ways, therefore, the operations of the NFL and the NBA correspond to the marketing strategies of other large trans-nationals including the Disney Corporation, McDonald's and Budweiser. It is along these cultural, economic, ideological and technological flows that sports migrants will continue to ply their athletic labour.

REFERENCES

Appadurai, A. (1990) 'Disjuncture and Difference in the Global Cultural Economy', *Theory, Culture and Society*, 7, 295–310.

Basketball Monthly, various issues.

Dezalay, Y. (1990) 'The Big Bang and the Law: The Internationalization and Restructuration of the Legal System', *Theory, Culture and Society*, 7, 279–98.

EBBA (1987) Correspondence from the Secretary of the English Basketball Association.

Featherstone, M. (1990) 'Global Culture', *Theory, Culture and Society*, 7, 1–14.

FIBA (1989) Correspondence from the Secretary of the European Basketball Association.

King, A. (1990) 'Architecture, Capital and the Globalization of Culture', *Theory, Culture and Society*, 7, 397–411.

Maguire, J. (1988) 'The Commercialization of English Elite Basketball 1972–1988: A Figurational Perspective', *International Review for the Sociology of Sport*, 23,4, 305–23.

——— (1990) 'More Than a Sporting "touchdown": The Making of American Football in England 1982–1990', *Sociology of Sport Journal*, 7,3, 213–37.

(1991) 'The Media–sport Production Complex: The Case of American Football in European Societies', *European Journal of Communication*, 6, 315–35.

Mennell, S. (1990) 'The Globalization of Human Society as a Very Long-term Social Process: Elias's Theory', *Theory, Culture and Society*, 7, 359–72.

Olin, K. (1984) 'Attitudes Towards Professional Foreign Players in Finnish Amateur Basketball', *International Review for the Sociology of Sport*, 19,4, 273–82.

Robertson, R. (1990) 'Mapping the Global Condition: Globalization as the Central Concept', *Theory, Culture and Society*, 7, 15–30.

Sklair, L. (1991) *Sociology of the Global System* (London: Harvester).

Smith, M. (1983) *Violence and Sport* (Toronto: Butterworth).

16

Travelling, Comparing, Emigrating: Configurations of Sport Mobility

Henning Eichberg

A PYGMALION CASE OF SPORT

'We can systematically comb thoroughly one continent after the other and help our friends in every country to leap in order to smooth their path towards the top of world football. This is their aim. That they might reach it, this is our task.' These were the conclusions of the elite German trainer, Dettmar Cramer (1978), summarizing his experiences from matches and training in 70 countries. He presented his views in 1978 in a special issue on football in the official West German parliamentary gazette, *Das Parlament*. Cramer exemplified his vision of the global embrace by the encounter with Saihon Sarr, a 16-year-old, barefooted schoolboy from Bathurst, capital of The Gambia, whom Cramer discovered in 1968. At that time Cramer was the FIFA coach to this West African country, and he introduced the boy into the Gambian national team. He wrote that:

> In August 1977 I travelled as coach of FC Bayern to Norway in order to study our UEFA Cup opponents in Mjöndalen, playing at home against the national champions, Lilleström. I did not believe my eyes when I saw an African forward from the home team whose movements seemed familiar to me. After the match we shook hands after a break of nine years. It was Saihon Sarr who had accepted an offer from Mjöndalen to play football there and at the same time to study sport in Oslo. He spoke fluent Norwegian and earned his money at a petrol station. He was 25 years old, married and could afford holidays in his own country. We had long conversations in Mjöndalen, later in Munich and after the return match in Oslo. We have become friends and say, facetiously and reflectively at the same time, 'To make friends is even more important than to score goals'. But there is, of course,

more than simply personal sentimentality in the game. German football trainers have done good things abroad, both for the youth of countries where they were engaged, for the respect of the Federal Republic and for German football (Cramer, 1978: 9).

The mixture of well-intentioned ideas surrounding this case of sport emigration is characteristic of the hegemony of western sports; to meet and to emigrate. Cramer's comments about Gambia – ('Most of the players are poor and the best of them are drawn to foreign countries') – reflect personal sentimentality and a systematic neglect of the neo-colonial dimensions of sports; individuals striving to reach the top of the world; the 'brawn drain' (Bale, 1991); individual achievement and cultural drop out; and identity and alienation.

The enthusiasm of the German coach was *not* directed towards the cultural gain of the Gambian people. His interest and engagement were systematically canalized in another direction. The old motive of Pygmalion – the pride and love of the maker – finds a new context. The analysis of the ideological 'Pygmalion syndrome' or 'achievement orientation–emigration–alienation' could – and perhaps should – lead to critical studies of the relations between sport ideology, cultural neo-colonialism and exploitation (Bale, 1991: 196–201). But this will not be the focus of the reflections which follow. The discussion of exploitation and cultural imperialism often bears the stamp of moral evaluation and voluntarism. I have no objection to this but it should not divert our attention from the analytical question of how the historical dynamics of sport colonialism can be understood and on which empirical base alternatives can be defined. Methodologically, this means that we should not continue the controversy on the level of ideology (whether pro-Cramer or anti-Cramer) but try an analysis which moves from the superstructure of ideas towards the base of body-cultural practices. Is it on this material level of social body configurations that the cultural contradictions, dynamics and changes can be identified? (Eichberg, 1978; 1989a; Carter and Krüger, 1990).

FITNESS, HEALTH AND DISCIPLINE: A GYMNASTIC CASE

Two other examples of sport mobility, travelling and meeting in movement culture, can be added to the case of Cramer and Sarr. It was in the 1920s and 1930s that Danish gymnastics suddenly received international attention. Based on the farmers' cultural revolution in nineteenth-century Denmark and the Swedish Ling system, gymnastics had become a popular mass activity, taught in the free folk academies and in local rural associations all over the country. The first school to specialize in gymnastics was the Ollerup Folk Academy, founded in 1920 by Niels Bukh.

Building on the gymnastics of Elli Björkstén from Finland, Bukh developed a system of movement, posture and staging of collective performances that came to dominate Danish gymnastics until the 1950s (Korsgaard, 1982; Eichberg, 1989b). Niels Bukh's school at Ollerup became especially well known both inside and outside the country as a result of its travels and demonstrations abroad. In 1931, a group of 25 young men and women under Bukh's leadership travelled round the world displaying their gymnastics in Danzig, Soviet Russia, China, Korea, Japan, Canada, the USA and England (Flensted, 1932; 1945; Krogshede, 1980: 201–18; Jörgensen 1940). The highlight of the journey was the Danish gymnastic demonstration in Japan, laying the foundations for the establishment of similar gymnastic forms in that country. A committee had been formed by representatives of the Japanese state, schools and gymnastic organizations to develop the Danish contact and its president, the high school principal Obara, expressed the 'hope that Japan should soon be able to foster a youth as fit, healthy and good as those in Danish gymnastics' (Krogshede, 1980: 203). The exchange in Japan consisted of mutual attempts to demonstrate precision and discipline, interest in each other, singing their own folk songs and national anthem and learning those of their hosts, learning some phrases from the partner's language, impressing each other with elaborate ceremonies of politeness, especially involving national flags. While the Danish side presented its bodily exercises in rank and file with utmost discipline and precision, the Japanese side competed with precise and enthusiastic 'banzai' shouts.

This event was regarded as a brilliant success by both sides. The Danish delegation, which was received in audience by the Japanese Crown Prince and the Prime Minister, met an impressive public reception at home and became, though a purely private initiative, a sort of national institution. The Japanese side immediately and successfully adopted Danish gymnastics. Thus, the present paradoxical situation – after some fundamental changes in Danish gymnastics since the 1960s – that to experience 'original' Danish gymnastics of the Niels Bukh type, one must look for it in Japan.

The case of the Danish–Japanese gymnastic meeting shows many similarities to the sporting model of Cramer–Sarr. The values of fitness, health and social discipline, expressed by the Japanese representative Obara and demonstrated by Niels Bukh's young people, are not alien to the world of sport. Both sport and gymnastics celebrate a form of internationality – and a cult of nationality at the same time. They could even join together for example in the framework of the 1936 Olympic games in Berlin where a mass demonstration of Niels Bukh constituted an essential gymnastic contribution to the monumental sports arrangement.

This combination showed, however, by remaining separate entities, that two different patterns of body cultural behaviour were meeting. Gymnastic performers can meet in display and demonstration, but rarely in sportive competition. If they do, gymnastics becomes transformed into something else, into a sport producing measurable results.

Is the difference at the configurational level relevant in comparing the dynamics of internationality, mobility and migration? Neither the Lingian nor the Bukhian gymnastic configuration would prevent a gymnast from emigrating. On the contrary, there existed some strong incentives for gymnastics teachers to emigrate – at least temporarily – in order to establish gymnastic schools abroad. Research on a broader base about this type of Danish emigration is still to be done, but two examples may be illustrative. From 1905 the Danish gymnastic instructor, H.G. Junker, held courses in England and became appointed the first male gymnastic inspector in that country. Later, in 1910, he established an institute of educational gymnastics in Silkeborg in Denmark, instructing several thousand English gymnastic teachers who could now replace the earlier army physical training inspectors and army sergeant majors in English schools (Borup-Nielsen, 1990). Earlier, gymnastics for English girls' schools had been modelled on the Ling system by the Swedish teacher, Marina Bergman-Österberg. Appointed as superintendent of physical education in girls' and infants' schools in London in 1881, she established a physical training college in Hampstead in 1885 and at Dartford in 1895, teaching Swedish gymnastics there until her death in 1915 (May, 1969). The migration of gymnastic teachers is, however, quite different from the migration of athletes; it is as different, perhaps, as the gymnastics configuration is from the sports configuration.

A FAIR OF THE SPECTACULAR: THE FOLK-GAMES

In April 1990 the Breton town of Karaez (Carhaix) was in a highly excited mood. It was to host a 'Première Journée Internationale de Jeux et Sports Traditionnels'. Almost 5,000 spectators, a remarkable percentage of the small town's inhabitants, crowded around the sports fields where the contests involving 500 active participants in 35 games and sports were to be held. Around the main fields, booths and stalls offered the traditional Breton crêpes, thin pancakes filling the air with their sweet odours, as well as books and papers from the Breton nationalist and left-wing cultural movements. Other stalls presented the Breton traditional games, mostly 'palet', casting games with plates and many varieties of balls and skittles, while some stalls and games were especially set up for children.

The same multiplicity unfolded on the main fields. An Irish and a Breton team played – maybe for the first time in history – a game of Gaelic football against each other. It appeared that some of the players were not quite acquainted with the rules, playing something between football, handball and fistball. The game provided the opportunity for great delight and laughter among the spectators. Icelandic glima-wrestlers showed their art, once as a folkloric demonstration dressed in national costume, and after this in a competitive style, now clothed in bright blue sportswear. Wrestlers from the British Isles showed a different but related style. Accompanied by the sound of the bagpipes, Scots in their kilts and men from Cumberland with their colourfully embroidered shorts tried to unbalance each other in the backhold fight.

The Basques presented themselves in quite another manner by demonstrations and competitions of extreme strength, hacking through tree trunks, lifting stone blocks of 200 and 250 kilograms and balancing heavy stone balls over neck and shoulders. The preparation and staging of the strong body is a spectacle and display in itself. The bulky body of the strongman is armoured by tight bandages. Acclamations, shouts and laughter accompanied the ceremony as well as the displays of strength.

The highlight of the Basque performance was, however, the competitive hacking down of two upright trunks. The trunks, three metres high, have to be notched in order to put in a plank on which to stand. From this high platform the top of the trunk is hacked down while the spectators watch with feelings of giddiness and tension; *incroyable* – incredible! In spite of warnings, journalists approach the place of action and are hit by flying splinters. Victory occurs when one trunk is hacked through twice, but the loser continues until he has finished, also to great public acclaim. This is not a sport; rather, it is an acrobatic display, grown out of labour and its transformation into an exercise of dramatized strength.

The same historical development can be seen in the Breton games such as casting straw bales over a rope, high in the air, or running in competition over straw bales, carrying heavy bags. If a participant in this hurdle race stumbled and fell down it was not seen as a mistake or a failure, as in sport. The laughter of the spectators showed that it was a valued part of the event, the deliberate display of the grotesque.

There is rarely an exercise illustrating this as clearly as the tug of war. Two teams of six strongmen stood against each other at Karaez, some of them about 50 years old and with grey hair, barefoot and directed by a stout and bald referee. When the start was commanded there rose again that strange relation between the tension of strong bodies and the tension of the public. The tug of war continued for some time without result but suddenly one of the participants accidentally fell over on to his back. Again, this is not a failure but an expected occurrence. The spectators burst into laughter, the tension is broken and soon one team has drawn the other over the line. The strongmen triumph but they are at the same time subjects of a popular culture of laughter. When some minutes later young Breton girls took up the rope, five against five, the pattern changed. Now the body language told quite another story.

The attention to folk games, to festivals and their body language, leads to observations which could bear comparison with other forms of body culture; of travelling, meeting and comparing. The documentation of the games by the organizers (Jaouen and Couedelo, 1990) and by the media (IFCW, 1990) give another, still valid, picture to the phenomenological observation in the field. Altogether, they need a theoretical discussion, which is at the same time comparative, contrasting and configurational.

CELEBRATING THE DIFFERENCE

All in all, the festival of the folk-games in Karaez represented a mass fair and a fascination with many features which are not represented in sports and gymnastics meetings. Evidently, it was neither the production of top class results nor the display of fitness, health and discipline that determined the configuration of folk sports in Karaez and gave them their particular fascination. The display of bodies surrounded by and integrated into the sound of traditional music, the smell of the crêpes and sugar, the crying and laughter of the children, formed a mixture of popular amusement continuing old traditions, of fair and circus and creating new forms fitting into the age of media amusement. The television, film and radio crews moving among the playing fields illustrated that there were not just pre-modern aspects of the arrangement.

Once more, the case demands reflections on the configuration of such a specific body culture and its societal significance in order to define its relevance for the understanding of migration and mobility in sports. At first glance, and looking at the recent literature of popular, traditional folk-games, it might seem as if they have all, one after the other, become part of a process of sportification. The Basque competitions of strength are regulated and manifest themselves in lists of records and measured results (Franco, 1978). The tug of war was once in the Olympic programme but was evidently regarded as too bizarre, representing a popular non-sporting tradition. It was therefore expunged from the Olympics after 1920. Since then it has struggled for recognition, forming national and international federations (the Tug of War International Federation [TWIF] in 1960), regulations for competition, classes of weight, etc. (Burat 1990; Möller 1990–91, 4: 30–32). The Breton games are likewise organized in a federation (FALSAB), and bear some incipient overtones of sportification (Floc'h and Peru, 1987). The same is true for Breton wrestling (*gouren*), using sport as a model for regulations regarding dress, record listing, rules, organization, ceremonies, etc. (Jaouen and Beon 1985). (The tendency is illustrated by a contrast: in the annual Monterfil Gallo festival of popular music and games, the games are in a non-sportive way integrated into the Breton popular culture of music, dance and fair.) The Icelandic glima wresting shows by its costume tendencies towards both the folkloric and sportive (Einarsson 1988). Both are removing the ancient art of fighting from everyday folk life and from the popular 'circus' fair.

Seen in this way, the popular games appear as 'traditional games', that is, games on their belated way towards sportification, hindered by some 'traditional' bounds, but nevertheless moving towards a modern pattern. Traditional games would in this perspective mean 'not-yet' sports.

The Karaez event, however, shows how unsuitable this terminology and its implicit scenario are. The festival of folk-games is not a 'not-yet' but *another pattern*. Whereas sport tries to construct a framework of standardization in order to homogenize the conditions for the production of results, the popular games festival stages the inverse: the *non*-standardization, the game of utmost *variety* (Möller 1984; 1990–91). There are no limits to the ways in which bodily displays can be varied. The folk-games are a festival of difference.

The popular games differ not only from sport but also from the configuration of gymnastics with its discipline in rank and file, its fixation with uniform precision, uniform dress and uniform movement. As Niels Bukh wrote in 1930:

catching another person, hindering a competitor, running with an artificial (often funny) handicap, going on stilts, etc. Many of these arrangements aimed to create stumbling (Möller, 1990–91; 2,3: 22–25, 52–8; 4: 93–107). An example is the race of shepherds and shepherdesses that has survived in parts of Württemberg. The famous shepherdesses' race at Markgröningen, documented since the fifteenth century, was characterized by the hindering of competitors (Tomschik, 1971). In effect, this was a race which involved the act of stumbling. In the process of sportification in the nineteenth century, the pioneers of sport were often in error about the real modern configuration of sport. Subjectively, they had the intention of renewing the old folk sports, that being the reason for introducing competitions like the three-legged race and the sack race.

The three-legged race, as held in the Berlin stadium in 1892, was run by pairs of runners having one of their legs bound together (Diem, 1971, 2:959). This gave a grotesque impression in accord with the popular stumble traditions but placed it outside the cult of the straight line of modern sport. The sack race was proposed in the first Danish book of sports, alongside running and stumbling with a bucket of water on the head (Hansen, 1893: 621–2). Against all the well-meaning intentions, it never became a modern sport but was downgraded to an amusement fit only for children. Evidently, the (non-formulated) configurational dynamics of sports were stronger than the restorative ideas of its founder generation. There was a gap between the empire of ideas and the historical decisive force of the body cultural base, erasing stumbling and popular laughter, erasing the grotesque and shaping the serious, streamlined modern sports body.

FOLK, MODERNITY AND FOLKLORIZATION

The case of stumbling can, therefore, illustrate the fundamental social relations in sports and body culture. The presence of children is another, related, indicator. In a festival of folk games, they play an important role, colouring the whole atmosphere whilst they are structurally excluded from the events of sport and gymnastics, respectively isolated in their particular class of age, weight, and 'minor' performance.

The stumbling, the laughter, the children – there is sufficient evidence in the practice of popular games that they are not just forerunners or incomplete traditional forms of modern sport and gymnastics, but form a configuration of their own, with its own societal significance. While sport is producing results and is by this mode of production evident as an institutionalization of the productivity syndrome in the industrial capitalist society (including state capitalism), the folk-games are non-producing, non-productive in the industrial meaning of the word. While gymnastics demonstrate discipline and self-discipline, the popular games stage the grotesque body as *not* being under the control of discipline. They can scarcely be used to illustrate a healthy and fit lifestyle. The bulky Basque stone-lifting athletes are a somewhat horrendous sight for advocates of hygienic discipline. The non-disciplinary aspects join, therefore, the non productive ones, giving the popular games their character of anti authoritarian wildness that was present in the ancient carnivalistic traditions (Bakhtin, 1968). Could this be a partial explanation of their recent success? Anyway, the specific configuration of the folk-games constitutes a contrasting picture against some fundamental tendencies in modernity – production and discipline – appealing, therefore, to the fascination of 'the exotic'. Folk constitutes a sort of inner exoticism.

The culture of *folk* in this meaning of the word is not identical with the *folkloristic*. On the contrary, folklorization has been a typical modern transformation process from the nineteenth century when older elements of folk culture – among them folk-games – changed into a representative staging of authentic identity. The folklore became, a national or regional representation, a scientific reconstruction, serious pattern, far from popular laughter, stumbling and children' involvement. 'Original' games and 'original' dances were to be per formed in 'original' costumes. There was no place for stumbling in the (often geometrical) choreographies of folklore. And there was no place for the non-serious carnivalism, the blasphemous mixture of styles, the amusement of children. Folklore became a modern contrast to the non-modern wildness of popular non-discipline.

Does this mean that the relation between folk culture and folklore one between pre-modern and modern? Once more, this would not describe the complexity of the historical process. Though there were several folkloristic traits in the festival of Karaez, the event as a whole witnessed a modern, if not trans-modern, actuality of the folk configuration. And this is true for other similar festivals and events the 1980s, whether the Eurolympics of National Minorities (first held in Friesland in 1985), the Inter-Celtic Festival in Lorient, or the Inuit Circumpolar meetings with the drum dance, rock music and Eskimo games (Eichberg, 1991). The most recent changes in the world sports, the dramatic breakdown of eastern European state sport, m also contribute to the development of renewed and trans-modern folk configurations in body culture. That is why close attention must now be directed towards all tendencies creating new configurational contradictions in the field of sports, be it the renaissance of national Slavic Sokol gymnastics (Blecking, 1991) or the reappearance of Hungarian, Georgian, Kazakh, and other, folk games (Chuzainov, 1990). For over a century, sportification has assumed a hegemonic tendency in movement culture. Now, new developments are catching our attention – and the attention of the media. A French observer commented on the Karaez folk festival, referring to the activity of the television teams between the playing fields: 'The spectacular has changed its place'. But has it?

What is the relevance of the changing process and its contradictions for the evaluation of migration processes in sport? The folk-game pattern determines the mobility of the actors in quite another way from achievement sports and hygienic gymnastics. The folk-games have a different kind of bond to their local and regional space from global sport and uniform gymnastics (Hellspong, 1989). As a celebration of difference, their meeting is a meeting of different patterns and styles. Thus, they do not favour the ubiquitous replacement of athletes.

On the other hand, folk-games are not excluding mobility as such; far from it. The Karaez example shows more than just accidental internationality. One of the specialists in Breton traditional games and games research is a Basque teacher, living in Brittany (Bedecarras, 1991). In the late 1980s, Breton gouren wrestling had spread to Friesland via Breton emigrants and Friesian teams now take part in tournaments of the International Federation of Celtic Wrestling. Breton gouren trainers have even reached Denmark where they began, around 1990, to instruct youngsters from gymnastic movements in non-sportive folk wrestling. Large-scale immigration from African and Asian countries to western Europe is now accompanied by much folk-cultural activity. The Punjab bhangra dancing in London is just one example (Hargreaves, 1989).

Quite another tradition of mobility could also obtain new significance in the near future – the circus. Folk games and popular sports have since ancient times had a professional supplement, namely the work of vagrant people (Hampe, 1902). These have been a source of permanent innovation and communication, helping to make the old European society much more culturally mobile than industrial prejudices will concede. Professionalization and mobility in the age of mass media can renew these 'underground' traditions in a surprising way.

The actual success of 'catch-as-catch-can', both as local (and mobile circus and on television illustrates the possibilities.

PRODUCTION, DISCIPLINE, VARIETY

The analysis of three cases, the German-Gambian football meeting c Cramer and Sarr, the Danish Niels Bukh gymnastics in Japan, an the Breton–International folk-games festival in Karaez, illustrate basi differentiations of modern sport and body culture. The categories c the classical sociological discourses in sports, mostly following dualisti patterns, are not sufficient to describe the complexity of this soci field. The hegemonic dualism of the nineteenth and early twentiet centuries between pedagogical gymnastics (as practised in Englis state schools) and sports (as practised in English private schools and i associations) neglects folk activities as the third form of body culture The same is true for the ideological differentiation between 'rationa sport' and 'romantic' gymnastics, or *Turnen* (Guttmann, 1978). Th evolutionist dualism between folk games and modern sports (Dunning 1973; Bale, 1989: 39) temporalizes the actual contradiction an excludes the significant model of hygienic gymnastics. The actua sports–political dualism between elite sport and mass sport banalize or harmonizes the structural–configurational conflicts.

Instead of these, Danish sociology of sport has, for a decade developed a categorical set of three points called the trialectics of bod culture (Eichberg, 1989). It has also been shown to be a usefu instrument in drawing a more appropriate picture of the social–spatia configurations of sports (Eichberg, 1988; Lyngsgaard, 1990). Could i trialectic approach lead to some fundamental differentiations o nationality and internationality, of migration and mobility? It is no possible to explore this in detail here, but the step from the trialectic of body culture to the differentiations of nationalism and to th trialectics of international migration can be briefly outlined. Bod culture in modern times has been structured by at least thre determinants. These are (a) the production of results; (b) socia disciplining; and (c) dialogical body language.

The hegemonic model in industrial culture has been the product oriented configuration of sport. It means to streamline movemen culture in the interest of results. Records and achievements i centimetres, grams, seconds and points are the decisive outcomes Technology, training and tests make up some of the characteristics o sportive production. It favours the worldwide construction of standar dized rules and homogeneous conditions in order to ensure a 'fair competitive production in centimetre-gram-second (c-g-s) or related scales. The mythical picture of self-representation is the pyramid of sport consisting of hierarchical order of ranking scales. The appropriate space for this model is the standardized sports hall adopting international norms. Sports containers of a universal shape and design dominate the diversity of the cultural and geographical environments in which they are found. Tracks in straight lines mark the shortest way for the streamlined body from the start to the goal. Among the cases described above, the Pygmalion case of international football represents the achievement pattern most precisely. But c-g-s athletics of the middle class is still more characteristic and the Olympic sport is the institutionalized paradigm.

From the beginning of modern industrial culture, the sport model has not been alone. Beside it, the exercises of school gymnastics, military drill, and medical preventative or health-related gymnastics developed, often in competing 'systems'. In different ways, they combined movements for fitness, health and social discipline. Thus, they may be called exercises in social hygienics. Their typical order was the movement in rank and file, on command or after common timing. But the recent tendency towards sport for all with its context of welfare hygienics has brought a number of innovations, with aerobics more in the older rank-and-file tradition and body-building modelled in more individualistic directions. The overall ideology is to find or teach the 'right' way of poise and movement as well as of nourishment, defined by the universal laws of nature, that is, natural science.

The classical space of social hygienic sports is the gymnastic hall. It is as rectangular and panoptical as the sports hall, but filled with specific exercise machinery. This is revived in the 'machine parks' of modern fitness studios. Among the three cases of meeting in sports, the case of Niels Bukh's gymnastics shows most of the characteristics of the social disciplinary model. The Slavic Sokol gymnastics (Blecking, 1991) as well as the communist mass displays, derived from them in the form of Spartakiades (Segal, 1977; Lane, 1981) and many of the patriotic sport displays of the third world countries, are other manifestations of this pattern.

However, the folk-games of Karaez showed a third configuration, the celebration of difference. Here the diversity of body experiences is put on stage, crystallized in the form of varying games, competitions, dances and musical displays. What fundamentally contrasts with the other patterns of sport and rank-and-file gymnastics is the element of the uncomparable. The folk body activities are non-streamlined and they do not follow the fitness cult of 'straight order'. Instead the games appeal to a great variety of juxtaposed experiences: rhythm and game, ecological experience of the outer world and meditative concentration on the inner world, expressiveness and festivity, ecstasy and silence, trance and laughter.

The spaces of folk-games and popular movement cultures can vary much more than the standardized sets in achievement sport and hygienic exercises. The games can take place where people are living, in the public square or in the road. Around 1900 the police had to battle against children's games to make way for traffic. But the space of folk-games can also be the green environment outside the urban area and the village. It can be in architectural structures transformed from their original functions, the churchyard and its graves in older times, the shut-down factory today. The labyrinth has been an ancient structure of dance and play, representing a contrast against the modern configuration of the straight line (Eichberg, 1989c).

THE TRIALECTICS OF NATIONAL IDENTITY

Having made the step from the unlimited multitude of real body cultures to the categorical set of trialectic analysis it has to be stressed that a concrete phenomenon never will be completely 'identical' with a configurational reconstruction. The analytical reconstruction – trialectics, configuration, contradiction – is simply an instrument for better understanding and comparison. Football, for example, is not only a sport of production, as in the case of the German–Gambian and Gambian–Norwegian meeting, but includes remarkable elements of folk-culture (Eichberg, 1990). Other sports can profitably be analysed under the concept of social hygienics. Danish gymnastics followed not only the hygienic model of 'scientific naturalness' but was also originally (in the nineteenth century) an element of folk culture and popular oppositional movement, if not of folk cultural revolution (Eichberg, 1989b; Korsgaard, 1982; 1986). And in the 1936 Berlin Olympics, Niels Bukh in some way entered the sporting world. Tug of war and gouren wrestling, though folk activities, show signs of sportification, and much of the recent interest in traditional games in the frame of sport for all is part of the expectations of social welfare

No real phenomenon is 'pure', but the construction of analytical categories is necessary to obtain a framework and a set of dimensions for comparison. In this respect, the analytical process can proceed from the configurational contradiction of body cultures towards their cultural-geographical significance, the trialectics of national identity and identification. One problem is that sport is internationalist while

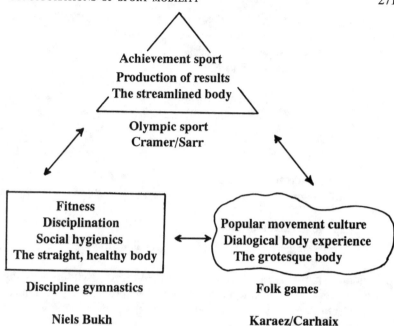

Figure 16.1   Trialectics of body culture

gymnastics and folk-games represent national forms (Figures, 16.1–16.3).

The evaluation of the football coach, Cramer, praising the 'respect of West Germany and German football', illustrates the fundamentally nationalistic character of sport identification (and maybe of every 'internationalism'). Identification in this model proceeds through achievement, understood as collective sports results, as well as in economic success, growth and expansion. 'We are the greatest' is the aspiration in this configuration of nationalism and is described in Olympic rankings or gross national product – a nationalism of production. It seems clear that this type of nationalism is dominant in liberal capitalist systems.

The case of Niels Bukh's gymnastics with its frequent use of parade-like exercises in rank and file, of national songs and national flags, evokes another type of collective community. National integration is here structured on the base of egalitarianism (as opposed to the structural inequality of achievement sports) and of pedagogical formation. The bodies show, by their individual straight backs and their choreographed straight lines, the collective fitness of the 'national body'. It was that which impressed the Japanese, not primarily the

Figure 16.2 Patterns of national identity

production of the Danish sport records. 'We are disciplined' is the body language of integrational nationalism, whether in the variant of French Jacobin nationalism (introducing mass gymnastic festivals and a national uniform for all) or of Prussian *Turner* discipline.

The *folk* model of identity is, in contrast once more, neither determined by economic productivity nor by the (centralized) power of discipline. *Popular identity* is growing from less controllable sources, from language and everyday life. The base of folk identity is a body language consisting of spatial orders (proximity and distance) and of temporal rhythms (Hall, 1984). Body language finds its institutionalized expression in dances, festivals, games and plays – forms of sensual dialogue and reciprocity in folk life. Laughter and variety, the grotesque body and the dialogue of teasing are important ingredients of folk culture and identification.

MEETING THE OTHER

'Nationalisms' need not be the same, therefore, when seen from their respective body cultural base. Likewise, the internationality in meeting, mobility and migration is not all of one kind. The pattern of sports, with its high degree of objectivity – records, rules, standardized equipment, homogenized environment – has a strong impact on the structure of migration: to meet the familiar; to meet the *same*. Everywhere in the world, the conditions of sport production should be absolutely the same and this demand for standardization produces strange debates about the international unit of measurement – the kilogramme, or kilopound or Newton? How to treat the tiny difference in air pressure between Berlin and Nairobi (Sperlich, 1979)? A whole meterology of sport can be based on this (Lobozewicz, 1981). Comparing results in a 'fair' manner means to meet in a homogeneous world of test, technique and training. This is the specific material base for the international migration of talents, following the suction from lesser to greater power, from lower standards of sport production to higher standards (Bale, 1991, Arbena, Bale and Sang in this volume). The imbalance of colonial sport imperialism (Mangan, 1986) is renewed on a new industrial base. The brawn drain is a logical part of what has been called the totalization of modern sports, the mediatization of the single athlete by a technological scientific economic system (Heinilä, 1982).

However, historical processes are never so simple, and neither is the phenomenon of mobility in achievement sport. The migration of the athlete from the 'poor' to the totalized world might be seen as being countered by another mobility – hooligan tourism (Williams et al., 1985; Dunning et al., 1988). The athlete's search for better conditions on the same scale is meeting the 'wild' search for an experience of otherness and the demonstration of one's own otherness: 'we are the animals!'. In this respect the hooligan – though a product of achievement sport – cannot be explained only in the framework of productive sport configuration. But this demands much more reflection in depth by also comparing the peaceful, carnivalistic counterpart of the hooligan, the Danish 'roligan' (Eichberg, 1990a).

Returning to the second element of the trialectics of sport mobility, it can also here be concluded that the migration in sports and in hygienic gymnastics is not the same. The meeting of Danish gymnasts with the Japanese is not, however, as easy to interpret. Unlike competitive sports, it was clearly not a comparison of results. But in some respects the gymnastics meeting established a common pattern of exercise too, with the subsequent paradox of Niels Bukh gymnastics today surviving just in Japan. The common body cultural pattern was the Danish model, thus functioning as a kind of export model (comparable with the Swedish gymnastics of Martina Bergman-Österberg in England). On the other hand, the gymnastic group from Denmark showed but a superficial touristic interest in the Japanese side of things and no curiosity in the otherness of the partner. They returned to Denmark with a good deal of national pride in their luggage, certainly also some Japanese and other flags exchanged for Danish ones and some gifts and souvenirs. But there was no cultural element from Japan to be identified in the subsequent practice at the

Ollerup Gymnastics Academy. So we could conclude that the pattern of internationality was marked more by the 'representation of the own' model than by a balanced exchange and dialogue.

This trait cannot be generalized for all kinds of social-hygienic disciplinary movement cultures. Surely, it is fitting for many of them and marks a certain egocentricity, contrasting the objectification tendency in achievement sport. But mutual international learning also takes place in hygienic exercises. This is, however, stimulated less by the search for otherness than by the search for the universal natural laws regulating the hygienic and disciplinary order among all people, fundamentally uniform as they are. Hence, what has little or no status in the patterns of achievement sport and social hygienic gymnastics is the meeting of the other, the experience of otherness. This is the focus of the popular or folk games, 'folk' meaning the celebration of difference, of the incomparable.

The meeting of the otherness can have two different dimensions. The *outer* dimension underlines the peculiarity of one's own group and the exotic appearance of the other group(s). This is the field of regional or local identity and differentiation. The exoticism means a game with steoreotypes: stereotyping the other (with those 'strange' games, kilts, music, etc.) and stereotyping the self. The importance of stereotyping, playing with stereotypes and 'joking' relations has often been shown in anthropology (Kleivan, 1971). The *inner* dimension of the otherness is related to the grotesque body in folk-games, the body stumbling, falling into the water, moving like an animal, the fool, the clown, the body to laugh at. Here one meets the *alter ego*. The disappearance of this dimension is an indicator of the folklorization of the folk culture. The game of folk identities thus loses its fundamental human trait: of being a *dialogue*; and there is no dialogue without questions about one's own identity. Folklorization as a reconstruction and representation of the self loses the grotesque body, the laughter and the dialogical openness. It illustrates, therefore, what is essential in the category of folk.

TOTALIZATION, DISNEYFICATION AND POSTMODERNITY

What could be the use of a new (trialectic) way of thinking about nationality, internationality and body culture? Is it just another academic game of making models and phenomenological designs? There is a political dimension in rethinking the internationality of sports. Primitive dualistic evaluations – which still prevail – have for a

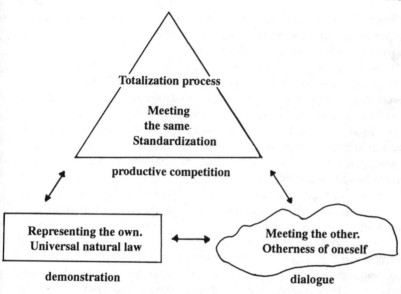

Figure 16.3 Configurations of mobility

long time prevented us from treating this field in a more appropriate manner. The exclusive dualism of nationalism versus internationalism has no empirical value at all. No nationalism can be conceived without the internationality of the wave of nationalism since the late eighteenth century. And no internationalism can be thought of without its national-cultural specific pattern (and an internationalism denying this is normally even more problematic: an unconscious enthnocentricism). Under these aspects and in a time of new actuality in the national question – in eastern Europe among other places – the rich empirical material of sport and body culture furnishes a treasure-house of potential analyses.

The analytical differentiation of nationalization and internationalization could thus also enter into the renewed debate about integration and dissociation on the economic level. Comparisons between Brazil and Denmark, between Java and Japan, have shown in detail how enormous economic potentials (Brazil, Java) have become ruined by their integration into a capitalist world economy whilst 'autocentric' development patterns (Denmark, Japan) 'have prospered even without a base of industrial raw materials' (Senghass, 1977, 1982). Similar comparisons have been outlined between autocentric sports development in Cuba and the dependency model of Jamaican sport (Bale, 1991: 196–201). But what is more, the totalization process of sport has ruined regional body cultures. Its study promises, therefore, an important contribution to the critical study of world systems in general (Heinilä, 1982; Galtung, 1982; Hietanen, 1982; Eichberg, 1984, 1990b).

Recent transformations of the international sports system make it even more urgent to reanalyse sport from its body cultural and configurational contradictions. If it is true that the cultural industry of mass media is transforming some relevant parts of professional sport into a spectacle dominated by entertainment interests and staged for television, then the limit of 'traditional' sporting modernity could be transgressed. The configuration of sporting modernity was determined by the production of better and better results. The logic of show sport is determined by the fascination of entertainment, by the staging of the spectacular; a gap is opening.

A difference of 0.001 seconds in running or swimming is not spectacular as such. It can be boring. What is spectacular is music accompanying sporting activities, cheerleaders dressed in a carnival manner, Disneylike figures parading around the sports field (see Maguire's chapter in this volume). If this Disneyfication is traced back historically, modern sport can hardly be seen as a major influence. It is circus. The drum, the laughter, the fool of pre-modern folk culture are making their comeback. In other words, the dynamics of post-modern media sport have to lead our analysis back to patterns of popular entertainment, to the configuration of folk, but which is exploited now by a new capitalist strategy. Different world systems are competing now: the totalization of (modern) sport and the Disneyfication of show sport. Do they integrate or, rather, do they dissociate?

All these questions also open up new perspectives on the traditional folk cultures. Events such as that at Karaez are not just pre-modern. The scenarios of their possible development and the scenarios of sport in general are no longer as clear and as linear as one would have thought in the perspective of modernity.

THINKING THE THOU

From a philosophical perspective, the comparative study of body cultures is also open to debate. Is the trialectical differentiation of body cultures, (as well as that of nationalism and internationality), simply an accidental, commonsense construction? The philosophy of the 'I', the 'It' and the 'Thou' could suggest that this is not the case. When Martin Büber (1973) designed a philosophy of the Thou as the third, this was called 'the Copernican turn of the twentieth century's philosophy' – and soon forgotten. Evidently, it did not fit into the dualistic patterns of modern western thinking. The categories developed above in an empirical, comparative way, would, however, obtain anthropological depth in the light of Martin Büber's philosophy. The It, the hegemonic structural element in capitalist society and in western thinking, can be seen embodied in the objectivity of the sport result, in production-oriented achievement sport. At its side, the I consists of the other strong element of western *Weltanschauung*, subjectivity. It is some way related to the bodily practice of hygienic self-cultivation and disciplined self-representation. Both It-related sports and I-related gymnastics are rather late historical products, developmentally based on the third, the relation of Thou. This, the principle of dialogue, could be seen embodied in the folk-practice of dance and game, of joking and laughter, of meeting diversity and otherness. The renewed actuality of this third relation would hint in the direction that the folk aspect, just like the Thou, is not – as it might seem under industrial capitalist conditions – merely a residue from ancient times but an anthropological dimension with trans-modern potential.

At the same time, the Büber philosophy will contain an admonition not to fall into the trap of another dualistic evaluation: folk games being the 'good' alternative against the hierarchical stress system of sport and the semi-fascist discipline of hygienic fitness gymnastics. Things are not so simple. I, It and Thou are analytical categories and so are the three patterns of trialectics in body culture. Moreover, the It and the I are necessary dimensions of the *conditio humana* too. In order to survive, the human being is subjugated by the necessity to say 'it' and to treat the environment or even other human beings as if they were 'things' – counting them, measuring them, talking about them, creating order among them . . . There cannot be meaning in abolishing one of these relations and returning to the 'great warm womb of the Thou'. But it gives meaning, politically and culturally, to study critically the structural imbalance between the 'compulsory dominance of the expanding It' (Büber) and the marginalization of the dialogical principle. Under this aspect, the cultural criticism of achievement sports and of fitness sports is a humanist necessity. And the similarly critical attention to the dialogical configuration of folk-games and popular body culture is more than just a supplement to academic – sociological, historical, geographical – specialization of disciplines. It is an(other) entrance to the conscience of human variety and human dialogue.

REFERENCES

Bakhtin, M. (1968) *Rabelais and his World* (Cambridge, MA: MIT Press).

Bale, J. (1989) *Sports Geography* (London: Spon).

(1991) *The Brawn Drain; Foreign Student-Athletes in American Universities* (Urbana, IL: University of Illinois Press).

von Barloewen, C. (1881) *Clown: Zur Phänomenologie des Stoplerns* (1984 edn) (Frankfurt/Main: Ullstein).

Bedecarrast, P. (forthcoming) 'La Soule: Approches Croisées', in Barreau, J.J. (ed.), *Cultures Corporelles en Procès* (Rennes: Presses de la Université Rennes 2).

Blecking, D. (1991) *Die slawische Sokolbewegung* (Dortmund: Forschungsstelle Ostmitteleuropa an der Universität).

Borup-Nielsen, G. (1990) 'Det springende punkt i engelsk gymnastikhistorie', in Hansen, J. (ed.), *Kropskultur og idræt–regionalt, nationalt og internationalt* (Odense: Universitetsforlag) pp. 91–6.

Büber, M. (1973) [1923] *Ich und Du* (Reprinted in *Das Dialogische Prinzip*, 3rd edn, 1973 (Heidelberg: Lambert Schneider) pp. 5–136.

Burat, T. (1990) 'Il tiro alla fune', *Lo joa'e les omo*, 7, 37–46.

Carter, J. and Krüger, A. (eds) (1990) *Ritual and Record* (New York: Westwood Press).

Chuzainov, K. (1990) 'Kazakh Popular Plays and Games' in Eichberg, H. (ed.), *Östeuropa–Idrættens Revolution?* (Copenhagen: Danish State Institute for Sports and PE) pp. 48–50.

Cramer, D. (1978) 'Hilfe auf dem Weg zur Spitze', *Das Parlament*, 28,22, 9.

Diem, C. (1971) *Weltgeschichte des Sports*, Vols I and II, 3rd edn (Stuttgart: Cotta).

Dunning, E. (1973) 'The Structural–Functional Properties of Folk-Games and Modern Sports', *Sportwissenschaft*, 3, 215–32.

Dunning, E., Williams, J. and Murphy, P. (1988) *The Roots of Football Hooliganism* (London: Routledge).

Eichberg, H. (1978) *Leistung, Spannung, Geschwindigkeit* (Stuttgart: Klett).

(1984) 'Olympic sport – neocolonialism and alternatives', *International Review for the Sociology of Sport*, 19,1, 97–106.

(1988) *Leistungsräume: Sport als Umweltproblem* (Münster: Lit).

(1989a) 'Body culture as paradigm', *International Review for the Sociology of Sport*, 24, 43-63.

(1989b) ' "Folkelig gymnastik": Über den dänischern Sonderweg in der Körperkultur', in Gutsche, K. and Medau, H. (eds), *Gymnastik: Ein Beitrag zur Bewegungskultur unserer Gesellschaft* (Schorndorf: Hoffmann) pp. 52–95.

(1989c) 'The Labyrinth – the Earliest Nordic "Sports Ground"?', *Scandinavian Journal of Sports Sciences*, 11,1, 43–57.

(1990a) 'Crisis and Grace', Colloquium Paper No. 66/90 (Florence: European University Institute).

(1990b) 'Forward Race and the Laughter of Pygmies: On Olympic Sport' in Teich, M. and Porter, R. (eds), *Fin de Siècle and its Legacy* (Cambridge: Cambridge University Press) pp. 115–31.

(1991) 'A Revolution of Body Culture? Traditional Games on the Way from Modernization to "Postmodernity" ' in Barreau, J.-J. and Jaouen, G.

migrants would form part of this enquiry. Sport migrants appear to be a new band of specialists who work outside the traditional professional and organizational cultures of the nation state. Problems of inter-cultural communication also arise for sport migrants—witness the 'babel-like' quality of global sports festivals or tournaments. For sport migrants such a social milieu involves a multi-layered form of inter-cultural communication centring on interacton with fellow players, coaches, officials, the crowd and media personnel. While some sport migrants may find the move from one culture to another relatively free of culture shock, others may not. The movement of eastern European ice hockey and basketball players to North America, for example, may also bring problems of adjustment to free market economic processes.

This labour migration may also engender hostility in the host country. Sport labour unions, such as in European soccer, have sought to protect indigenous workers by arguing for the application of quotas and qualification thresholds to potential migrants. During 1993, the English Professional Footballers' Association (PFA) called for tighter controls and checks on the playing credentials of foreign players (*The Mail on Sunday*, 24 January 1993, p. 95). An attempt by FIFA, the world governing body of soccer, to remove restrictions on foreign players in European leagues prompted the threat of an Europe-wide strike by professional players (*The Guardian*, 25 November 1992, p. 16). Following a meeting held in February 1993 between the PFA, the football authorities and the Department of Employment, foreign players became subject to tighter restrictions (*The Guardian*, 27 February, 1993, p. 16). This resistance is matched by those concerned with the development of national teams. The presence of overseas players could deny indigenous players access and thus lead to personal and a national underdevelopment. In contrast to these sentiments, major European soccer club owners seek to strengthen their position at every opportunity. The ascendancy of AC Milan exemplifies this process. Its owner, Silvio Berlusconi, argues for no restrictions on sport migration. As part of this process, which he sees as already under way, Berlusconi concluded that 'the concept of the national team will, gradually, become less and less important. It is the clubs with which the fans associate' (*World Soccer*, April 1992, p. 10). Given this approach, the fortunes of the national team become secondary. Corporate success is what counts.

4 Cultures, Self-identities and National Identities

Questions of attachment to place, notions of self-identity and allegiance to a specific country are significant in discussion of sport labour migration. The global sports economy ensures that highly rational and technical criteria determine the status and market value of migrants. The new generation of sport migrants may, as a result, have little sense of attachment to a specific space or community. One has only to think of the 'rebel' cricket and rugby union tours to South Africa to understand how sport migrants can likewise act as mercenaries for 'big business'. In addition, performers may not share the same cultural identity as the 'native' followers of the national team they purport to represent. Here, the pluralization of national identities (stemming from the impact of globalization processes) is at work. It is not clear whether this process will gather further momentum or if a strengthened national emphasis (as a form of resistance to globalization processes) will result in a selection policy that would amount to a form of 'ethnic cleansing'. A study of this area may provide important insights into the broader process of globalization and national identities.

On the other hand, a new order of globally recognized sports migrants appears to transcend national identity and assume the form of international icons. Such figures stand outside the dominant invented traditions of the nation state, and also assume a transnational significance beyond their sporting prowess. For example, athletes such as Muhammad Ali, Arthur Ashe, Martina Navaratilova and Ruud Gullit each highlight issues relating to ethnicity and gender to sections of global audience.

We believe that this collection has raised important issues regarding the global movement of athletes. It was our intention to capture both the current state of play and also provide some impetus for further research into this area. This research base should, we hope, also inform the generation of policies that would make the experience of talent migration less exploitative and somewhat more enriching for the migrants themselves.